Internationalization of

China's

Privately Owned Enterprises

Determinants and Pattern Selection

Internationalization of
China's
Privately Owned Enterprises
Determinants and Pattern Selection

Wen Xiao
Liyun Liu

Zhejiang University, China

World Scientific

ZHEJIANG UNIVERSITY PRESS
浙江大学出版社

Published by

World Scientific Publishing Co. Pte. Ltd.

5 Toh Tuck Link, Singapore 596224

USA office: 27 Warren Street, Suite 401-402, Hackensack, NJ 07601

UK office: 57 Shelton Street, Covent Garden, London WC2H 9HE

and

Zhejiang University Press
No. 148, Tianmushan Road
Xixi Campus of Zhejiang University
Hangzhou 310028, China

Library of Congress Cataloging-in-Publication Data
Xiao, Wen (Economist)
    Internationalization of China's privately owned enterprises : determinants and pattern selection /
by Wen Xiao (Zhejiang University, China) & Liyun Liu (Zhejiang University, China).
        pages cm
    ISBN 978-9814635639
    1. Free enterprise--China. 2. Investments, Foreign--China. 3. International business enterprises--
China. 4. Entrepreneurship--Government policy--China. I. Title.
    HB95.X56 2015
    338.8'8951--dc23
                                    2014044964

British Library Cataloguing-in-Publication Data
A catalogue record for this book is available from the British Library.

This edition is jointly published by World Scientific Publishing Co. Pte. Ltd. and Zhejiang University Press. This edition is distributed worldwide by World Scientific Publishing Co. Pte. Ltd., except Mainland China.

In-house Editors: Lum Pui Yee/Dipasri Sardar

Typeset by Stallion Press
Email: enquiries@stallionpress.com

Printed in Singapore

Contents

Preface

The economic globalization in which developed countries play dominant roles and Multinational Enterprises (MNEs) are the major market participants, has introduced tremendous changes in all economic sectors. However, developing countries dominate the incoming "New Economic Globalization", and therefore China adopts the strategy of "going global" to meet this challenge and has played a leading role in the new globalization. China's opening-up originated from the introduction of foreign capital. As a developing country, China cannot just participate actively in the global division of labor, which is dominated by developed countries in the form of introduction of capital. In addition, China cannot remain a competitive power in the international market just in the form of trade. Therefore, a strategy of internationalization has become an inevitable choice for China so as to facilitate the internationalization process of indigenous China's enterprises.

Since China adopted the "going global" strategy in 2001, China's internationalization activities have been active, though gradually. In the early internationalization process, state-owned enterprises (SOEs) were the main participants. However, constrained by their link to their government, their overseas investment activities have been hampered by the so-called "red phobia". Foreign countries and regions have imposed restrictions on overseas investment by China's SOEs in industries like technology, energy and resources, which are closely related to national government, and hence the internationalization process of China's SOEs began to slow down. In contrast, China's privately-owned enterprises (POEs) are less related to the government, and they make full use of their advantages to become the main force of internationalization in the circumstances of rising global protectionism. In the post-financial crisis era, China's POEs have adjusted their goals and strategy of internationalization accordingly and hence their internationalization process has leapfrogged. Therefore, it is a key research issue to develop a theoretical framework based on China's experiences to explain the determinants and patterns of China's POEs' internationalization.

According to the existing research literature, research attention has been focused on the internationalization practice of European and American enterprises. Demand conditions, technological development, industrial structure, domestic rivalry, company strategy, market imperfections or transaction costs, psychic distance, organizational learning, networks, market potential, localization advantage, managerial decisions, previous international experience of owners and entrepreneurs are all believed to be relevant determinants. However, these factors may not necessarily influence the internationalization of China's POEs, which results from a government-led internationalization process of POEs. Institutional factors may exert great influence on the internationalization of China's POEs, which is confirmed by the research in this book.

This book reviews the existing theoretical research of enterprise internationalization, analyzes its determinants and pattern choice, and finally proposes the argument of "bounded entrepreneurship". When initiating their business, indigenous Chinese entrepreneurs are constrained by their low levels of education and experience and by unfavorable institutional arrangements, which results in their limited rationality, and hence leads to different internationalization patterns of China's POEs from those of developed countries.

Based on the literature review, this book conducts some empirical analysis and case studies on the determinants of China's POEs' internationalization by using six various approaches. This book concludes that the existing theories for enterprise internationalization from developed countries can only provide a partial explanation of the internationalization process of China's indigenous POEs, as their owners are constrained by their limited education and lack of international experience and by China's unique institutional barriers. The argument for bounded entrepreneurship is proposed to explain the unique internationalization patterns in the context of China. Thus, we argue that Chinese entrepreneurs in private sector have limited capabilities in assessing the degree of integration and homogeneity of the domestic and foreign markets and limited entrepreneurial cognition of international business opportunities and hence tended to start their businesses in the home market. Given the lack of business networks and experience about foreign markets and operations, they did not "wait for a windfall" but strove to obtain the information by other means, such as attending exhibitions. Given the bounded entrepreneurship, some of them carried out inward-oriented internationalization activities to learn technological and managerial knowledge before they started outward-oriented activities. Given the limit technological knowledge, they pursued a combined strategy of differentiation and cost leadership. A technology-innovation-driven strategy will lead to a better performance. Finally, the timing of internationalization alone may not be sufficient to interpret a firm's performance.

Taking into account the impact of the financial crisis on the global economic structure and economic balance, this book makes full use of the latest enterprise questionnaire survey data to identify the determinants in the overseas investment patterns and the performance of China's POEs. This book conducts a regression analysis of the overseas investment pattern selection and the performance by selecting as explanatory variables enterprise scale, domestic impetus, host country's incentives, enterprise's internationalization experience and other relevant factors. We conclude that an enterprise's internationalization experience, the Chinese government's incentive policies and host country's market potential are the decisive factors for the overseas investment pattern selection, which verifies the fact that the internationalization process of China's enterprises is bounded by government regulation. At the same time, in terms of the internationalization performance, regression results show that the enterprise's international-ization experience is the most important determinant, and confirm that accumulation of the internationalization experiences has made a positive contribution to the internationalization of China's POEs. The firm-level econometric analysis also confirms that the institutional factors play a significant role in the internationalization of China's POEs.

Based on the theoretical research and micro-econometric analysis, this book selects several well-known POEs in China to conduct detailed case studies. It explains the internationalization pattern selection for China's indigenous POEs from the aspects of process, strategy, determinants, etc.

The innovations in this book lie in the following three areas: (1) To propose a theoretical framework for internationalization of China's indigenous POEs on the basis of "bounded entrepreneurship" which is consistent with

China's situation. The existing research literature makes use of the evidence of developed countries to explain the determinants and pattern selection for enterprises' internationalization. However, owing to insufficient education and management training, China's entrepreneurs pay more attention to business opportunities for rapid development of the internationalization process. (2) This book makes full use of firm-level data in the questionnaire to explore the determinants and pattern selection of the internationalization of China's POEs, which is of great pioneering value. The micro firm-level data from the questionnaire survey can greatly improve the reliability of results. (3) Based on a detailed case analysis of several well-known POEs, this book proposes internationalization pattern selection for China's POEs. The internationalization process of enterprises from developed countries like European countries and USA is mainly influenced by market forces. However, bounded by the institutional arrangements, the internationalization process of China's enterprises is mainly influenced by the institutions. Therefore, this book develops a new approach to make use of the firm-level data to conduct detailed case studies, and the argument for "bounded entrepreneurship" has been extended the theoretical framework of the internationalization of China's indigenous POEs, which is of significant importance, both theoretically and practically.

Wen Xiao

Acknowledgments

We would not have been able to complete this work without the support provided by the Center for Research of the Private Economy, Zhejiang University and China's Council for the Promotion of International Trade. We wish to thank Mr. Liu Xiaming and Mr. Lin Gaobang for their comments and suggestions. We owe great gratitude to the innumerable scholars whose careful research informed our work. We are also indebted to Dr. Zhou Minghai and Dr. Tang Zhaoxi who inspired us with questions and challenges. Many colleagues in Zhejiang University have read some parts of our work, and their comments have led to the hopefully much better version. We also would like to thank Mr. Chen Yijun for his careful review of our work. Deep thanks to Mr. Pan Jiadong for the tremendous efforts he has devoted to the job of case studies.

Chapter 1

Introduction

China's private economy has experienced a very rapid growth since it adopted the policy of economic reform and opening up to the outside world at the end of 1978. The private sector has played a crucial role in the Chinese economy, especially in the coastal regions. China's opening up and integration into the world economy has facilitated the growth of its private sector. Related to this, the issue of internationalization of China's POEs has attracted much attention. We will present a theoretical basis for the research on the internationalization of Chinese privately-owned enterprises (POEs).

1.1 What is Internationalization?

There are several explanations in the literature of internationalization. One explanation argues that internationalization, as a mode of overseas investment, can be explained by internalization, ownership and location advantages (Williamson, 1975; Dunning, 1988). Another argues that internationalization is a continuous evolution (Melin, 1992), and the increment in knowledge and market investment will introduce a higher participation of firms in the world economy (Johanson and Vahlne, 1977). Welch and Luostarinen (1988) analyze the evolution of the internationalization concept. They define internationalization as "the process of increasing involvement in the international market", and they believe that internationalization may include international expansion of inward and outward aspects (Welch and Luostarinen, 1993). Moreover, Johanson and Vahlne (1977) propose the argument that the internationalization process can be seen "as the consequence of a process of incremental adjustments to changing conditions of the firm and its environment". They indicate that international activity involves a decision to commit current resources to a foreign operation. Its involvement in the international market is closely related to the market they enter and their entry mode selection. Welch and Luostarinen (1988) believe that international involvement can be reflected in the firm's products, organization, personnel and structure.

Beamish (1990) defines internationalization as a process in which firms are increasingly aware of the vital importance of international trade to their future development, both directly and indirectly, and then trade with other nations. This argument is fairly comprehensive, because it has integrated the above three arguments into a uniform framework. First, Beamish's definition of internationalization has combined the internal organizational learning and investment patterns. Therefore, it realizes internationalization is related to both behavioral science and economics. Second, it is process-based, which means that internationalization is a dynamic process. Third, the definition not only covers the "outward" aspect, but also the "inward" aspect, internationalization behavior such as imports, counter-trade, etc., have been included. Finally, there is an implication that relations developed in the internationalization process will probably exert some impact on the firm's growth and its expansion to other countries.

Obviously, there is not a universally-accepted definition of the internationalization of enterprises. Most scholars prefer to use the word internationalization to describe the outward international business activities of an enterprise or group (Luostarinen, 1970, 1979; Johanson and Wiedersheim-Paul, 1975; Johanson and Vahlne, 1977; Piercy, 1981; Turnbull, 1986). Some other scholars, like Welch and Luostarinen (1988), define internationalization as the process in which the enterprises gradually increase their international involvement. There are some scholars who believe that enterprise internationalization should include both inward internationalization and outward internationalization.

According to the existing literature on internationalization, we interpret internationalization as the process by which enterprises engage in international business activities, and increase integration in the world economy. This definition leads to two modes of the internationalization of enterprises, both inward and outward, where the inward mode is the initial stage of internationalization, whereas the outward mode is the advanced stage. It includes a wide variety of modes: imports and exports of merchandise, technical cooperation, joint ventures, licensing, franchising, management contracts, subcontracting, project operation, foreign direct investment, etc. Moreover, this definition of internationalization regards the internationalization of enterprises as a process. It believes that enterprises' integration in international business, namely the degree of internationalization, can be easily measured. For instance, we can assess the degree of internationalization by measuring the ratio of overseas sales to total sales, and we can also assess the degree of internationalization from how enterprises carry out their international business activity, where the outward foreign direct investment (OFDI) is regarded as the advanced stage of internationalization. In the subsequent chapters, we examine the degree of internationalization of China's POEs using both the ratio of international sales to total sales and the international business modes they adopted.

In addition, there are various other internationalization modes. However, we choose to focus on exports of merchandise and foreign direct investment in this book. Exporting is the most prevalent internationalization mode for China's POEs to take, whereas foreign direct investment is the advanced stage of internationalization, therefore both these two modes can, to a large extent, represent the internationalization mode of small and medium-sized enterprises.

To proceed with our research of internationalization, we must have an appropriate tool to evaluate and compare the internationalization level of different enterprises. Obviously, we can obtain some quite simple measures from the definition of "internationalization", such as the ratio of export sales to total sales, the ratio of imported technologies to total utilized technology, the ratio of overseas assets or overseas sales to total assets or total sales, etc.

The data and material used in these methods are readily available. However, we badly need to develop a specific index system to evaluate the internationalization of China's POEs, as internationalization contains a hybrid content and structure, with inward and outward internationalization, in a diverse form. In particular, China's POEs have their own characteristics in the process of internationalization.

The issue of internationalization has attracted much attention from scholars and institutions. At present, the Trans-Nationality Index (TNI) (UNCTAD), Degree of Internationalization Scale (DIO) (Sullivan, 1994) and the Trans-Nationality Spread Index (TSI) (Gillies, 1998) are the three typical measures.

TNI denotes the performance of internationalization. We use the Multinational Index of UNCTAD to examine the internationalization performance by measuring the weighted average of the ratios of enterprise sales abroad to total sales, overseas employees to total employees and overseas assets to total assets. This index is not complicated and its data is available.

The formula is:

$$TNI = (FSTS + FETE + FATA)/3,$$

where FSTS (Foreign Share in Total Sales) denotes the ratio of overseas sales to total sales.

FETE (Foreign Employment in Total Employment) denotes foreign employees as a percentage of total employees, which is reflected in the ratio of employees devoted to overseas operations to total employees.

FATA (Foreign Assets in Total Assets) denotes the ratio of overseas assets to total assets, meaning assets devoted to overseas operations divided by total assets.

It is relatively easy to obtain the data of this index, but it also has the following shortcomings: Firstly, it cannot be applied to examine the degree of internationalization for enterprises who commit to inward internationalization, or enterprises who commit to both inward and outward internationalization; secondly, the enterprise's motivation for internationalization is not fully accommodated. In practice, enterprises have various purposes of internationalization: Some aim at expanding the foreign market; some aim at mitigating the shortage of domestic resources; some aim at transferring profits. The TNI will underestimate the degree of internationalization of those enterprises who aim at seeking resources, because overseas sales are not their main purpose, but the TNI takes the ratio of foreign sales to total sales as a factor; thirdly, the TNI separates local/domestic business activities from overseas business activities, but the scope of business activities overseas has been ignored. For example, an enterprise with a high TNI may carry out its international business activities in only one or two countries, whereas an enterprise with a low TNI may engage in international business activities in dozens of countries.

1.2 China's Radical Internationalization Development

1.2.1 Transformation in development mode of foreign trade

Since 2002, China has made efforts to accelerate the transformation of foreign trade development mode, thus effectively promoting the sustainable development of foreign trade.

The scale of trade in goods has expanded rapidly. From 2003 to 2011, China reached an annual average growth rate of 21.7% in the total export and import of goods where the annual average growth rate was 21.6% for exports and 21.8% for imports.[1] In 2011, the total import and export volume of goods in China was USD3,642.1 billion, an increase of 4.9 times compared with 2002,[2] which placed China second overall in world trade. China has been the largest exporting country and second largest importing country in terms of trade for three consecutive years.

New progress has been made in market diversification. Positive achievements were made in the market diversification and the geographic distribution of international markets was further optimized. In 2002, the US, the EU, Japan, and Hong Kong (SAR of China) accounted for 57.2% of total volume of imports and exports. This figure dropped to 52.9% in 2005 and further dropped to 45.1% in 2011.[3] The proportion of emerging markets and developing countries such as ASEAN and BRICs countries in the foreign trade of China kept increasing. In 2011, the proportion of ASEAN and BRICs countries to China's total value of imports and exports increased to 10.0% and 7.8%, respectively, while Latin America and Africa respectively increased to 6.6% and 4.6%.[4]

Positive transformation occurred in the structure of trade in goods. From 2003 to 2011, the annual average growth rate for general trade

---

[1] http://finance.chinanews.com/cj/2012/11-07/4309025.shtml.

[2] http://www.stats.gov.cn/ztjc/ztfx/kxfzcjhh/201208/t20120821_72840.html.

[3] http://www.mofcom.gov.cn/aarticle/ae/ai/201211/20121108422673.html.

[4] http://www.stats.gov.cn/ztjc/ztfx/kxfzcjhh/201208/t20120821_72840.html.

reached by 24.2%, surpassing the annual average growth rate for 17.7% of China's processing trade.[5] In 2011, the volume of general trade reached USD1,924.58 billion, an increase of 6.3 times compared with 2002, and its proportion to the total volume of imports and exports rose from 42.7% in 2002 to 52.8% in 2011; the volume of processing trade was USD1,305.2 billion, an increase of 3.3 times compared with 2002, and its proportion dropped from 48.7% in 2002 to 35.8% in 2011.[6] And meanwhile, positive results were made in the transformation and upgrading of the processing trade; the industrial structure has transformed its reliance soly on labor-intensive goods to a triple structure attaching equal importance to the intensity of labor, technology and capital, and the extension of processing and manufacturing was gradually implemented; the industrial structure was continuously improved and the industrial chains were continuously extended; the proportions of mechanical and electrical products and high-tech products in the processing trade rose from 64.7% and 27.1% in 2002 to 78.1% and 50.5% in 2011, respectively.[7]

Structure of trade in goods was further optimized. In terms of exports, China transformed its reliance on primary products to industrial products in the 1980s, then textiles and other light industrial products to electromechanical products in the 1990s. Since 2003, the export proportion of high-tech products represented by electronic and information technologies has kept increasing. The proportion of manufactured goods exported to the total export volume increased from 91.2% in 2002 to 94.7% in 2011; that of mechanical and electrical products to the total volume increased from 48.2% in 2002 to 57.2% in 2011, and that of high-tech products in the total volume rose from 20.8% in 2002 to 28.9% in 2011. Compared with 2002, the export quantity of automobiles increased by 37 times in 2011[8]; the export of ships increased by 22 times, making China the largest ship exporting country by overtaking Republic of Korea. A breakthrough was made in the export of aeroplanes and satellites. In addition, the export volume of more than 50 kinds of products such as

---

[5] http://finance.chinanews.com/cj/2012/11-07/4309025.shtml.

[6] http://www.stats.gov.cn/ztjc/ztfx/kxfzcjhh/201208/t20120821_72840.html.

[7] http://www.mofcom.gov.cn/article/difang/jiangxi/201212/20121208498357.shtml.

[8] http://www.mofcom.gov.cn/article/difang/jiangxi/201212/20121208498357.shtml.

notebook computers, mobile phones, TV's and containers ranked first in the world. The proportion of exports of highly hazardous resource-intensive products with high-energy consumption decreased gradually.

In terms of imports, the import of advanced technologies, equipment and key parts and components kept increasing and that of bulk resources and energy products kept expanding. In 2011, the import volume of mechanical and electrical products' high-tech products reached USD753.29 billion and USD462.99 billion respectively, accounting for 43.2% and 26.6% of the total import volume respectively, and increasing by 3.8 times and 4.6 times compared with 2002; the proportion of the import of high-tech products in the international market rose from 6% in 2002 to 14% in 2011, ranking the second in the world. In addition the proportion of the import of inedible materials and mineral fuels, lubricating oil and relevant materials rose from 14.2% in 2002 to 32.2% in 2011.[9]

Transformation and upgrade of traditional labor-intensive industries were accelerated. The total export volume of the light industry, textile and pharmaceutical industry in 2011 was USD575.13 billion, increasing by 35 times compared with 2002; the trade structure was continuously optimized, and the quality and benefits kept improving along with the stabilization of exports and imports. An increasing attention to research, development and innovation was paid and an increasing number of enterprises expanded their businesses to research, development and design in the form of self-establishment or outsourcing. For agricultural products, the export volume in 2011 was USD60.1 billion and the import volume was USD93.9 billion, increasing by 2.3 times and 6.6 times respectively compared with 2002.[10] According to the statistics released by the WTO, the export of China's agricultural products ranked fifth in the world, while imports ranked the third[11]; concurrently, the commodity structure of the import and export of agricultural products was changed so that labor-intensive products with comparative advantages gradually took the leading position in exports while imports concentrated on land-intensive products.

---

[9] http://www.mofcom.gov.cn/article/difang/jiangxi/201212/20121208498357.shtml.

[10] http://www.mofcom.gov.cn/article/difang/jiangxi/201212/20121208498357.shtml.

[11] http://www.mofcom.gov.cn/article/difang/jiangxi/201212/20121208498357.shtml.

Positive achievements were made in the expansion of imports. Since 2003, China's imports have played an increasingly important role in promoting the industrial structure, guaranteeing the supply of domestic necessities and boosting the domestic consumption. The scale of imports increased by 4.9 times from USD295.2 billion in 2002 to USD1,740 billion in 2011 with an annual average increase of 22.6%, basically the same as 22.7% for exports; China's imports as a percentage of global imports went from 4.4% in 2002 to about 10% in 2011, ranking from the sixth to the second in global imports; the import of bulk products such as minerals, energy and agricultural products accelerated rapidly, and its proportion of total imports increased from 16.7% to 29.2%.[12] Meanwhile, the active expansion of imports effectively promoted the improvement in the trade balance. China's foreign trade surplus was USD30.43 billion in 2002, with it reaching a historical high of USD298.1 billion in 2008. It fell to USD155.14 billion in 2011, and its proportion of GDP dropped from a record high of 7.5% in 2007 to 2.1% in 2011.[13]

The quality strategy was comprehensively advanced. In recent years, the Ministry of Commerce has carried out activities such as the "Year of Improving the Quality of Foreign Trade Commodities" and organized special campaigns against the export of counterfeits that infringe upon intellectual property rights and other activities to further regulate the production and operational environment for foreign trade; enhanced research and promotion in the international market for export products and conducted special training for improving the quality of foreign trade commodities; prepared and released quality safety manuals concerning 29 categories of key export commodities in the fields of light industry, medical care, textiles, food, native products and animal by-products; opened a service platform (website) for the quality of foreign trade commodities to constantly improve the level of public service. All the efforts mentioned above have effectively maintained the good image of "made in China", promoted the cultivation of export brands, protection of intellectual property and continuous improvement of commodity quality and accelerated the transformation from "made in China" into "created by China".

---

[12] http://www.mofcom.gov.cn/article/difang/jiangxi/201212/20121208498357.shtml.
[13] http://www.mofcom.gov.cn/article/difang/jiangxi/201212/20121208498357.shtml.

1.2.2 Rapid development of foreign cooperation

In 2001, the "going global" strategy, as a basis of foreign investment and cooperation, was promoted as a national strategy and was written into China's 10th Five-Year Plan for National Economic and Social Development. Since 2003, the Ministry of Commerce of the People's Republic of China (MOFCOM), together with other related departments, has gradually improved the policy support system, service guaranteeing system and risk-control system for the "going global" strategy, and guided and encouraged enterprises to actively and steadily carry out foreign investment and cooperation, creating the environment for continued development in foreign investment and cooperation.

The scale of OFDI has significantly expanded. The scale of China's overseas direct investment increased from USD2.7 billion in 2002 to USD74.65 billion in 2011, with an annual growth rate of 26.9%.[14] Since the outbreak of the international financial crisis in 2008, global investment has decreased by a large margin, but China's has enjoyed a steady growth in overseas investment. The outflow and stock of China's overseas investment in 2011 ranked 6th and 13th in the world respectively, with it being just 26th and 25th respectively in 2002.[15] At the end of 2011, the OFDI stock was USD424.78 billion, with 18,000 enterprises setup abroad and total assets amounting to USD2 trillion.[16] The contract value of contracting projects and the realized turnover increased from USD15.05 billion and USD11.19 billion in 2002 to USD142.33 billion and USD103.42 billion in 2011, up by 30.4% and 31.3% year on year.[17] From 2002 to 2011, the contract value of contracting projects and the realized turnover amounted to USD737.41 billion and USD464.61 billion, respectively. In 2011, the accumulated contract value and turnover reached USD841.6 billion and USD539 billion, respectively.[18] According to China International Contractors Association,

---

[14] http://www.chinadaily.com.cn/business/2012-08/30/content_15720945.htm.

[15] http://finance.chinanews.com/cj/2012/10-30/4288823.shtml.

[16] http://english.mofcom.gov.cn/aarticle/newsrelease/significantnews/201209/20120908320386.html.

[17] http://www.mofcom.gov.cn/article/zhengcejd/bq/201210/20121008410161.shtml.

[18] http://www.mofcom.gov.cn/article/zhengcejd/bq/201210/20121008410161.shtml.

in 2011 China's foreign labor service cooperation industry expatriated 452,000 labor service personnel, representing a 10% year-on-year growth. By the end of 2011, the cumulative expatriated workers had reached 5.88 million.[19]

Increasing innovations occur in the investment pattern. Overseas mergers and acquisitions (M&A) are on the rise. From 2003 to 2011, investment in overseas M&A totaled USD130.86 billion, accounting for 51.6% of the total value of OFDI.[20] Aiming at obtaining an overseas marketing network, technology, brand, energy and resources, a series of M&As have been conducted smoothly, such as Geely's purchase of Sweden's Volvo, Lenovo's buying of the IBM PC business, Sinopec's buying of stock equity in Switzerland's Addax Company. Breakthroughs have been made by enterprises in large-scale overseas operations and investment projects. The collective investment mode has been developing steadily and the overseas trade and economic cooperation zones have made great progress. China now has established 16 cooperation zones in 13 countries, among which 9 zones have passed acceptance tests by host countries, including the Zambia–China Trade and Economic Zone, the Thai–Chinese Rayong Industrial Zone, the Ussuriisk (Russia) Trade and Economic Zone. The Zones attracted nearly 300 enterprises with over USD3 billion actualized investment value.[21] Foreign investment, contracted projects and resource exploration are in a coordinated development. China's investors carried out investment projects in resource fields such as oil, gas and mineral exploration, and transportation and infrastructure projects such as highway and port construction. Collaboration between enterprises has been increasingly strengthened. Several enterprises can undertake projects as a group by making full use of their particular advantages, so as to enhance the competitiveness. In overseas investment cooperation, China's enterprises have invited foreign enterprises to collaborate on the projects and share common interest.

---

[19] http://english.mofcom.gov.cn/aarticle/counselorsreport/asiareport/201202/20120207968987.html.

[20] http://economy.big5.enorth.com.cn/system/2013/09/10/011297168.shtml.

[21] http://finance.chinanews.com/cj/2012/10-30/4288823.shtml.

The range of investment fields gradually broadened. China's OFDI has extended its investment regions and industries, covering 178 countries and regions. Hong Kong (SAR of China), Virgin Islands, Cayman Islands, Australia, Singapore, etc. became China's main destinations for foreign investment. China's foreign investment frequently involved business services, the wholesale and retail trade, mining, transportation, manufacturing, etc. The markets for foreign contracting projects were diverse. While consolidating the traditional markets in Asia and Africa, non-traditional markets in Latin America, and Central Asia were constantly being opened up. Positive progress has been made in opening up developed countries. The proportion of high-tech foreign contracting projects increased. Housing construction projects as a percentage of newly signed contracts dropped from 30% in 2002 to 20% in 2011.[22] The proportion of petrochemical, power and electronic communications projects that will bring more exports and high profits accounted for nearly 50% of newly signed contracts.

Furthermore, the quality has been further enhanced. China's enterprises have constantly improved its global management. About 69 enterprises from mainland China were selected by "Fortune 500" in 2011. Huawei, Lenovo, Haier and other enterprises began to take on a multinational corporation shape. Local enterprises were increasingly active in foreign investment. Till the end of 2011, local non-financial OFDI amounted to 23.8% of total foreign investment; 60% of the turnover of foreign contracting projects were completed by local enterprises and 86.6% of total expatriated workers were from local enterprises.[23] Foreign contracting projects were on a large-scale shape. The number of projects with a contract value of more than USD50 million increased from 53 in 2002 to 498 in 2011, in which projects with a contract value of more than USD100 million increased to 226.[24] Angolan social housing, Tehran Metro Line 4, the refinery at Cienfuegos, Cuba, and other major projects were implemented, which played an important role in improving people's livelihoods, transportation and production capacity for host countries. The large-scale enterprises increased their strengths. At the end of 2011, 3,165 enterprises were

---

[22] http://news.ifeng.com/gundong/detail_2012_10/30/18672806_0.shtml.
[23] http://finance.chinanews.com/cj/2012/10-30/4288781.shtml.
[24] http://finance.chinanews.com/cj/2012/10-30/4288781.shtml.

qualified to conduct foreign contracting projects, in which Huawei, China State Construction Engineering Corporation, and China Sinohydro have performed outstandingly. There were 50 China's enterprises enrolled into the Top 225 International Contractors by Engineering News-Record (ENR) Magazine in 2011, an increase of 11 enterprises compared with 2002.[25] China's foreign contracting projects have transferred their emphasis from quantity to quality. EPC contracting has become the main method. Planning and design played a leading role in the implementation of contracting projects, and franchising has already made progress in the operation and management. Supporting policies and measures that safeguard the service cooperation have been put forward. The increasing overseas labor disputes have been effectively curbed.

1.3   An Inevitable Choice for Privately-Owned Enterprises (POEs)

The private economy has become of extremely vital significance for the socialist market economy in China, but unfortunately there is not a universally-accepted definition of private economy, nor of private enterprise. Scholars have briefly tried to explain the definition of private enterprises combining aspects of both the management unit and ownership. We define the POEs from the aspect of the management unit. The private sector is different from state-owned or state-run, government-owned or government-run sectors in China's context. The private sector includes the following six parts: (1) individual and private enterprises; (2) township enterprises; (3) private technology enterprises; (4) joint-stock enterprises that are not state-controlled; (5) foreign-funded enterprises that are not state-controlled; (6) state-owned (or publicly-owned) but privately run (ownership remains unchanged, but the management unit changes) enterprises. Hence, our definition of privately-owned enterprises covers private enterprises, some collective enterprises, some joint-stock enterprises, and a very small amount of state-owned enterprises (contracted or leased to the private enterprises or individual enterprises).

Economic globalization has introduced internationalization which is obviously the inevitable choice for the further development of

---

[25] http://finance.sina.com.cn/roll/20110909/093510460464.shtml.

China's POEs. Economic globalization has unprecedentedly promoted the free allocation of commodities, capital, technology, talent and services and the free mobility of goods and production factors in the world market, which has strengthened the economic relations of all countries, cooperation among enterprises, as well as increasing competition. Under the circumstances of deep economic globalization, few enterprises (including the private enterprises in China) could ignore the international market, and should integrate themselves in the international market. Generally speaking, when an enterprise starts its international business activities, it is the beginning of its internationalization process, even if it cannot eventually grow to be a truly multinational corporation. Though the internationalization process may be very long, the fact that the enterprise moves towards internationalization cannot be denied. With the deepening of China's reform and opening up and its entry into the World Trade Organization, private enterprises possessing comparative advantages in the value chain have been increasingly involved in the process of economic globalization in the form of international investment, production, sales, service and other international economic activities. Based on the following two reasons, we conclude that China's POEs can proceed with their development in the context of economic globalization only when they have accomplished internationalization.

First, the POE can make full use of the comparative advantages only when it strengthens its integration in the international market, and further integrates itself into the process of economic globalization. By taking advantage of markets and resources both at home and abroad, absorbing foreign advanced technology and management experience, training and introducing qualified personnel, grasping external information, China's POE can better seek a ready market, prevent and avoid risk, and be provided with a much wider space for their future development.

Second, only when the POE integrates itself into trade liberaliza-tion and economic globalization, the global value chain, as well as implementing an international operations strategy, can it transform from being "opportunity-oriented" and "cost-oriented" to "strategy-oriented" and "value-oriented" and eventually improve its comparative advantage and competitive advantage. Provided more and more of China's POEs choose to go global in the form of foreign investment and operation,

China can promote its economic structural optimization, its transformation of the economic growth pattern, and its economic development and opening up.

Thanks to the past 30 years and continued reform and opening-up, some POEs not only urgently need to go global, but are also in a good condition to go global. By the end of the WTO transition period, China's economy has been further integrated into the world economy, which will create good conditions for POEs to make full use of both domestic and overseas markets, resources both at home and abroad, and participate in international competition and the international division of labor. POEs face enormous challenges and opportunities. In the new era, to achieve the economic and social development, their private enterprises must accelerate their internationalization process, actively participate in international competition, and promote their international competitiveness during the internationalization process. We conclude that POEs are able to accelerate the implementation of internationalization strategy using the following basic conditions:

First, the basic conditions have been created for the POE to engage in international business. Although it is inferior to large and medium-sized state-owned enterprises in terms of overall strength, it possesses obvious advantages in some areas. The first is that China's POEs are endowed with market intuition and flexible mechanisms, and hence they are able to respond quickly to market changes and integrate themselves to operations of large enterprises. Furthermore, China's POEs are closely related to the local economy, and they usually focus on the production of labor-intensive products which can fully exploit local resources. The second is that POEs can promptly satisfy the growing demand for diversification. POEs are apt to find market opportunities and promptly satisfy the diverse demands of customers by developing new products. Therefore, POEs are born with the characteristic of flexibility in some industries and certain products. Third is that POEs have a good foundation for technological innovation. Although China's POEs cannot provide strong financial resources for investment in research and development, they have a high degree of interest for innovation in technology which is highly related to their survival and development. Therefore, they have played a dominant role in China's technological innovation. In addition, many China's POEs have their own specific technical advantage, which is embodied in the fact that they keep their foothold in the squeezed market, monopolized by large enterprises.

Second, China's entry into the WTO has created more chances for the internationalization of POEs. China's entry into the WTO on the one hand marked the milestone of a new era for opening up in which China has transformed the previous strategy of "bring in" to a better coordination in pursuing both the "bring in" and "go global" strategies; on the other hand, China's entry into the WTO has brought a new competitive pattern of so-called "internationalization of the domestic market, the internalization of international competition". Whether consciously or subconsciously, China's POEs have to actively engage in international operations so as to participate in the international competition.

Third, economic globalization has accelerated the process of internationalization of China's POEs. Currently, with the development of science and technology, and the increasing development of the international division of labor and economic globalization, the traditional division pattern that was based on natural resources and products has collapsed, while a worldwide specialization network is forthcoming. Under the circumstances of globalization, enterprises are required to become international enterprises, and this is an irreversible trend that no country or enterprise can avoid. The WTO's first Director-General Renato Ruggiero once said that to stop globalization is just like stopping the earth from rotating. Therefore, China's POEs must face the challenges of economic globalization, and choose to "go global" without hesitation.

Finally, the knowledge economy and network management have provided an extensive space for China's POEs to carry out international business activities. One characteristic of the knowledge economy and information economy is "irrelevance to scale". Namely, large enterprises no longer exploit their advantage of scale to provide goods or services; private enterprises can provide goods or services with the help of information technology. In the information era, those who have advantages in knowledge, information and talents, can eventually conquer the market. In this respect, the gap between large enterprises and private enterprise is not as huge as the gap existing with respect to capital and technology. Microsoft started its business decades ago with only two men and thousands of dollars. However, because of knowledge, information and personnel, it has now developed into a world-famous enterprise. The rapid development of information technology and network management has expanded the marketplace for private enterprises to participate in the global competition.

This book is about how to figure out the determinants and patterns for the internationalization of China's POEs. Based on the existing literature review, we analyze the status quo and the policy evolution of China's POEs' internationalization, and then present a comparative study of the internationalization of various industries. Furthermore, we evaluate the major determinants and pattern of the internationalization of China's POEs by an empirical approach. We present theoretical explanations to the determinants of the internationalization, after we have conducted a comparative analysis of individual cases. Finally, we propose some suggestions for the internationalization of China's POEs.

This book conducts a combination of research methods using both empirical studies and case studies. Data has been collected from questionnaires issued to about forty of China's POEs, and we process the data and conduct an empirical analysis on the determinants and the pattern of internationalization. In addition, we conducted a field investigation of 16 of China's POEs, before we start the empirical analysis. In doing so, we obtained detailed information to support our conclusions.

We collected data mainly from in-depth interviews supplemented with archives to "provide stronger substantiation of constructs and hypotheses" (Eisenhardt, 1989). The archives were obtained from company reports, the press as well as company websites. The time length for an interview was between 1.5 and 2.5 hours.

Interviews were tape-recorded unless the interviewees objected. To ensure the accuracy of the interview data, we not only checked the factual information and opinions provided by the interviewees against the archives, but also asked some important questions in alternative ways to see whether the answers were consistent. As suggested by Eisenhardt (1989), we also made use of multiple investigators in the majority of our interviews to increase the likelihood of capitalizing on any novel insights that may be in the data and enhance the creative potential of the study. All interviews were conducted during June, July and August 2006.

We conducted a comparative case study of 16 China's indigenous, POEs as a multiple-case design which is more compelling and the overall study is more robust than a single-case design (Herriott and Firestone, 1983; Yin, 2003). Multiple cases are considered as multiple experiments. This design follows a "replication" logic, and is different from a "sampling" logic (Yin, 2003, pp. 46–47). Consistent with Eisenhardt (1989), we chose multiple cases within roughly each category in terms of their industry, geographic location, years of business and degree of internationalization (number of foreign countries/regions with which the enterprise has conducted business) to allow findings to be replicable within categories. Thus, if common patterns of internationalization emerge from different types of enterprises within this private section of the Chinese economy, then our findings would be more generalizable.

Following the idea of analysis by induction, we constantly compared the main propositions with the existing theories of enterprise internation-alization, which have been highlighted in this field with our multiple cases to "confirm, challenge or extend the theory" (Yin, 2003, p. 40). Given our research question, we developed six propositions in the preceding section. Our unit of analysis is the China's indigenous, POE that has internationalized. Our approach of linking data to propositions is the idea of "pattern matching" described by Campbell (1975), relating several pieces of information from the same case to some theoretical propositions. We kept on trying to ask related questions based on the existing theories originating from the experience of enterprises in developed countries, and the experiences of developing countries would probably introduce challenges and alternative answers to the existing theories.

Chapter 2

Literature Review of Enterprise Internationalization

2.1 Progress of Enterprise Internationalization

Enterprises internationalization theory is to research the enterprise's international operations. Researchers have proposed different theories of how enterprises extend from a closed environment into an open market. In these theories, many factors are regarded as the determinants of the pattern selection of enterprise internationalization. Anderson (2004) summarized that demand, technical development, industrial structure, domestic competition, strategy, market imperfection or transaction costs, organizational learning competence, networks, market potential, localization advantage, managerial decisions and previous experience of founders/entrepreneurs are relative influential factors. These theories lead to the following questions from an enterprise growth perspective. What causes the enterprise to internationalize? How does a domestic enterprise grow into an international or multinational one? Why can some enterprises maintain their internationalization growth strategy successfully while other enterprises cannot? In empirical research, various factors influencing international development have been applied in case studies and research based on surveys. These factors include organizational learning (Anderson and Skinner, 1999), social or business networks (Chetty and Holm, 2000; Anderson, 2002; Chetty and Wilson, 2003; Coviello, 2006), social capital (Yli-Renko *et al.*, 2002), entrepreneurship (Anderson, 2000), international marketing orientation (Knight and Cavusgil, 2004), resource base (Westhead and Wright, 2001; Dhanaraj and Beamish, 2003), clustering (Maitland *et al.*, 2005) and localized capabilities (Mariotti and Piscitello, 2001). Anderson mentioned that the importance of each factor above-mentioned depended on the degree of internationalization and the maturity of the specific industry.

2.1.1 Theoretical and empirical study of enterprise internationalization

Adam Smith (1776), David Ricardo (1817), Ohlin (1933) proposed the factor requirement for internationalization. They analyzed the important influence of the difference between the technical level and factor endowment on enterprise internationalization in a country.

After World War II, with the development of multinationals, the study of international enterprise operations focused more on FDI. Burenstam Linder (1961) pointed out the demand conditions of foreign direct investment (FDI); technical advance was the determinative factor of FDI (Vernon, 1966); market imperfection was an important reason for FDI (Hymer, 1960; Kinleberger, 1969); Dunning argued the presence of ownership advantage, internalization advantage and location advantage of FDI. This research led to extended FDI theories such as monopolistic advantage theory, product life cycle theory, internalization theory, the eclectic paradigm of international production. Overall, these theories mainly analyze the following three questions: What are the conditions to compete and grow internationally? What motivates the enterprise to invest abroad? What influences investment location selection? Many empirical studies have examined the framework of the above theories and verified their correctness. However, these studies are mostly based on FDI rather than the process of enterprise internationalization.

From the middle of the 1970s, the Uppsala school represented by Johanson and Vahlne suggested that each procedure of internationalization could not be regarded as a separate stage so that the analysis should focus on the whole process. They developed an independent theory to explain the evolutionary process and proposed a stage theory of enterprise internationalization. They pioneered the theoretical study of enterprise internationalization using enterprise behavior theory. The substance of stage theory in enterprise internationalization is enterprise behavior theory and enterprise growth theory. It is a process where the enterprises acquire, recognize and utilize the international market and operational knowledge gradually. They also emphasized "learning by doing". International growth depended on different learning opportunities including imitative learning, cooperation with other enterprises and introduction of professional personnel (Forsgren, 2002). Some researchers also analyzed the failure of multinational Mergers and acquisitions (M&A) repeatedly in the late 1990s from a learning ability perspective. Haleblian and Finkelstein (1999) estimated the relationship between acquisition experience and a firm's performance and suggested it appeared as a "U" shaped relationship in which the more experience the acquirer has, the more likely the firm's performance is likely to improve, especially when the acquisition occurs in the same industry. Very and Schweiger (2001) divided the learning in the M&A process into "target learning process" and "experience accumulation process". It requires more learning because during the stages of the acquisition process the acquirer faces various problems, which increase the M&A risk. The Uppsala internationalization theory was criticized by Turnball (1987), Andersen *et al.* (1993). However, it is considered the most influential theory in this field whose correctness is verified by quite a number of empirical studies in different countries (Bilkey and Tesar, 1977; Cavusgil, 1980; Karafakioglu, 1986).

After Johanson and Vahlne, enterprise internationalization became an independent field with lots of relevant theories and empirical studies emerging. It has become the focus of international business literature, especially in the past decade. There are some relevant theories including entrepreneur strategy-selection theory, international resources-based views, International New Venture (INV) theory, etc.

Root (1982), Reid (1983), and Turnball (1987) suggested that internationalization was a proactive strategy selected by entrepreneurs. Bell (1995) divided the entrepreneurs' behavior in the internationalization process into three aspects: targeting the market segment, following the client and following industrial tendencies. McDougall *et al.* (1994), Oviatt and McDougall (1994), Knight and Cavusgil (1996), Madsen and Servais (1997) and Anderson (2000) studied the survival strategy of enterprise internationalization and mention that it is positively related to the entrepreneurs' previous experience and personal network. Small enterprises with talented market intuition, flexible mechanisms and adaptability can follow leading entrepreneurs to make full use of processing technology, information technology and the global network to internationalize quickly. However, this literature is mostly based on new industries and new high-tech sectors. The theory can explain a tiny part of enterprise internationalization. Many empirical studies have established a link between proactive internationalization and entrepreneurs' attitude, motivation, position, experience and networks (Anderson, 2000, 2002; Oviatt and McDougall, 1994, 1997; Preece *et al.*, 1998; Westhead and Wright, 2001).

The size of the firm, planning and technological depth are the determinant factors and resource base of internationalization (Dhanaray and Beamish, 2003; Wolf and Pett, 2006; Yeoh, 2004). The reputation and network are very important to enterprise internationalization (Kotha *et al.*, 2001). Human and financial capital are key resources of enterprise internationalization (Westhead and Wright, 2001).

INV theory (Oviatt and McDougall, 1994) is an important advance in enterprise internationalization literature, which combines transaction costs, corporate governance structure, entrepreneurship and resources-based views to explain the emergence of new international ventures. The changes in technology, society and economy promote enterprises to enter the international market soon after being established which means they do not necessarily follow the evolutionary pattern. This theory is supposed to be a challenge to the traditional enterprise internationalization stage theory which actually is an important complement to the stage theory, because it implicitly or explicitly proposes some aspects Johanson and Vahlne had ignored.

2.1.2 Research on internationalization of China's enterprises

Low Sui Pheng and Jiang Hongbin (2003) estimated 35 international contractors' performance in China with indexes including international revenue as a proportion of total revenue, international business sales, foreign operation structure, degree of engagement in a specific industry and the whole internationalization index. The results ascertain that 10 Chinese international contractors are real global enterprises. This study also mentions that traditional multinational enterprise theory may not fully explain the development of Chinese international enterprises.

Child John *et al.* (2002) analyzed the concept of psychic distance based on material from a Hong Kong (SAR of China) business study. In three out of five cases, the Hong Kong enterprises located their first overseas investment in Southeast Asia where the psychic distance between Southeast Asian countries and Hong Kong (SAR of China) is relatively close. When business is expanded to Britain, many special factors contributed to explaining why the psychic distance was shortened or bridged.

Tsang and Eric (2001) studied the FDI in China of Chinese family enterprises located in Singapore and investigated their international progress from the aspects of knowledge and learning. The result supports their argument about the characteristics of Chinese family enterprises that influence the procedures of FDI.

It is very hard to track the challenge China has brought to the world market, because those state-owned companies, professional exporters, competing networks and technology giants are employing unpredictable internationalization patterns to engulf the world market (Zeng and Willianmson, 2003). State-owned enterprises, such as Haier Group, Huawei Technologies, Lenovo Group, Sichuan Changhong Group, established global markets with their advantage as domestic leaders. Professional exporters including BYD batteries and CIMC attempt to enter the overseas market with economics of scale. Competing networks such as Guangdong Chenghai toys, Zhejiang Shengzhou ties, Wenzhou lighters, etc., opened up the world market through the agglomeration of lots of closely related small professional companies. Technology giants including Beijing Yuande Biomedical Engineering Co., Ltd., Datang Micro-Electronics, etc., entered new emerging sectors like bioprocessing with the innovation of state-owned research institutions.

Chinese researchers have paid their attention mainly on the analysis framework, internationalization pattern and motivation analysis, case studies, thematic studies, performance analysis, countermeasure analysis, etc.

In terms of the analysis framework, Tong Lu and Zhaoyang Li (2003) proposed an enterprise internationalization pursuit mode — "Time and Internationalization Degree", a two-dimensional mode based on a survey of 112 firms. Some research results in the same period are as follows: Sixin Xie and Qiuzhi Xue (2004) proposed internal and external pattern of internationalization; Minchun Han (2004) proposed internal and external relation model; Feiqiong Chen (2004) proposed new enterprise internationalization pursuit model, i.e. time, internationalization degree and enterprise competitiveness three-dimensional model; Xin Wu (2005) estimated the internal and external internationalization pattern choice; Bin Wu and Tao Zhen (1997) proposed two stages theory; in order to maximize profit, the enterprise improves its comprehensive level and then seizes the profit; Guoming Xian and Rui Yang (1998) proposed technology accumulation and competing strategy theory based on learning FDI; Yaming Ma and Yangui Zhang (2003) created technology diffusion model, i.e. pursuing competitive advantage by FDI; Jianqing Yang (2004) argued industry development goal, i.e. upgrading domestic industry structure by outward FDI; acquiring technology and industry upgrading and establishing a new industry development strategy through counter-gradient investment.

In terms of the internationalization pattern and motivation analysis, Yan Liu (1992) analyzed the motivation from both foreign and domestic aspects; Jian Xie (2005) proposed the Wenzhou private enterprise "Bringing Home" and "Going Global" mode, namely "marketing networks–vertical integration–joint ventures–international supply chain"; Li Lin (2003) analyzed Wenzhou private enterprise "Going Global" mode: Cooperation in exports-overseas professional markets-international chain stores-foreign R&D center-cooperation with giant overseas production bases; Xiayang Wang and Honghui Chen (2002) estimated the resource and network internationalization; Ron Ma (2003) proposes a new mode of OEM and multinational purchasing; Changlin Zhao (2003) studied the internationalization of Nanjing private enterprises; Li Lin (2004) suggested "Bring Out" mode: "Order-competition-key chain-export and investment are mutually driven"; Xiayang Wang and Chuanhao Tian (2005) analyzed network internationalization; Jingyan Fu (2005) analyzed the impact of enterprise clusters on internationalization; Wei Zhao (2006) and Xiao Ren (2006) discussed the general process and influential factors in the literature; Zengtao Wang (2005) used TCL to analyze the influential factors of manufacturing internationalization. Qingbao Liu (2003) and Haiqiong Li (2005) examined the negative factors of private enterprise internationalization; Sanqing Wu (2005) used empirical methods and combines relevant literature on international enterprise operations. He tests the representative Pearl River Delta SMEs and creates measures to estimate the importance of influential factors. With factor analysis, he finds the influential factor structure of SMEs internationalization operations. So far, it is the only domestic study on enterprise internationalization utilizing empirical data and quantitative methods.

Case studies have been conducted on Wanxiang Group; Yong Jiang (2003), Cunhui Nan (2004) and Xuesong Zhang studied the Chint Group. These case studied introduce the background and cause of internationalization in detail and draw some beneficial conclusions.

In terms of thematic study, Chunding Li (2005) discussed network marketing, Lingya Li (2005) argued knowledge management, and Yujie Zheng (2005) proposed brand internationalization, all made studies that emphasized the particular level and detail of enterprises.

In terms of performance analysis, Qinghua Xia (2003) analyzed the relationship between international strategy and performance; Zhongwen Peng and Yonghui Li (2004) studied the benefit of internationalization.

In terms of countermeasure analysis, Huizhong Ren (2002) analyzed the necessity, primary situation, challenges and strategy orientation. The challenges include misunderstandings, financing difficulties, information block, limited innovation, low-level internationalization, inadequate experience and knowledge; Mingqi Xu (2003) analyzed the challenge and countermeasures; Youzhen Zhao (2003), Ping Zhao (2005), Yuchun Xiao (2005), Yuliang Zhu (2005) studied the situation, problems and countermeasures.

2.1.3 Conclusion

The research at home and abroad provides a rich literature with high reference value. Foreign academic circle contributes greatly to the influential factors of enterprise internationalization in theory and verifies them by empirical study. Domestic study is still discussing the factors qualitatively, while lacking profound and rigorous theoretical deduction. It is lacking in model construction and data analysis with econometric instruments and subsequent accurate quantitative examination. The research gap is reflected in the two following aspects:

First, existing theories are not compared and tested systematically with data from China.

Process Theory of Internationalization (PTI) and Internationalization New Venture (INV) theory are the most typical theories. Our scrutiny shows that most influential factors of enterprise internationalization are covered by PTI and INV. When researchers review or develop both theories, they all estimate or compare the impact of those factors (Andersen, 1993; Forsgren, 2002; Chetty and Campbell-Hunt, 2004; Autio, 2005; Zahra, 2005; Zahra *et al.*, 2005; Coviello, 2006). However, these estimates and comparisons are not supported by data from China. Table 2.1 estimates and compares the two most typical enterprise internationalization theories with data from China.

Second, representative theory framework is not proposed in combination with the development of the internationalization of Chinese enterprises.

The internationalization of Chinese enterprises is developing and might be immature. The government plays an important role in the internationalization process which leads the patterns to be complicated and multi-featured. In this context, can we synthesize the Western pattern to illustrate the Chinese pattern or can we develop a new theory to explain this?

In short, there has been lots of literature about enterprise internationalization in developed countries that were examined based on different theories. However, there has been little foreign study on the internationalization of Chinese enterprises, though domestically lots of papers have been published on the topic. Unfortunately, domestic study mainly lacks systematicity and depth, needing further investigation. The special experience of China's privately-owned enterprises (POEs) provide an excellent opportunity for the development of the theory and an empirical test. Are the influential factors of internalization in foreign research results also applicable to POEs? Can foreign relatively mature theories explain the internationalization process of Chinese enterprises, especially China's POEs? How to propose a framework different from traditional theories in combination with the features of Chinese POEs? This book will explore and attempt to answer these important questions.

Table 2.1. Estimation and comparison of enterprise internationalization theories.

Theoretical dimension	PTI	INV
Underlying theories	Behavior theory, theory of the growth of the firm	Entrepreneurship, resource-based view of the firm, governance theories
Generation of normative implications	Moderate	Moderate
Scope	Internationalization process	Initiation of internationalization — early internationalization process
Internationalization strategic posture	Reactive, reacting to unsolicited export orders	Proactive, opportunity-seeking
Nature of opportunity	Market demand	Supply push
Firm's objective	Survival, long-term profitability	Value creation, growth
Resource access and control	Internalization, internal development	Selective ownership, mobilized through networks
Access to foreign market information	Constrained information channels, market information accumulates through market commitment	Market information easily accessible through various channels
Fungibility of foreign market assets	Foreign market investments tend to be asset specific, not easily reallocated	Resource fungibility assumed for resources committed to foreign market activities
Speed of foreign market commitments	Commitment decisions are slow because of the need to integrate experiential market knowledge with firm knowledge	Mobile knowledge resources can be rapidly combined with fixed assets in target markets
Value creation logic	(Implicit) Value-creating assets are concentrated in the domestic country	Value creation based on cross-border resource combinations
Nature of path dependency	Each market entry creates a market-specific path dependency for growth	Early internationalization instills a path dependency for international growth
Degree of environmental dynamism	Stable, moderate dynamism	(Predominantly) Dynamic high-technology sectors

(To be Continued)

Table 2.1. (*Continued*)

Theoretical dimension	PTI	INV
Relationship between individual and firm's knowledge	Firm's experience supersedes individual experience	Individual experience and entrepreneurial vision drive international commitment decisions
Locus of decision making	Firm's decision-making system	Entrepreneur(s)
Resource endowment at the time of internationalization	Firm is a going concern whose resources and reservoir of experiential knowledge have been shaped by domestic experience (domestic imprinting)	Firm's experiential knowledge is co-created with foreign market experience (international imprinting)
Criteria for choosing foreign markets for entry	Manageability: Minimize difference between existing scope of activity and the new market entry	Opportunity: Maximize the size of market potential by selecting the market that offers the greatest growth potential
Nature of opportunity window	Long, durable	Short, transient
Nature of competition	Against local players in the foreign market	Against global players
Integration of country's markets	Country's markets distinct, separated by high barriers to entry	Significant international integration between country's markets
Importance of management's pre-firm experience	Does not matter because firm's collective experience supersedes individual experience	Crucial factor for early and rapid internationalization
Size of internationalization steps	Small	Mostly large
Effect of rapid market change	Slows down internationalization because of rapid obsolescence of firm's knowledge	Speeds up internationalization because of the need to move fast to seize opportunity
Selection of entry modes	Sequential progression from low-control modes to high-control modes	No predetermined sequence, but firms tend to prefer alternative governance mechanisms, such as alliances

(To be Continued)

Table 2.1. (*Continued*)

Theoretical dimension	PTI	INV
Importance of resource size	Large resources are important to accommodate resource-consuming internationalization moves	The quality of resources, sustainable resource distinctiveness in particular, is more important than the size of initial resource allocation
International dispersion of Value-creating resources	Value-creating resources concentrated in the domestic base	Value-creating resources dispersed across national borders
Implication for growth	(Implicit) Growth causes the firm to internationalize	Internationalization is necessary for growth
Implication for survival	(Implicit) Late internationalizers are more likely to survive internationalization moves than early internationalizers	In internationally integrated markets, internationalization may constitute a necessary condition for survival

Source: Autio (2005).

2.2 Schools of Enterprise Internationalization

Enterprise internationalization, an understanding and summary of the enterprise internationalization process, is one of the important issues for international enterprise study. It answers these basic questions: First, what is an enterprise internationalization process? Is it gradual or quick? Is it evolutionary or revolutionary? Second, what determines the internationalization pattern selection? Historically, most enterprises are founded and developed in the domestic market. But how could a domestic enterprise become an international or multinational one? Why can some enterprises maintain their internationalization growth strategy successfully and other enterprises not achieve their expected goals? Is it a linear or nonlinear relationship between the degree of internationalization of an enterprise and the performance? Enterprise internationalization theories attempt to answer these questions.

2.2.1   By international trade approach

In general, the international operation of an enterprise starts from international trade, which was also the earliest form historically. Adam Smith (1776), David Ricardo (1817), Hechscher and Ohlin (1891) proposed the requirements of internationalization early. They analyzed the important impact of the difference in the technology level and factor endowments on enterprise internationalization in a country from an international trade perspective.

In *The Wealth of Nations*, Smith (1776) suggested the theory of absolute advantage based on the regional division of labor. The comparative advantage of products comes from the relative difference of labor productivity between different products (Ricardo, 1817). The products with relatively high labor productivity have a comparative advantage while those with relatively low labor productivity have comparative disadvantages. Each country should produce and export its comparative advantage products while importing its comparative disadvantage products. It would make both parties benefit from comparative advantage. Ohlin (1933) proposed the Factor Endowments Theory on the basis of two former economists. It elaborated on the comparative cost from the perspective of production factors (land, labor and capital) and also explained the difference in factor cost along with the proportional difference between countries in land, labor, and capital reserves.

With the development of international trade practice, the effectiveness of classical trade theory is constantly challenged by reality. First, it assumes that production factors cannot flow freely between nations. However, one of the important features of international operation is the international flow of production factors. So the hypothesis can hardly hold. Second, it assumes that each trader can obtain complete information about international trade. It does not conform to incomplete information in reality. Third, classical trade theories do not assume that technology, production tips, management, knowledge and market experience are very important production factors which can become a comparative advantage.

2.2.2   By FDI approach

After World War II, with the development of multinational enterprises, the study of international enterprise operation focuses more on FDI. Burenstam

Linder (1961) pointed out the demand conditions of FDI. Technological advance is the determinant factor of FDI (Vernon, 1966). Market imperfection is an important reason for FDI (Hymer, 1960; Kindleberger, 1969); Dunning argued the ownership advantage, internalization advantage and location advantage of FDI. These studies led to multinational enterprise's FDI theories such as monopolistic advantage theory, product life cycle theory, transaction cost and internalization theory, the eclectic theory of international production, etc.

In monopolistic advantage theory proposed by Hymer and Kindleberger, the market is imperfect, which makes an enterprise have a monopolistic advantage such as product diversity, economies of scale, market barriers and so on. Its imperfectness leads the multinationals to have a monopolistic advantage. Thus the multinationals obtain competitive advantage against local firms from which they can benefit more than local enterprises through FDI. Taking advantage of imperfect competition is the fundamental motivation of the FDI of multinationals. Hymer summarized two requirements of FDI: First, monopolistic advantage, which could offset the disadvantage when competing with the local enterprise; second, the existence of an imperfect market, which leads it to obtain and maintain the advantage. Hymer's tutor, Kindleberger, listed four types of market imperfectness: (1) Product market imperfectness including product diversity, trade mark and price cartel, etc.; (2) Factor market imperfectness including the advantage of proprietary technology and managerial experience and the diversity of the capital market, etc.; (3) The imperfect competition in economies of scale and external economies; the enterprise with economies of scale can reduce costs and improve competitiveness; (4) Market distortion caused by policies, tariffs, interest rates, exchange rates, can cause market imperfectness. Their study broke the traditional assumption that the market was perfect when studying international capital flow. They indicate that the monopolistic advantage is the determinant factor of its FDI. But this theory cannot explain FDI in developing countries where enterprises take no monopolistic advantage.

The product life cycle theory developed by Vernon (1966) defined the product life cycle as innovation, maturity, and standardization in three stages. During the stage of innovation, the developed industrialized countries first invent and produce new products introduced in the domestic market. Then they are exported to developing countries and gradually capture a share in the international market. At the stage of maturity, the importer can produce the congeneric product as the technology spreads worldwide. Meanwhile there is also a lot of transnational investment and technology output. During the stage of standardization, the cost decreases dramatically in foreign countries and its original country of invention may import the product. The developed countries gradually give up this product and develop a new one to start a new cycle of product life. The product life cycle theory shows that multinational direct investment activity is a necessary step within the theory. This theory studies the international investment activity of multinationals from a dynamic perspective in combination with the monopolistic advantage of the enterprise, the marketing of the product life cycle and location factor. It also successfully explains the rapid development of FDI in developed countries in the East after World War II.

In 1976, the British scholars Buckley and Casson brought transaction cost theory to the study of multinationals and developed internalization theory systematically. The enterprise faces all kinds of market impediments in the operation. The transactions take place among subsidiaries instead of in the open market to overcome external market impediments or to offset market failure. The multinationals appear when it becomes an internalized market and the process transcends borders. External market failure, trading difficulty for intermediate products and high external market transaction costs lead to a form of market internalization. The enterprise becomes a multinational when its process transcends the borders. From this point, the process of market internalization of a multinational is its developing FDI process and the motivation that urges it to develop. This theory, which is a good contribution, brings the theory of market transaction internalization into international direct investment study and first indicates the motivation of international direct investment from an organization's development perspectives. The theory emphasizes the significance of the protection of intellectual property in enterprise competition which brings the theoretical analysis closer to the international direct investment of multinationals in reality. To some extent, it explains all kinds of FDI after World War II. However, the internalization theory only studies the motivation and basis of international direct investment of multinationals in its subjective aspects, without sufficient consideration of changes in the international economic environment, which means it is relatively one-sided and limited.

An eclectic theory of international production developed by Dunning, a British expert on research of multinational company suggested that an enterprise could develop its FDI with ownership advantage, internalization advantage and location advantage. Ownership advantage refers to an enterprise that has, or can obtain, factor endowments of production, productive technology, creativity, patents, trademarks, management skills, etc., which enterprises in other countries can hardly obtain. Internalization advantage means the capacity to keep ownership advantage within and benefit from it to avoid the impact of an imperfect market. Location advantage means factor endowments in the home country, an investment environment and profitability with the combinations of ownership advantage. Dunning mentioned that ownership advantage and internalization advantage were just two necessary requirements of FDI while location advantage was the sufficient condition. The selection between technology transfer, exports and FDI is based on the different combinations of two advantages. The eclectic theory of international production explains the subjective conditions of international FDI of multinationals using multivariable analysis. However, the condition underlining the possibility for the enterprise to invest aboard with two simultaneous advantages is too deterministic. Thus, it cannot explain the rapid development of FDI in developing countries without having two simultaneous advantages, especially direct investment toward the developed countries.

In sum, these international investment theories mainly analyze the following three questions: What are the conditions of engaging in international competition and achieving growth in their process towards internationalization? What motivates the enterprise to invest abroad? What is the influential factor in investment location selection? Many empirical studies examine the framework of the above theories and have proved their correctness.

2.2.3   Theories concerning internationalization of developing countries

Among enterprise internationalization theories especially for developing countries, the theory of small-scale technology (Wells, 1983) and state of localized technological capacities (Lall, 1993) are excellent. The foundation of these theories is still the classical comparative advantage theory and modern comparative advantage theory. They suggested that comparative advantage and comparative benefits were ubiquitous. Even in developing countries there might be some advantages for foreign investment.

The theory of small-scale technology suggests that the competitive advantage of multinationals in developing countries comes from low cost, which is closely related to the market characteristics in their home countries. First, small-scale technology services small-scale markets. A common characteristic of manufactured goods in low-income countries is small demand. Thus, large-scale technology cannot obtain economies of scale because of the small demand. Many developing countries acquire comparative advantage through developing technology for small-scale markets. The characteristic of this small-scale technology suitable for small-scale production is always labor-intensive with lots of flexibility. Second, developing countries have a greater advantage in national products. Distinctive national culture reflects another feature of foreign investment of developing countries. The primary reason for these overseas investments is to meet immigrant groups' demands. When the amount is really large, this type of investment has a greater advantage than others. One example is that the overseas Chinese community's food requirements have driven partial overseas investment in East Asia, Southeast Asian countries and regions. Third, high quality, inexpensive marketing strategy: Multinationals in developing countries capture market shares through high-quality, inexpensive goods. Multinationals in developed countries always spend much on advertising to set an image and create a brand effect while their counterparts in developing countries take a low value product marketing strategy with less advertising.

The state of localized technological capacities suggests that the formation of technology in developing countries contains internal enterprise innovation activities that become its specific advantage. The following conditions make them form and develop their own specific advantage: First, the technical knowledge gained in developing countries is related to its factor price and quality which are different from those in developed countries. For instance, the technology owned by developing countries always has the characteristics of intensive labor and less capital i.e. labor-intensive techniques. Second, the goods produced by developing countries suitable for their own economy and demand are also suitable for similar income-level countries. So enterprises in developing countries could form a specific advantage based on FDI at a low level. This advantage can drive them to develop FDI toward other developing countries. Meanwhile, innovation in mature technology can also prompt them to invest in developed countries. This specific advantage strengthens under the influence of the two following factors: One is that enterprises in developing countries can get cheap and skilled labor from the home country; the other is that enterprises can be family firms or privately-owned firms. This ownership structure brings extra advantages in management. This theory focuses on the micro level to prove the possibility of competing and operating with competitive advantage internationally for enterprises in developing countries.

2.2.4 By a resource-based view

In the middle of the 1970s, a group of northern European researchers (Carlson, 1975; Forsgren and Johanson, 1995; Johanson and Wiedersheim-Paul, 1975; Johanson and Vahlne, 1977) developed the stage theory of enterprise internationalization based on enterprise behavior theory called the Uppsala Internationalization Model. This model has two propositions: (1) The enterprise internationalization process should be a developing process; (2) This process is a sequential pattern in which enterprises gradually increase incremental commitment in the foreign market. Johanson and Vahlne examined four typical Swedish engineering enterprises for further case study. When comparing the process of their overseas operations, they found that these enterprises had strikingly similar steps in overseas operation strategy, i.e. the initial link with foreigners began from casual and sporadic exports. With the increase in export activities, the parent firm controlled more foreign market information and channels. Foreign markets become stable with the help of foreign agents. It is necessary for the parent firm to establish subsidiaries with the increasing demand and overseas business. In the end, the parent company starts to invest abroad and establish an overseas manufacturing base under mature market conditions. The enterprise internationalization should go through four sequential phases: (1) no regular export activity; (2) selling via an agent;

(3) establishment of a sales subsidiary; and (4) establishment of a production subsidiary.

These four phases form a continuous and evolutionary process that shows the degree of engagement in overseas market and internationalization of a firm respectively. Two aspects reflect the evolution: First, the sequence of geographical expansion of a market, from a local market, regional market, national market, close overseas market to a global market. Second, the evolution pattern of multinational operations. The most common pattern is from domestic operation, indirect exports via a broker, direct export, and overseas sales division to overseas production. Foreign enterprise operation from the first phase to the fourth phase illustrated the increase in resource commitments and the change of capacity in controlling overseas markets information channels. Obviously, in the phase of occasional exports, the enterprise provides few resources to the export market and the control of market information is scattered and irregular. In the phase of exporting via an agent, the enterprise has a fixed overseas market information channel and in the meantime it has to commit some resources. It is necessary to increase the variety and amount of resources when it starts to establish an overseas sales subsidiary. At the same time, it can directly obtain market information and acquire knowledge and experience. After establishing a production base, the enterprise ultimately becomes more involved in overseas markets.

The Nordic school explained the evolutionary feature of enterprise internationalization using market knowledge. Market knowledge consists of two aspects. One is general enterprise operation and technology, i.e. objective knowledge from education and books; the other is knowledge and experience of a specific market, called experience knowledge only from experiential practice. The amount of market knowledge of decision-makers directly affects the understanding of opportunities and risks in foreign markets and then affects the operational decision. When the operators lack market information, their risk-averse nature makes them minimize the commitment to an overseas market. The consequential decision proves that after a period of overseas operations, the entrepreneurs obtain and accumulate market knowledge and experience. In return, the overseas operation increases the decision-maker's market knowledge that becomes a new base for acquiring and exploiting opportunities. It encourages the enterprise to commit more resources to overseas markets.

The Nordic researchers used psychic distance to analyze the sequence of selecting overseas markets. The psychic distance is defined as the sum of factors preventing the flow of information from and to the market. Examples are differences in language, education, business practices, culture, and industrial development. When faced with different foreign markets, the sequence is from close to far in psychic distance. For example, Swedish companies always target neighboring countries such as Denmark, Norway and Finland. The reason is that it is more likely one can operate successfully in a relatively familiar environment than in a completely new one. In short, the Nordic school believes that the operation of multinationals observes two principles: Firstly, when faced with different overseas markets they select some countries whose market conditions and cultural background are close to the home country; namely, the overseas operation of multinationals has its cultural recognition. Secondly, in a specific market the enterprise always follows the evolutionary route from export via an agent to direct investment.

The overseas operation of multinationals should go through the above evolutionary process (Johanson *et al.*). But in some cases, it will skip some phases. First, it is possible to skip the phase of overseas operation when overseas investment is negligible compared to the total assets; second, under similar conditions an enterprise can skip some phases in order to utilize the experience acquired in other markets.

The stage theory of internationalization sparked a lot of attention. Many empirical studies have been done and opinions vary about the results. Some research proved that the operation of some medium and small-scale export enterprises show distinct stages. Some studies such as the export behavior of Swedish firms (Carlson, 1975), the export behavior of medium and small-scale firms in Wisconsin (Bilkey and Tesar, 1977), the export strategy of Japanese firms (Johanson and Nonaka, 1983) etc., supported the stage theory empirically. Others (Benito and Gripsrud, 1992; Bonaceorsi and Dalli, 1992; Ali and Camp, 1993) examined the theory and reached an identical conclusion: This theory was mainly applied to the internationalization behavior of medium and small firms, while in the case of large diversified enterprises the stage feature of internationalization was not significant.

Other test results illustrate that this theory can explain the international operation of "market-chase" multinationals very well. However, it is not significant to explore enterprises with other motivations such as resource-acquisition, tech-improvement, international-strategy, etc. The theory suggests that there is a linear relationship between the market knowledge of firms (or entrepreneurs) and the degree of involvement in overseas markets. But some researchers also challenge it. The study of US service firms shows that the relationship between market knowledge and market involvement appears U-shaped (Erramilli, 1991). Entrepreneurs always overestimate the risk in overseas markets when they lack experience of international operations so that the investment in overseas markets is minimal. However, when they acquire some experience, they could underestimate the difficulties in investing carefully. Finally, when entrepreneurs acquire sufficient international market experience they are able to overcome all kinds of difficulties and invest more abroad.

Some specific points of the stage theory of enterprise internationalization have drawn our attention. First, it emphasizes the dialectical relationship between knowledge and experience of the operators and their overseas operations. It reveals a simple truth that it will limit the international operation if a firm's decision-maker lacks overseas market knowledge and understanding. However, an important method of knowing the overseas market is to acquire practical experience in the overseas market. It takes international operation as a dynamic learning and feedback process. This learning process and operation complement each other. It is more important to understand the information exactly, knowing the market operation and grasping the opportunity, not just accumulating information. The more practical the experience, the quicker the entrepreneurs gain market knowledge, and the more likely they are to make correct judgments about investment and other larger decisions. Second, it emphasizes the direct impact of cultural differences on international operations. Especially for those small and medium-sized enterprises (SMEs) lacking experience in the international market, it is easier to succeed if the language, cultural background and level of economic development of the market are close. And it is essential to expand the scope for business in overseas markets and strengthen the confidence and capacity in international competition. Of course, the psychic distance will narrow with time. Third, this theory implies that trade might be a minimum risk with maximum success when firms consider expanding into the international market.

However, the explanation of the stage theory of internationalization is limited as a general theory. First of all, it is only suitable for analyzing the export process of manufacturing industry enterprises. Export and production cannot explain the multinational investment of service industries like finance, security, etc. Second, the exposition is too simple and partial even in the analysis of the multinational operation of the manufacturing industry. The international operation of enterprises depends on the operator's understanding of overseas markets that is a necessary condition. Whether or not an enterprise can succeed to compete internationally is the result of internal and external factors. Successful multinationals must satisfy the following requirements: The first is ownership advantage. This comes from owning and employing specific assets such as capital, technology, management, organization, human capital, and information. Second, this can lower costs and boost the profit from overseas investment through shifting assets. Third, the investment environment (infrastructure, policy and legal system, resource endowment, market size and its structure) can meet the needs of strategic development. So, international operation is a complicated decision-making process not simply controlled by individual factors.

Finally, we discuss the mode of foreign market entry. Exporting is a relatively safe mode of operation from the perspective of reducing investment risk. But for some enterprises, overseas operations are determined by international investment motivation. There are four motivations roughly including recourses investment, market-oriented investment, profit investment and strategic development-oriented investment. Obviously, the sequence of overseas market entry is different according to different motivations. Many enterprises start their internationalization by exporting. In addition, the mode of overseas market entry depends not only on their own strategy but also the operational environment in the host country. Direct investment is an effective mode of operation between high trade barriers.

2.2.5 Theories of enterprise export behavior

As a result of "stage theory", many researchers studied the exports and direct investment of enterprises based on that idea and proved that the mode of international market entry is a continuous process.

Table 2.2.   Export behavior comparisons.

Stage of export development	Johanson and Wiedersheim-Paul (1975)	Bilkey and Tesar (1977)	Cavusgil (1980)	Czinkota (1982)
Stage 1	No regular export activities	No interest in exporting	Domestic marketing	No interest in exporting
Stage 2	Export via independent agent	Accept overseas orders, but do not exploit foreign market actively	Former export stage: Collect information and estimate potential export market	Have interest in exporting
Stage 3	Sales subsidiary	Exploit foreign export market actively	Acquire export experience: Export goods to neighboring countries	Exploit export market
Stage 4	Production/ manufacturing abroad	Export goods to neighboring countries	Export actively: Export directly more goods to other countries	Acquire export experience
Stage 5	—	Experienced exporter	Various direct investment	Small experienced exporter
Stage 6	—	Exploit other foreign export markets actively	—	Large experienced exporter

Source: Paliwoda (1995).

Table 2.2 lists four kinds of export firm behavior proposed by six researchers. They differ in the division of stages but have the same approach to evolutionary development in multinational operations, namely they all mainly analyze the enterprises' behavior at each stage. This actually contains the assumption that the first step of a manufacturing enterprise's multinational operation is exporting, and then other forms of direct investment follow.

University of Michigan Professor Cavusgil (1980, 1982) divided the process of enterprise internationalization into five stages: (1) domestic marketing stage, mainly engaging in domestic production and marketing;

(2) former export stage, beginning to have interest in international markets, consciously collecting information and conducting an international market survey, irregular exports; (3) involved experimental stage, mainly engaging in indirect exports and beginning small international marketing; (4) active commitment stage, exporting goods to other countries directly; (5) international strategy stage, setting strategic planning based on the global market.

A study (Bilkey and Tesar, 1977) based on more than 400 Wisconsin SMEs in the manufacturing industry showed that they assembled significantly at the export stage.

The first stage: No interest in exporting, but occasionally receiving foreign orders;

The second stage: Foreign orders increase gradually, but no active exploitation of foreign market;

The third stage: Exploit foreign export market actively;

The fourth stage: Export goods to neighboring countries based on existing experience;

The fifth stage: Acquire export experience, begin to expand the export geography and adapt exports according to the change in exchange rate and tariffs;

The sixth stage: Expand exports into the global market.

The common link between the theory of export behavior and the stage theory is that the process of enterprise internationalization is continuous and evolutionary, and information acquisition, learning from experience and management are important factors in multinational operations. The theory of export behavior results from the statistics of lots of enterprises, rather than purely logical deduction. Thus, it is closer to reality and more practical. But the theory of export behavior is just a descriptive analysis about enterprise export stages which cannot absolutely explain the whole process of multinational operations.

2.2.6 Driving theory of multinational operations

According to the "Field Theory", enterprise management is a "Force Field". It is the result of the interaction of all kinds of "push factors" and "resistance factors" inside and outside the enterprises which affect the development of enterprises. There are resistance factors such as fear of risks, learning inertia, limitation of learning ability, etc., which hinder the development of multinational operations; there are also push factors such as fierce competition urging the enterprise to continuously improve its strength, the accumulation of experience strengthening the enterprise's confidence in OFDI, etc.

The enterprise situation at any time can be considered as a balance between the push factors and resistance factors. The development comes from the increase in push factors or the decrease in resistance factors. There are several theories driving the operation of internationalization, corresponding to the decrease in resistance factors:

- The first is order-driven theory. Lots of surveys show that the initial export is driven by the overseas customers' initial orders that cause the enterprise to export directly. These orders provide firms that never exported before with key market information. It also reduces the risk attached to the initial exports and becomes the impetus for international marketing.
- The second is customer-driven theory. There are behavioral features in the overseas operation. Some overseas service operations like banking, insurance, advertising, etc. are usually driven by customers who need the relevant service after entering the international market. So the enterprises that provide a service before entering the international market are following the customer's demands, naturally. This mode drastically reduces the uncertainty of marketing abroad, decreases the market exploitation costs and provides a good platform to expand international marketing. Thus, it has minimum risk. For instance, in the car accessories industry, manufacturers usually follow the main manufacturers in entering the international market.

The process of internationalization of Pennsylvania's Lorenz, which produces automotive lighting, is a typical customer-driven example. In 1993, it was just a small local company employing 350 people with less than USD50 million in annual sales. In September of 1994, it became a multinational and invested USD8 million to establish a subsidiary in Hungary. It built up its base outside Budapest and setup a real estate company with the local government. It also utilized the military base left by the Soviet Union. In 2001, there were 150 employers in the Hungarian subsidiary with more than USD10 million sales.

　　Its relatively less risky international operation pattern enabled it to develop from a domestic company to a multinational one. In the USA Lorenz's main customer is Ford. With the reform and opening up of Eastern Europe, Ford decided to setup factories in Hungary to supply the Eastern European market. In order to ensure quality, Ford invited its US supplier to exploit the market. For some small companies like Lorenz, following a world famous company provided a shortcut to international operations. Their sales were ensured in Hungary. It accepted Ford's supply contract for years which reduced the risk of market uncertainty and marketing costs. It could use Ford's resources to quickly develop its awareness, reputation, credit capacity, negotiating position, etc. So, its successful foreign investment in Hungary was directly related to using Ford's resources and business connections.

- The third is competition-driven theory. In an oligarchical industry, some competitive enterprises will soon follow the first one to enter the international market. In fierce market competition, the newcomer avoids being eliminated. It will not allow another enterprise to monopolize the overseas market. The main enterprises in the industry will compete in any market. The typical examples are McDonald's and Kentucky Fried Chicken, Coca-Cola and Pepsi Cola, who compete all around the world.

　　The competition-driven theory explains an enterprise's international operations from the motivation of the international market, which partially clarifies the enterprise's international marketing in practice. However, according to this theory, international marketing is a reaction to external stimuli and thus analysis of the internal motivation is neglected. It cannot absolutely explain the motivation of all international marketing.

2.2.7　Strategic management theory

The process of enterprise strategic management includes confirming basic tasks, assessing external environments and internal situations, goal setting, planning, implementation, procedure-control. Its main functions are strategy setting, strategy-implementation, appraisal and operational management.

　　Generally, strategic management starts by confirming the basic task of an enterprise that mainly answers two questions: What is the enterprise's business? Why does the enterprise exist? The enterprise can determine the direction of its advance by answering these two questions. The internal environment analysis aims at assessing the advantages and weaknesses of its finances and human resources. Assessing the financial situation helps a multinational company to evaluate the enterprise's capacity for expansion and investment and determines where to cut costs and strip assets. Internal and external analysis helps to confirm both short- and long-term goals. Its strategic planning is divided into several major parts and each branch and department has its own goal and responsibility. The implementation process begins after that. The enterprise will regularly evaluate the progress of the strategic implementation and amend the original plan. A multinational finding some products are not profitable must stop the production or supply, and develop new products to meet the new emerging demands.

Strategic planning is a process of evaluating the environment and inner advantage, setting long-term and short-term goals, implementing the plan to achieve the goals sequentially. The strategic management model of enterprise internationalization suggests that multinationals rely highly on the strategic planning process because of its general direction and specific guidance for operations. It is very difficult for multinationals to plan, implement and appraise without strategic planning. The multinationals have different strategic predispositions in operation that helps to explain some specific decisions.

Chandler (1962) proposed two famous arguments: Structure Follows Strategy and Structure Determines Strategy. Following that, famous managerialists (Strandskov, 1985; Axinn, 1988; Melin, 1992; Mintzberg, 1994; Welch and Welch, 1996) proposed the theory of strategic management of enterprise internationalization, combining enterprise strategic management theory and enterprise international operation strategy. It suggests that multinationals have different strategic predispositions in operation such as ethnocentric, polycentric, regiocentric and geocentric.

The multinationals with an ethnocentric predisposition formulate and implement strategic planning according to the parent company's values and interests. Profitability is the primary objective. The multinationals with this predisposition are operated abroad in the same way as they are domestically, most of which sell the same products at home and abroad.

The multinationals with a polycentric predisposition formulate their strategic planning to meet the host country's demands. The overall planning will reflect each local demand when in a different cultural situation. They need to make their basic task acceptable to the host country's culture. The goals of affiliated companies are determined by themselves according to local demand and the profit is reinvested in the host country for expansion and development.

The multinationals with a regiocentric predisposition value both profit and acceptance by the public, appearing as a combination of ethnocentricity and multicentricity whose strategy can meet the local and regional demands simultaneously. For instance, a company doing business in the European Union is of concern to all the member countries.

The multinationals with a geocentric predisposition view their operation from a globalization perspective. The largest multinationals adhering strictly to this predisposition produce global products with local characteristics and employ the best available managers no matter where they come from. Just as its name implies, a multinational will be globalized. However, it might be polycentric or regiocentric if its scale is small or the operation is limited to a specific culture and region.

In sum, the strategic predisposition can greatly affect its process of formulating the planning process, and then affect the enterprise internationalization strategy and market entry mode. Some multinationals care more about profit and growth than setting up a comprehensive strategy that can be to their own advantage. Some pay more attention to a product produced on a large-scale that can compete in terms of price throughout the whole country or region instead of that only suitable to a specific local demand. Others sell products to countries with a similar culture so that they can use the same marketing policy in the whole region. These policies and predispositions greatly affect the enterprise's strategy.

2.2.8   Resource-based views of enterprise internationalization

The resource-based view derives from *The Theory of the Growth of the Firm* (Penrose, 1959). Penrose proposed the basis view that the growth of the firm is a collection of resources. The expansion of the firm depends on the interaction between internal resources and the external environment.

Table 2.3. Multinationals' strategic predisposition in operation.

Type	Ethnocentric	Polycentric	Regiocentric	Geocentric
Basic task	Profit	Acceptance by the public	Profit and acceptance by the public	Profit and acceptance by the public
Management mode	From top down	From top down (each region sets goals respectively)	Region and its affiliated coordinate	Coordinate at each level
Organization structure	Product-divided layer	Region-divided layer and autonomy of nation-divided	Organize region and product with matrix	Organization network
Strategy	Globalization	Country-divided responsibility	Regional integration and country-divided responsibility	Globalization and country-divided responsibility
Culture	Home country	Host country	Region	Global
Technology	Mass production	Volume production	Flexible production	Flexible production
Marketing strategy	Product development depends on domestic demand	Local product development based on local demand	Local standardization rather than interlocal	Global product with local features
Profit strategy	Repatriated to home country	Left in the host country	Distributed in region	Redistributed globally
Human resources	Controlled by a native of home country	Locals in charge of important positions	Train regional managers and nominate them in charge of important position	Seek and train best personnel globally and nominate them in charge of important positions worldwide

It emphasizes the effect of productive resources, especially the management. The quality and availability of internal resources limit the direction and level of expansion. However, Penrose mentioned that if the enterprise grows according to expansion planning which is limited by the scale of the veteran management team, after the completion and implementation of the planning, the management should be released and used for the next step. Enterprises always think that there are lower costs and less risk to concentrate on existing products. But they might expand into a new business to pursue growth (Penrose, 1959). The direction of the growth of the firm is affected by the external environment and internal resources that are also used to pursue expanding opportunities, and especially by the quality of the management.

If the enterprise cannot imitate or copy the source of the special ability of an ascending enterprise, the difference in the efficiency of each enterprise will continue (Lippman and Rumelt, 1982). Their core view is that the competitive advantage of enterprises means special and inimitable resources. It first introduced enterprise strategy as a resource that can bring a Ricardian Rent to economic analysis. *A Resource-Based View of the Firm* published in US Strategy Management (Wernerfelt, 1984) signaled the origin of the theory of this approach. It suggested that the enterprise's internal environment that determined the market advantage was more significant than the external one. The organizational competence, resources and knowledge inside enterprise explain how enterprises acquire excess earnings and maintain competitive advantage. Later, Barney (1991) contributed to the resource-based view. "The Core Competence of the Corporation" (Prahalad and Hamel, 1990) published in *Harvard Business Review* combined the resource-based view and enterprise practice that gave this approach a lot of attention.

Strategic management literature often refers to the resource-based view and takes the theory of the growth of the firm as its foundation. However, the resource-based view does not draw the same attention in the international business domain despite the fact that it has been spread in recent studies. It is still in its infancy. The impact of the resource-based view is reflected in many fields, especially in multinational management, strategic alliances, market entry and international entrepreneurship (Peng, 2001).

Foreign Investment and the Growth of the Firm (Penrose, 1956) applied the resource-based view to multinationals. It also emphasized domestic expansion, as did the resource-based view. With few exceptions, an overseas subsidiary is a dependent enterprise: "Once the overseas subsidiary is established, it has its own life and its growth depends on the internal resources and opportunities the new environment provides." In Penrose's argument, the link between parent company and overseas subsidiary is just ex post thinking: "Don't forget that the parent firm committed management and technology resources to ensure that the overseas opportunities exist and can be taken up." The operation of an overseas subsidiary is dependent and it is more suitable for it to be regarded as a dependent enterprise once it has been established apart from some important exceptions. The most important exception is finance. The necessary management resources for expansion existed inside the overseas subsidiary (Penrose).

This raises a question as to what advantage an enterprise can get from creating and maintaining a multinational? As to Penrose's argument, the parent enterprise and its overseas subsidiary are regarded as one enterprise after the establishment of the subsidiary. How is this structure sustained? Obviously the internal capital market cannot explain it because domestic expansion can also create the same advantage. Why does it assume an overseas advantage? Her analysis of multinationals is implausible.

In a resource-based perspective Wolf (1977) first studied multinationals based on Penrose's result. He suggested that the growth of the firm had many directions including domestic specialization, domestic industry diversification and foreign geographic diversity. As Penrose mentioned, the promoting factors of growth are from both internal and external environment. Some factors may promote the enterprise to diversify. Market saturation can make the enterprise diversify in the domestic market. Other factors may lead to geographic diversity including multiple overseas expansions. Wolf drew a conclusion that FDI and domestic diversification were a choice of growth by making use of idle resources. So, international expansion and domestic diversification have a common foundation.

Firms might hope to exploit access to an intangible asset such as technology and marketing (Caves, 1982). But the restrictions of management resources limit the opportunities that the enterprise can pursue at some points (Penrose, 1956). As a foreign operation involves the fixed cost of entering a new market, such as an information-search cost, the enterprise tends to expand in the domestic market first (Caves, 1982). When the domestic market is saturated and diversified chances disappear, the possibility of continuous expansion will decline. Eventually firms find that overseas investment has become an attractive expansion opportunity. It is also profitable when considering the additional information costs of overseas expansion. In similar conditions, it still expands into these new domains to share the costs. Enterprises first tend to enter some overseas markets where there is no disadvantage in language and culture. Caves and Penrose both suggest that each enterprise is a set of resources that is more suited to some specific expansion directions. In the same circumstances, the enterprise tends to select the opportunities that can make best use of its productive resources. The empirical study also supports this view (Caves, 1982). Firms tend to become large in the domestic market and then expand abroad (Horst, 1972). Meanwhile the overseas market should be similar to the domestic market. For instance, US firms expand into Canada.

Traditionally, international business has been considered a monopoly stage for big companies. Traditional theories also suggest that SMEs consider expanding abroad when they grow up. However, in recent years more and more SMEs have become active in the international market. With the development of the resource-based view, their unique competitive advantage in international operations is realized gradually. Taking reasonable account of their resource advantage will promote their international operations. The resource-based view becomes an important study in perspective.

The key view of the resource-based approach is that the profit of firms comes from firm-specific resources that exist inside. It is very hard to imitate this invisible and intellectual property (Wernerfelt, 1984). The capability of SMEs' entering overseas markets is related directly to their accumulation of tangible and intangible resource reserves (Bloodgood, 1996). Bloodgood also suggests the enterprises with precious inimitable, irreplaceable resource reserves have more advantages and are more likely to internationalize than competitors.

From the resource-based view, each firm is a set of unique resources and capabilities. The internationalization of an SME is determined by the interaction of internal resources and external environment. The internal resources are crucial factors, especially the management resource. It is more likely for an SME to exploit overseas markets with the reduction of trade barriers, globalization and the application of modern communication and information technology. By comparison, the internal resources are more important. The motivation and competitive advantage of SME's internationalization consist of firm-specific resources including export experience, flexible strategic adjustment, entrepreneurship, absolute control by entrepreneurs, expertise, experiential knowledge about global opportunities and internationalization.

Westhead and Wright (2001) argued that the four resources influencing SMEs' internationalization include general human capital, financial resources available for handling emergencies, the founder's management ability and experience and knowledge. The empirical study shows that the SME's previous experience of exports encourages them to initiate international operations. Affluent capital and information, the founder's age and rich professional knowledge also promotes the SME to internationalize. The general human resources and financial resources for handling emergencies do not contribute to SMEs international operations significantly.

As described in the stage theory of enterprise internationalization (Johanson and Vahlne, 1977), some SMEs may go through a long-term, evolutionary process to become a multinational. However, this argument has recently been challenged by empirical studies. Some SMEs internationalize more quickly than the model predicted (Knight and Cavusgil, 2004; Lu and Beamish, 2001). How could these SMEs succeed in exploiting the overseas market without going through different stages mentioned in the stage theory of enterprise internationalization? One reason is that they have superb tacit knowledge about global opportunities (Peng *et al.*, 2000) and the ability to exploit it more effectively (Mitchell *et al.*, 2000). The resource-based theory suggests that the knowledge of internationalization might offer the enterprise competitive advantages in foreign markets because of the difficulties of acquiring tacit knowledge (Liesch and Knight, 1999, p. 385).

The resources-based view recently has challenged the stage theory of enterprise internationalization. Some enterprises following the steps suggested by the stage theory must overcome lots of "inertia" in the final internationalization because of their early domestic orientation (Autio *et al.*, 2000). By contrast, those who internationalize early have fewer such obstacles. Thus, the SMEs without domestic orientation perform better than the competitors which internationalize long after their foundation. Contrary to the inherent disadvantage of SMEs' internationalization suggested in the stage theory, they might have an inherent advantage in the process of internationalization.

2.2.9 Theory of INV

Oviatt and McDougall represent the study of the theory of INV. Changing economic, technological and social conditions in recent years have reduced the transaction costs of multinationals interchange and increased the homogenization of many markets so that the conduct of international business is easier to be understood for everyone. The knowledge acquired in the domestic market easily influences the expansion of the international market. So, it is possible for entrepreneurs to combine the domestic and international market as a whole and begin to internationalize in the initial period.

A new international venture is a business organization that exploits multinational markets to obtain enormous competitive advantage from its foundation. Due to the lack of enough resources controlled widely by the ownership, the new venture tends to use few resources for survival and is founded with an internationalization strategy. A large-scale is not needed when the venture possesses assets or resources for transaction exchange. Its advent challenges the viewpoint of traditional theories that "the multinational must be a large enterprise". The INV theory suggested that the experience of entrepreneurs before the enterprise was founded is crucial. The entrepreneurs are cautious about whether to combine the resources from different markets just because in earlier activities they developed some such as network, experiential knowledge, etc. Only when they do have these resources from different markets can they combine a particular set of resources across national borders and form a specific new international venture. So, a network as part of the founder's competence is one of the four parts of INV theory. Although the entrepreneurs can enter the international market by controlling licenses and privileges, the network is still a more efficient choice to occupy and internalize resources for the internationalization of new ventures.

They also mentioned that the communication and transportation channels between two countries had limited the information collected about the international market. But recently, with the development of channels and the homogeneity of international markets, the process of enterprise internationalization has been simplified and shortened. These changes reduce the impact of the psychic distance to a minimum so that the enterprise can by-pass the internationalization stage, or even all stages together.

The INV theory particularly focuses on the special resource-technical knowledge in international competition. The multinational is at a disadvantage in the operation compared with local enterprises. It has to possess firm-specific experiential knowledge by creating differentiation or cost advantage to overcome the existing advantages of local enterprises. So, the firm-specific experiential knowledge is the basic resource of differentiation and cost advantage strategy. According to Porter's theory, the product can be differentiated through the distribution system, marketing, etc. Differentiation strategy requires the enterprise to choose product quality that is different from the competitor. On the other hand, cost advantage derives from the economies of scale, exclusive technology, priority in obtaining raw materials and so on.

2.3   Determinants and Pattern Selection

2.3.1   Network model of enterprise internationalization

The network model of enterprise internationalization offers an explanation to the multinational operation of many SMEs in an industry. After the middle of the 1980s, the network approach prevailed in the West. The enterprise is analyzed as a decision unit in traditional enterprise competition theory. The network approach suggests that any enterprise only survives in a certain social relationship while the industry is in a social relationship network among enterprises. The operation is not completely achieved by the simple exchange of goods. There are "hub" and "satellite" enterprises in any industry. In the auto industry, the relationship between an automobile company and its suppliers is just like that between the "hub" and "satellite". For the common benefit, both invest in the mutual relationship to develop together.

The network model of enterprise internationalization was proposed by Swedish scholars (Hagg and Johanson, 1982; Hammarkvist, 1982; Johanson and Mattsson, 1988). They analyzed the multinational operation of intra-industry enterprises. Johanson and Mattsson discussed the enterprises internationalization in the network in *Internationalization in Industrial Systems — A Network Approach*.

The network model suggests that the industry system that is also called "a network of relationships" consists of many enterprises that engage in production, sales, and service, etc. The division of labor indicates mutual dependence among enterprises. They also cooperate through interaction in the network.

The relationship network is stable and at the same time, it is also dynamic. Each enterprise in the network preserves the relationship with others under given conditions. But this will change as time goes by and the circumstances change. The network model emphasizes the inside "complementarity". Its existence means a kind of "special dependence" between enterprises different from that in traditional theory.

Intra-industry activity of the enterprise such as establishing, maintaining and developing a network relationship is a cumulative process that determines its "market position". From a microcosmic perspective, there are three features of market position: (1) the role compared with others; (2) the importance to others; and (3) the closeness with others.

Therefore, the key proposition is that the existence of a single enterprise depends on the resource controlled by others that is obtained by the position in the network. According to the network model, the internationalization of an enterprise is a process of establishing and developing its relationship in the international market network. There are mainly three accesses: (1) international trade and investment with the aim to expand network scope; (2) regional economic integration with the goal to eliminate operational barriers; and (3) global economic integration. The degree of internationalization depends on its position in the international production (market) network. A highly internationalized production network means a lot of close links between enterprises in the international division of labor.

The traditional FDI theory suggests that the ownership advantages enable the enterprise to operate internationally. The stage theory of an enterprise mentions that it will face a more complicated international environment in multinational operations, as internationalization is an evolutionary process. This theory emphasizes the learning and accumulation of overseas operational experience that is the key factor in a successful internationalization. The network model of enterprise internationalization puts the emphasis on the impact of competition and cooperation in enterprise internationalization from a network perspective. It extends the study from the enterprise itself to the relationship and interaction among enterprises. The network model of enterprise internationalization explains enterprise internationalization behavior well in a networked economy.

This model offers enterprises a new perspective to set development strategy. It discusses the relationship between enterprises and the market and how it influences the competitive position directly from a dynamic perspective.

2.3.2   The innovation-related internationalization models

The Innovation-Related Internationalization Models were first proposed by Rogers (1962). Enterprise internationalization is a result of a series of innovations. The enterprise is an evolutionary system that has a variation-introduction mechanism at any time, introducing created variations. They are more suitable than any entity in the system and stay in the system after selection by the mechanism. The system advances constantly in this process. Technological innovation becomes the core of business that provides the system with new variations, making it adaptable to the constantly changing environment.

The evolution of technological innovation is a very important part of Schumpeter's economic theory. But Richard R. Nelson and Sidney G. Winter in 1982 proposed the evolutionary model. *Understanding Technical Change as an Evolutionary Process* published in 1987 clarified the nature of evolution further and formalized the theoretical model.

According to the model, the process of evolution includes the following parts: first, the variation-introduced mechanism; second, the entity-selected mechanism. Nelson and Winter's analysis was based on three assumptions:

(1) In the evolution system, there are some feasible entities not existing in the system. They have a chance to be introduced into the system by a creator and are more suitable than the existing ones.
(2) Technological innovation is the core of business, which should be formalized by principles. Different roles lead to different interpretations

of the principles. There are many uncertain factors in the enterprises' living environment because they keep innovating and the market condition changes. Enterprises must adapt to these factors or be eliminated. These assumptions exclude the beliefs that the enterprise maximizes its profits, the entire industrial sector is balanced as a whole, etc.

(3) As in the new classical model, the actors are assumed to be purposeful and full of wisdom. They operate the enterprises according to decision-making rules. But in the evolutionary model of technological innovation, the emphasis is mainly on the other aspects of decision-making rules. The enterprises have a set of patterns whose general features show up at any time. On the other hand, it can be understood that a series of actions in the past creates these patterns that are followed by enterprises.

Czinkota (1982, 1991) and Cavusgil (1980, 1982) applied the evolutionary nature of technological innovation in the analysis of the process of enterprise internationalization. The enterprise international operation was the result of the interaction of the external "push mechanism" and the internal "pull mechanism". The push mechanism includes the change in market structure and operational environment, etc., while the pull mechanism refers to the institutional innovation and the form of ownership advantage. It determines whether the enterprise can enlarge its involvement in the international market based on the initial period of international operations (like indirect exports).

The innovation-related internationalization models suggest the impact of the internal mechanism on the development of international marketing from an institutional innovation perspective. It is better than the driving theory of multinational operations that only analyzes the external factors. However, it is unilateral to investigate the influence only from one internal innovation factor, because there are many internal factors influencing the development of international marketing apart from innovation.

2.3.3 Integration and responsiveness model

Prahalard and Doz proposed the integration and responsiveness model in 1987, which mainly analyzes the impact of economic integration on the enterprise's behavior. The factors of global strategy integration include:

(1) The importance of multinational customers: The multinational as a provider should satisfy and complement the integrated requirements of customers in different countries, respectively.
(2) The appearance of multinational competitors: It illustrates the possibility of competing globally and forming an opinion when assessing competitors' reactions across borders.
(3) The investment intensity: Any aspects of high investment, such as studying and developing robotic systems, requires an increase in global coordination to share the investment costs as soon as possible.
(4) The technology intensity: The multinationals are encouraged to produce in fewer sites especially where there is strict intellectual-property protection. It also increases the necessity of coordination as a whole.
(5) Lower costs: It requires a higher level of coordination to make full use of low-cost resources and economies of scale.
(6) Universal demand: If a certain product needs little or no adaptation for different countries, integration is coming.
(7) Acquiring raw materials and energy: Some enterprises that produce aluminum, paper, etc., are required to locate close to the material resource. Integration and coordination are crucial because the markets need various specifications of the final product.

In the economic integration, the enterprises will set a local-responsiveness strategy:

(1) The differentiation in demand: The enterprise is required to pursue a local-responsiveness strategy when it has to satisfy totally different demands.
(2) The differentiation in the distribution channels: The various marketing approaches in different countries require a local-responsiveness strategy.
(3) Availability of substitute goods and adaptability: It requires a local-responsiveness strategy when substitute goods emerge or the existing goods have to adapt according to the local demand.

In a highly centralized market structure where the local competitors are very important, it is the best entry strategy, and perhaps the best sustainable strategy. That means that the multinationals must respond according to the local demand or withdraw. These factors are synthesized in an integration-responsiveness diagram. The enterprise can choose one strategy and shift to another when the circumstances change.

2.3.4 International environment factor model

USA Professor R.N. Farmer and B.M. Richman proposed the Farmer and Richman model after studying the influence of the international environment on operational efficiency. There are three basic principles in this model.

First, efficiency is a function of environmental factors and operational skills. The environment is an external condition that determines the efficiency while operational skills are internal. Thus, the efficiency varies with different environments and operational skills.

Second, the environment influences the operational skills directly. It not only affects the operation process directly, but also affects the process indirectly through influencing the operational skills. Its impact is very complicated so that the environment can affect each element of operational skills simultaneously. For instance, the goal and its implementation is one element of operational skills that is affected by society, politics, law and the economy.

Third, environmental factors are both international and domestic. The domestic environment affects the international one. In the international operation, relationship issues arise first. They constitute the international environmental factors. Every sovereign state treats a foreigner and foreign enterprises differently than own citizens, to some extent. These special provisions are related directly to the factors that will affect the operation.

Farmer and Richman suggested that the impact of the environmental factors on multinational operation was direct and crucial. When a multi-national is operating in a country, the domestic environmental factors influence the process directly. Meanwhile, they determine the quality of enterprises that affects the efficiency indirectly. On the other hand, international environmental factors affect the performance of the enterprise directly. So it is the effect of the domestic environmental factor, international environmental factors and the operational skills together that determine the efficiency of multinational operations.

The elements of the Farmer and Richman model:

(1) International environment factors (I)

I-1 Social factors

1) Concept of nation.
2) Attitude toward foreigners.
3) Character and level of nationalism.

I-2 Political and legal factors

1) Political conception.
2) Laws and regulations for foreign enterprises.
3) Participating in international institutions and international treaties.
4) Subordinative political and economic groups.
5) Export and import restrictions.
6) International investment restrictions.
7) Repatriation restrictions.
8) Exchange controls.

I-3 Economic factors

1) General international payment policy.
2) International trade status.
3) Relationship with international financial institutions.

(2) Domestic environment factors (C)

C-1 Education factors

1) Illiteracy rate.
2) Popularity of specific professional, technical training and general secondary education.
3) Popularity of higher education.
4) Development planning of special business personnel.
5) Attitude toward education.
6) Education and demand.

C-2 Social factors

1) Attitude toward operator or enterprise operations.
2) Attitude toward relationship between lower and upper classes.

3) Status of various social organizations.
4) Attitude toward operational performance.
5) Hierarchy and social mobility.
6) Attitude toward material interests.
7) Attitude toward technology.
8) Attitude toward risk-taking.
9) Attitude toward change.

C-3 Political and legal factors

1) Relevant laws and regulations.
2) Defense policy.
3) Foreign policy.
4) Political stability.
5) Political institutions.
6) Changes in the law.

C-4 Economic factors

1) Economic institutions.
2) The central banking system.
3) Fiscal policy.
4) Economic stability.
5) Capital market structure.
6) Market scale.
7) Investment in public infrastructure.

(3) Operational skills factors

B-1 Planning and innovation

1) Enterprise's goal and its implementation.
2) The way of using planning.
3) Planning and its time period.
4) Planning scope of enterprise activity.
5) Alteration to planning.
6) Methods, technology and tools for planning and decision making.
7) The extent and validity of employees' participation.
8) Manager's decision-making behavior in the planning process.
9) Utilization of planning method.
10) Utilization of science.

11) Innovation, level and speed of operational innovation and venture in specific period.
12) Access to change and introduction of technology in operation.

B-2 control

1) Strategic actions and control based on function.
2) Control technology.
3) Characteristics and structure of feedback system for control purposes.
4) Timing and formality for correcting mistakes.
5) Personnel control.
6) Integrated control system and prediction.
7) Effectiveness of control system for operation planning.

B-3 Organization

1) Scale of central enterprise and its affiliates.
2) Degree of centralization and decentralization.
3) Degree of specialization or division.
4) Span of control.
5) Formation of organization and activities, consultation and service.
6) General customers and specialists.
7) Functional permission.
8) Organizational chaos and conflicts of permission and responsibility.
9) Leadership in decision making.
10) Informal organization.
11) Organizational function and elasticity in creating or handling change.

B-4 Personnel

1) The method of employment.
2) Promotion standards.
3) Technical standard appraisal.
4) Nature and utility of work introduction.
5) Nature and scope of salary and welfare.
6) Nature, scope and time of training.

7) Development of informal personnel.
8) Policy of temporary dismissal and general dismissal.
9) Freedom to dismiss employee.
10) Freedom to employ and maintain personnel with necessary proficiency and competence.

B-5 Direct, lead and motivate

1) Autocracy of operation, or employees' engagement.
2) Technology and method for motivating managerial staff.
3) Technology and method for motivating employee.
4) Technology for monitoring.
5) Bureau and technology for exchanging opinions.
6) Opinion exchanging effectiveness between employees.
7) Access to motivation for improving competence.
8) Interest and consistency of personnel, working groups, departments and staff.
9) Reliance, assistance, conflict and distrust between various employees.
10) Dissatisfaction, absence and turnover.
11) Restrictive work habits, time and energy wasted in negotiating and conflicting with unproductive group.

B-6 Marketing policy

1) Product line (diversification, specialization, change and quality).
2) Channel and customer location.
3) Pricing.
4) Promotion and primary marketing point.

B-7 Production and purchase

1) Produce or entrust others to produce, satellite factory utilization.
2) Quantity, features and location of primary material supplier.
3) Timing of purchasing primary material.
4) Average stock-sales ratio (inventory of primary material, semi-finished products and finished products).
5) Minimum, maximum and average scale of production unit.
6) Stability of production.
7) Factors set used in primary product.

8) Primary productive technology.
9) Automation and mechanization.

B-8 Research and development

Status and features of research and development (product development and improvement, the utilization of new material, new productive technology and the utilization of technology).

B-9 Financial

1) Form and cost of financial scheduling (capital, debt, long-term loans, and short-term borrowing).
2) Capital source.
3) The main purpose of capital.
4) Capital reserves.
5) Profit distribution.

B-10 Relationships

1) Relationship with client.
2) Relationship with supplier.
3) Relationship with investor and creditor.
4) Relationship with union organization.
5) Relationship with government.
6) Relationship with community.

In sum, the operational environment influences the strategy directly. The Farmer and Richman model segments the environment that contributes to analyzing the impact of the internal and external operational environment on international operation in detail.

Economic Environment of International Business (Raymond Vernon and Louis T. Wells, 1990) explored several key issues such as commodity, currency, technology, services, investment, etc., which affected contemporary multinationals' activities. It studied the multinationals' role, international competition, risk-avoidance method, operational strategy, operational mode and organization structure determined by operational strategy and external environment, the dependent and restrictive relationship with the host country and homeland from the three aspects of the internal environment, national environment and international environment.

The common features of multinationals: (1) connected mutually by common ownership; (2) relying on common resources such as currency, credit, information, systems, trademark and patents; and (3) controlled by common strategy. They emphasized that the overseas information collection network influenced the international expansion greatly. "In international business the competitiveness generated from an effective information collection network is significant. It is reflected obviously in the important decisions such as acquiring some new overseas resources or expanding into a new market and in some daily overseas operations". "Some studies on the behavior of multinationals in the US proved effectively that the existence of a spread network contributed significantly to the goal of establishing a branch abroad. Those who introduced new production lines would finally establish overseas branches. However, the time lag in introducing a product abroad will be shortened after acquiring relevant experience. It is more obvious when in a country where the enterprise has got enormous experience."

2.3.5   Four-element model of enterprise internationalization

The four elements model of enterprise internationalization was proposed by Danish scholars Torben Pederson and Bent Petersen in 1998. Pederson and Petersen insist on a basic point that the international growth of an enterprise is an evolutionary process. Their model is different from other theories in the following aspects: Firstly, the evolutionary process is determined by "internal resource factors" and "external market factors"; secondly, the pace of resource commitment differs drastically. And the difference is attributed to "the level of evolution". The basic principle of this theory is that the pace of resource commitment synchronizes with the knowledge accumulation of specific overseas target markets. The overseas market expansion is related directly with the competence for acquiring, integrating and utilizing the resources. Also, the overseas market expansion keeps the same pace with the increase of its sales or market share while still being limited by the degree of market competition.

Torben Pederson and Bent Petersen suggested that the international operation was affected directly by market knowledge, quantity of production factors, market share and market competition structure. It is an

Table 2.4. The quantification and introduction of variables in the model.

Variables	Constructs	Items
Dependent variable	Gradual resource commitment	Years from first activities in the market to establishment of subsidiary To what extent can investments not be transferred to other markets? (1–7 scales) Sales volume in the foreign market
Independent variables	Market knowledge	What was the knowledge about market conditions before establishment? (1–7 scales) Before establishment how difficult was it to obtain sufficient knowledge about the foreign market? (1–7 scales)
	Resource base	Number of foreign subsidiaries (log) Number of foreign employees as proportion of total employment (log) Worldwide turnover of companies (log)
	Market volume	Did the subsidiary establishment await the realization of a certain sales volume in the foreign market? (1–7 scales) Exploitation of sales potential was an important motive for establishing the subsidiary (1–7 scales)
	Global competition	The intensity of local competition (1–7 scales) The extent to which affiliate activities are integrated with parental activity (1–7 scales) The importance of the local competition for the global competitiveness of the company (1–7 scales)

Source: Pedersan and Petersen (1998, p. 495).

evolutionary process for enterprises (entrepreneurs) to acquire overseas market knowledge. The pace of acquiring and accumulating depends on the operator's learning capability and consciousness. The entrepreneurs' cognition and understanding of specific overseas market conditions including market scale, market characteristics, operation mechanism, relevant laws and regulations are prerequisite. The enterprise could reduce the uncertainty efficiently through knowing the overseas market and then reduce the operational risk. The overseas operation (pace, mode, performance) is also influenced directly by the ownership, except for experience and knowledge. The production scale and quantity of factors determine the potential capability to operate internationally. From an external environment perspective, the larger its market shares, the more capable it is to expand into overseas markets. The intensified intra-industry competition also encourages the enterprises to capture the global market.

2.3.6 Inward–outward cross model of enterprise internationalization

Two Finnish researchers, Lawrence S. Welch and Reijo K. Luostatinen, suggested in *Inward–Outward Connection in Internationalization* (1993) that "the inward process might precede and influence the development of outward activities, in such a way that the effectiveness of the inward activities could determine the success of outward internationalization".

Chinese researcher Neng Liang also proposed two patterns of enterprise internationalization. Internationalization largely means how to confront the international competition in the local market. Thus internationalization can be divided into "outward" and "inward" patterns in two aspects. The outward-internationalization includes direct or indirect exports, technology transfer, foreign contract arrangements, overseas joint ventures, foreign subsidiaries and branches; the inward-internationalization refers to imports, purchase of patents and technology, processing and compensation trades, domestic joint ventures, foreign subsidiaries or branches, etc.

The home market has been a portion of the international market. After internationalizing in the domestic market, the relationship reflected in the process of inward and outward internationalization is the substance of these two standpoints.

The implementation of an international operation is an evolutionary process from simple importing and exporting, establishing foreign agents, setting up a foreign branch to form an international marketing network. It is a complex system. Its operational area extends from a country to several countries, even the global market. The international operation strategy model mainly includes the following three types:

First, single entry strategy. In the initial stage of international operation strategy, the factors that the enterprise should consider are still simple. The SMEs commonly exploit this strategy without careful investigation of the target market. Also, it requires low resource commitment and it is easy to avoid risk. At present, this strategy that is implemented easily is taken by most Chinese SMEs.

Second, stage strategy. The enterprise gradually accumulates the relevant knowledge of international operations to capture the market share steadily. The international operation modes evolve through domestic operation, indirect exports via an agent, direct exports, establishing an overseas sales branch and producing abroad sequentially. It enables the enterprise to adapt to the changing external environment from low risk to high risk, from little control to great control.

Third, system selection strategy. After analyzing the target market, the enterprise formulates some optional international operation modes based on its resources. It chooses one mode after considering all the factors, including the target market competition situation, the demographic characteristics of potential consumers, the political situation and development of the capital market. It is a complex system. The lofty requirement with regards to the quality of the enterprise hinders SMEs from implementing this strategy.

Chapter 3

Policy Evolution

A significant strategy for China's internationalization is to encourage domestic enterprises to go global. China, as a developing country, is initiating its outward foreign direct investment, in view of the fact that foreign direct investment policy institutionally safeguards the enterprises' international business. Therefore, perfect foreign direct investment policy mix is of significant importance, both in theory and practice, to facilitate the development of China's OFDI as well as to accelerate its internationalization process.

3.1 Initial Development of China's Private Economy

China's domestic enterprises emerged strongly before the 1930s, as China's domestic enterprises enjoyed considerable development. After the 1930s, however, their prosperity was choked because of Japan's aggression against China and the civil war afterwards. In addition, the planned economy adopted since 1949 put an end to its further development.

In 1949, the gross industrial output value by the state-owned enterprises was CNY 3.68 billion, while the gross output value by privately-owned and individually-owned enterprises was CNY 10.05 billion, which occupied more than 70% of the total. However, the output value of the private enterprises shrank to CNY 0.69 billion in 1957, only holding less than 1% of the total.[1] Statistics from National Bureau of Statistics are shown in Table 3.1.

---

[1] *The Abstract of China's Statistics* 1985, China Statistics Press.

Table 3.1. 1949–1978 gross industrial output value by ownership (billion CNY, %).

Year	State-owned enterprises Output (billion CNY)	%	Collectively-owned enterprises Output (billion CNY)	%	Public and private partnership Output (billion CNY)	%	Private enterprises Output (billion CNY)	%	Individual enterprises Output (billion CNY)	%	Sum Output (billion CNY)	%
1949	3.68	26.2	0.07	0.5	0.22	1.6	6.83	48.7	3.23	23	14	100
1952	14.26	41.5	1.12	3.3	1.37	4	10.52	30.6	7.06	20.6	34.3	100
1957	42.15	53.8	14.92	19	20.63	26.3	0.04	0.1	0.65	0.8	78.4	100
1965	12.56	90.1	13.84	9.9	—	—	—	—	—	—	139.4	100
1978	34.16	80.8	81.44	19.2	—	—	—	—	—	—	423.1	100

Note: Statistics are from *The Abstract of China's Statistics* (1985).

As Table 3.1 shows, private and individual enterprises had almost disappeared in China after 1957, until 1978 before the Reform and Opening up Period. During these two decades, state-owned enterprises substantially dominated and championed the development of China's economy.

3.1.1 Initial development of China's private and individual enterprises

Before 1949, China was an economically-sluggish big country with rather disproportionate development, which mainly focused itself on traditional agriculture. Due to warfare and the Kuomintang's government, draconian inflation as well as the chaos of the market had debilitated the privately-owned economy. The People's Republic of China was setup in this context and a powerful state-dominated economy was built through confiscating the property of the bureaucrats. Hence, as the dispensable part of "five economic compositions", the privately-owned economy experienced protection, exploitation, and restriction.

With the disappearance of the fake social purchasing power as well as the compression of social demand in the "Unified Finance", the whole nation took on the picture of a stagnant market with flat demand after April 1950. And hence the Financial and Economic Commission followed the instructions of the Central People's Government Council to regulate "industry and commerce" after May. It essentially aimed to grant deserved status to the privately-owned economy to promote its development in the cities. The following were the main steps:

(1) Expanding the processing orders for and purchase of goods from privately-owned industry. The state increased the ratio of the processing orders and purchase of goods to privately-owned enterprises (POEs)' industrial output, which not only reinforced the state-owned economy's domination in the privately-owned economy, but also expanded the demand for the private economy.

(2) Dividing the business scope of public and private operations.

State-owned enterprises focused on the wholesale sector and thus properly reduced its business in retailing, and its business only covered grain, clothing, coal, cooking oil, salt and so forth.

(3) Regulating the price policies.

Taking production, transportation and selling into consideration, the government kept a rational price difference between wholesale and retail as well as the producer and the seller, making the privately-owned businesses profitable.

(4) Adjusting loans policy, reducing deposits and lending rates, issuing loans to the privately-owned industry.

Banks augmented their credit to privately-owned industry, which was of vital importance to social well-being and issued loans to private commerce that were beneficial for the urban–rural trade.

(5) Reducing the tax burden.

The agriculture tax was reduced. For the commercial tax, not only the categories but also the tax rates were cut.

(6) Adjusting employee–employer relations.

The government made it a practice that the democratic rights of the working class were supposed to be ratified, for the sake of productivity. Labor meetings were held in order to tackle disputes between employees and employers through negotiation. There was a slogan at that time: "lower wages, humanize relations, solidify relationships and get over difficulties."

(7) Modulating production and marketing relationships.

It aimed to reduce the imbalance between production and sales, namely the privately-owned industry's disorderly production and the blocking of the urban–rural distribution network. The Financial and Economic Commission decided to report timely market information, like supply and demand, so as to help privately-owned entrepreneurs be informed of market conditions, thus avoiding risks.

The privately-owned economy soon got rid of its troubles after the modulation. From the autumn of 1950, markets had begun to flourish with a substantial rise in market transactions. Both the boosting of the market and the restoring of the exchange between urban and rural areas had stimulated the development of the privately-owned industry, making its output increase dramatically. For example, in 1951, in the so-called "Golden Age" of privately-owned industry, the gross industrial output of private enterprises saw a 39% rise over the previous year.

"The Modulation" had made contributions to the rapid recovery of the national economy both in 1950 and 1951. Although a large investment sum was used to setup state-owned enterprises in 1952, private enterprises still occupied more than 50% of the total gross industrial output. In the meantime, the privately-owned economy had been encouraged and regulated to maintain further development through both direct and indirect administration as well as by the reorganization of privately-owned finance.

During the recovery of the national economy, the urban privately-owned and individual economy had also undergone many major changes in the management system. In a macroscopic way, the state strengthened its regulation of the privately-owned economy including its exploitation, restrictions and transformation, and readjusted public–private relations. While from the microscopic perspective, the internal management system in POEs took on a new look, as well as its employee–employer relations. At this time, based on the policy of "Exploitation, Restriction and Transformation", the government divided the privately-owned economy into two parts. First is the individual economy with private capital. And second, a control system containing four kinds of control measures was established, namely with administrative management, economic levers, self-discipline in industrial organization and mass participation. Through the above-mentioned means, division and cooperation could respectively be achieved under the leadership of the state-owned economy.

As for the administrative legislation, first of all, owners in industry and commerce, especially those whose industries were highly associated with the national economy, were re-registered successively after liberation, and their ownership, capital, characteristics of enterprises and business scope were ratified. Second, the government promulgated and then implemented several restrictions aimed at transforming private finance and business as well as the statutes aimed at combating market speculation. Third, the government controlled the individually-owned and privately-owned economy by the approval of business operations. Shortly after the foundation of the PRC, only after approval by the Administration Department of Industry and Commerce could an enterprise engage in business, either individually owned or privately-owned. Meanwhile, an enterprise had to apply to the Administration Department of Industry and Commerce and get permission if it wanted a suspension or termination.

Apart from the direct measures such as the above-mentioned administration, legislation and mass participation taken to regulate the privately-owned economy, the government also made full use of economic levers such as taxation, interest rates and industrial organization to manage and regulate the privately-owned economy.

As a relatively effective method of regulating the economy adopted by the government, the taxation lever found its place after the foundation of the PRC. There were three instances when this lever was widely used. First, the government adopted high tax rates and fines for delayed payments to control inflation and decrease social pressures in March 1950, namely the Unified Financial Policy Period. Second, through reduced tax rates and simplified taxation in June 1950, the government stimulated the privately-owned economy so as to maintain development. Third, after the "Five Antis" in 1952, the government used the taxation lever again in a second adjustment to revitalize the market. What is more, in order to implement the policy of prior development for the state-owned economy and to actively foster a cooperative economy, the government differentiated the tax policies, imposing lower tax rates on the state-owned economy and cooperative economy than on the privately-owned economy, and heavier taxation on commerce than on industry within the privately-owned economy.

3.1.2   The difficulty in the nationalization reform era

Known as "Government–Private Joint Ventures", enterprises that were a cooperation between the government and private sector had emerged as early as during the Westernization Movement in the late Qing Dynasty. Under the rule of the government of Qing Dynasty and the Kuomintang, "Government–Private Joint Ventures" had been an important way for bureaucratic capital to control the national capital and bureaucrats to embezzle the state-owned assets. After the PRC was founded, a batch of enterprises became public–private ventures by the process of confiscating the bureaucrats' capital. In the meantime, many POEs were suffering and hence expected government investment (transforming loans into investment).

Before 1953, the Central Committee of the Communist Party was very prudent about public–private partnership, strictly conforming to three principles, namely "be in urgent need of development, be in conformity with national investment plans, capitalists be real volunteers for partnership". The reason why the Financial and Economic Commission did this was as follows: For one thing, the government had to think about the efficiency in the use of funds due to the shortage of capital at that time. For another, to avoid the misinterpretation and turmoil caused by this partnership, we had to do it in this way since the Kuomintang once used it to devour the national industry.

In June 1953, Li Weihan, the secretary in the United Front Department of the Central Committee of the Communist Party, conducted a survey and then proposed that it was a good solution to transform the capitalist enterprises through public–private partnership. The proposal was accepted by the Party, and adopted as the development policy to eliminate private capitalism in the form of national capitalism. As for the POEs, the tension was felt in their employee–employer relations because of the "Five Antis" in 1952. After 1953, along with the shortage of raw materials and chocked sales channels, the POEs also suffered lack of management autonomy and capital shortages. In this context, the government decided to carry out public–private partnership to achieve the following results. First, disputes between employees and employers were dispelled because of this partnership. Second, enterprises' sales were treated equally with state-owned enterprises since their merger into the national plan. Third, national provision of capital satisfied their great needs.

The POEs faced more ordeals because of natural agricultural calamities in 1954. As for the supply and allocation of raw materials, the supply of industrial raw materials was in shortage except those for agricultural products. As for the supply of capital, the nation implemented "To Save for a Loan" policy for privately-owned industry to make sure their loans were less than their deposits. In fact, there existed a capital shortage in the whole nation, which made it harder to help POEs. Privately-owned industrial enterprises suddenly lost their original supply and sales channels since private wholesalers were substantially transformed. After two years of public–private partnership, the remaining private industrial enterprises were those on a small scale, using sluggish technology and having low profits. For the above-mentioned reasons, neither local government non-state-owned commercial institutions, from an economic perspective, would invest in raw materials and capital in those enterprises.

In order to tackle the above-mentioned problems, the Central Committee of the Communist Party endorsed the "Report on Meeting of Expansion of Public–Private Partnership and Symposium of Privately-owned Industry Problems" in April 1955. The report put forward the "Overall Consideration, Comprehensive Arrangement" policy to reform capitalism. That is, in the process of partnership, the focus should be on the whole industry with big enterprises taking the lead before small and medium-sized enterprises. Advanced enterprises assisted those lagging behind, so as to reshuffle, merger and eventually make a public–private partnership. The projected idea of overall reconstruction and rearrangement of privately-owned industry was, in fact, the starting point of public–private partnership for all industries.

During the National Federation of Industry and Commerce Conference later on, Vice-Premier Chen Yun explained further about public–private partnership for all industries and fixed interest rates. Then the conference documented "Declaration to All-China Industry and Commerce", which required private owners to respond actively to accept socialist transformation. From January 1956, the country highlighted the transformation from a capitalist industry to a socialist one. From 1952 to 1956, the barriers that POEs faced were mainly internal disputes between employees and employers as well as the external harsh industrial environment, which were totally caused by a series of controls over raw materials, sales channels and credit to POEs. The political situation, public opinion and ideology also further contributed to these results. For further analysis, the POEs at that time were not adapted to the economic mode set by the government, which also conflicted with the strategic targets of fast and prior development of heavy industry. If POEs competed for the limited resources within the planned economy, they might prevent the realization of the goals of the single planned economy.

The external industrial environment, i.e. market fluctuations and imbalance between supply and demand were inevitable for POEs. For example, the government had begun to comprehensively control important raw materials, all kinds of purchasing and finance since 1953, which in fact cut down the link between POEs and the market. The POEs were embedded in the market economy, and they could hardly survive without the market. With the comprehensive growth of the planned economy, it was impossible for POEs to live on in the absence of free trade.

Since then, from the start of the "Anti-Rightist" campaign from 1957 until 1978, before the reform and opening up, not only was the privately-owned economy illegal on the mainland, but also the independent workers, who originally were private-enterprise owners, were discriminated against. This leftist ideology, as well as the planned-economy-centered economic pattern reduced China's economic development. This consequently hampered the sound development of a market economy, and thus energetic POEs lost the opportunity to thrive.

3.2 Temporary Decline of China's Private Economy

In 1956, the "Public–Private Partnership" adopted by China was accomplished in only a year. Ten years afterwards, POEs almost disappeared, which indicated that China had entered the age of complete public ownership. In these ensuing 10 years, private enterprises almost disappeared because of the criticism of a "Small-Scale Spontaneous Force" by "The Great Cultural Revolution" as well as the anti-capitalist movement (or "cut the capitalist's tail"). During this historic period, the research of POEs had to be interrupted due to an absence of documents and information.

The death of private enterprises directly led to a shortage of consumer goods in the second half of 1956. In such conditions, some original urban and rural businessmen re-established the private and self-employed economy that they named as "Underground Factories" at that time, and thus automatically reduced the supply and demand gap. As a result, the private and self-employed economy resurged in 1957. According to the statistics, there were some 700,000 people in the private and self-employed economy and small vendors of about 600,000 to 700,000 thousand in the first half of 1957.[2]

Since the "Anti-Rightist" movement in 1957, however, opinions changed about the bourgeoisie and privately-owned economy after the socialist transformation. In the three years of the "Great Leap Forward" from 1958 to 1960, the remaining parts of the private and individual economy were wiped out due to the superstition of "Large in Size and Collective in Nature". In 1961, the Central Committee of the Communist Party issued "Several Provisions on Improving Commercial Work (Draft)". One important part of the draft was to setup a rural trade market and to restore the cooperation of stores and groups, raising their business enthusiasm. In the meantime, "Several Provisions on Policies of Urban and Rural Handicrafts (Draft)" was endorsed and it also allowed the development of individual handicrafts. Once the policies were deemed as not working, the individual economy was soon invigorated regardless of the severe situation and shortage of materials at that time, and hence its size surpassed that of 1957.

But it did not last long. From 1964, the "Socialist Education Movement" emerged in urban and rural areas, which aimed to crack down on speculation. The movement then fiercely spread until the outbreak of "The Great Cultural Revolution" in 1966. During the 10 years of "The Great

---

[2]The Central Literature Research Division (1995). Important Literature Collection about the New China (Volume 11). Beijing: The Central Literature Press.

Cultural Revolution", not only were people scared of "capitalism", but also the individual economy sharply declined. There was a severe shortage of commercial service centers in cities and the whole economy badly wanted a new supplement.

All in all, before the reform and opening up period, due to the influence of the planned economy, the state-owned and collective economy was dominant, only leaving a little space for a private and individual economy. The SMEs were restricted to development in this context. Moreover, the industrial and regional policies adopted by the government contravened those enterprises. From the 1950s to 1970s, China's industrial policies had taken the development of heavy industry as a priority, which produced a sluggish heavy industry in the 1950s. This policy, however, had adverse effects for the shear reason that it needed large capital investment as well as capital-intensive enterprises on a relatively large-scale. The policy meant the accumulated capital went to large and medium-sized heavy industry, and thus constrained light industry and the service industry that led to low investment. At the same time, the regional policy was unfavorable to the development of small and medium-sized private enterprises. During the period of the 1960s and 1970s, according to the principles of "Preparing for War", China carried out a policy of "three central lines" (central regions of China) by large-scale construction and much capital investment in three central lines of national defense to promote the economic development of central regions along the Beijing–Guangzhou railway and the northwest and southwest China. Although the large-scale construction made a certain contribution to the local economy, most of the projects had no knock-on effect on economic development, and also stifled the development of SMEs.

3.3   The Development in the Post-Reform Era

Breaking out of their confinement in 1976, POEs gained political support for development. At that time, the employment pressure in cities, which was originally high, substantially increased due to the return of as many as 30 million young people. Quite a lot of them started their own businesses in order to support their families. While in the countryside, some farmers began to trade food, fruit and so on because China adopted the household contract responsibility system. The individual economy then began to sprout and gradually formed a spectacular group of self-employed. However, the time when contemporary China's POEs truly developed was not until after 1979. At the Third Plenary Session of the 11th CPC, the Party shifted the focus from the class struggle to economic development, adopting policies to reform the management system for industry with collective ownership. It also implemented some policies on industrial policy, management methods, supply and markets, loans and taxation to encourage the development of township enterprises and individual enterprises. As a result, individual enterprises, collective enterprises and township enterprises, where private enterprises were dominant, boomed. The development of China's private enterprises showed two distinctive features in this period. For one thing, as the main force of small and medium-sized enterprises, township enterprises had prospered since 1984. For another, from 1979 to 1983, while the number of township enterprises declined from 1.52 million in 1978 to 1.35 million in 1983, the number of employees increased from 28.27 million to 52.08 million.[3] In July 1981, the State Council issued "Some Provisions on the Non-Agricultural Individual Economy in Towns" explicitly indicating that the individual economy generally referred to the operation of an individual or family, or with no more than five apprentices after permission from the Department of Industrial and Commercial Administration. Since then, as an important part of private enterprises, self-employment has grown. But at that time the self-employed were not so popular. Some in the privately-owned economy still badly wanted to be under the umbrella of state-owned units, only to be called "redcap" enterprises. The 12th Party Congress in 1982 pointed out that a "socialist state-owned economy must dominate the whole national economy" and that the proper development of the private sector economy should be encouraged only by national regulations both in town and country. The news was inspiring since it was the first time that the private economy was supported by the party's national congress. Furthermore, the scope spread from towns to rural areas. However, "proper"

---

[3] Zhang and Li (2001).

hinted at the restricted development of the private-sector economy for it was still weak when compared to the whole national economy. The private economy was still primarily composed of handicrafts, in the form of small-scale family businesses. In other words, besides some "redcap" enterprises, the self-employed accounted for the most important POEs during this period. When facing market risks, they not only resorted to family relationships but also resorted to Guanxi to maintain the enterprises. Some POEs were even forced to be "redcap" when confronted with the continuous risks of "capitalism or socialism" as well as "anti-capitalism".

The State Council stipulated three private ownership structures, namely sole investment, partnership and limited liability in a report titled "Temporary Provisions on Private Enterprises" in June 1988. At the same time, clauses about private enterprises were added to the "Constitution of the People's Republic of China" at the First Session of the 7th National People's Congress. As a result, private enterprises with 90,600 registrations were officially recognized by the national economic and political system. Of course, the debate over "capitalism or socialism" still remained a big obstacle to the development of China's POEs. Excitingly, private enterprises began to become competitors of state-owned enterprise. The planned economy provided enormous room for the development of POEs that guaranteed their market share. Then a group of private enterprises introduced second-rate, third-rate equipment and technology from abroad to enhance production, thus completing their primitive accumulation of capital.

In early 1992, the "South Speech" delivered by Deng Xiaoping at the 14th Party Congress in October created a more favorable environment for China's POEs. In September 1993, the Second Session of the 9th National People's Congress endorsed amendments to the Constitution, clearly stating that within the limits prescribed by law, the self-employed and the private economy were indispensable parts of the socialist market economy. After that, the POEs burgeoned. Meanwhile, in the context of reform and opening up policy, China began to adopt policies to encourage domestic enterprises to go global and join competition in the international market, which provided experience for those enterprises to further expand into the global market.

Right now, China's enterprises have spread their multinational business to over 160 countries and regions with resources and trade as their main investment scope. Furthermore, apart from the traditional import and export operations, China's enterprises have expanded their international business in various forms. Many enterprises have setup branches or facilities abroad to implement international business management. Some even established R&D centers which marks the new stage of multinational operations that China's enterprises have entered. The internationalization process of China's enterprises can be divided into three stages.

The first stage was from 1979 to 1985, which was defined as the early period of internationalization of China's enterprises. The State Council promulgated 15 economic reform measures in 1979, including provisions that allowed running enterprises abroad. This provided a powerful politic reliance and motivation for the formation of multinational companies as well as their business. During this period, 185 overseas joint ventures were established worth USD296 million in total, including Chinese investment of USD178 million. As for these enterprises, they located their investment in 45 countries and regions with most of them being in developing countries or Hong Kong (SAR of China) and Macao (SAR of China).[4] The following are some examples. In November 1979, the Beijing Friendship Commercial Service Company and Commercial Co., Ltd., made a joint venture with the Jinghe Co., Ltd., in Tokyo. In March 1980, China Shipping Industry Corporation, China Charting Corporation and Hong Kong Global Shipping Group founded the International Joint Shipping Investment Co., Ltd. In July 1980, the Bank of China along with the First National Bank of Chicago, United States, Japan Industry Bank and Hong Kong Huarun Group setup the first Chinese-foreign joint venture financial enterprise — Zhongzhi Industry and Finance Co., Ltd. What is more, China's enterprises found their way into The Netherlands, Yemen, Australia and Belgium to build joint ventures through foreign direct investment. Those were the earliest overseas enterprises by China after reform and opening up. With the deepening of the reform, Chinese enterprises have gained expertise in multinational operations.[5] But, generally speaking,

---

[4] The Abstract of China's Statistics 1985, China Statistics Press, 1985.

[5] Zhao Youzhen. The Internationalization of Medium and Small Sized Firms — Theory and Practice. Shanghai: Fudan University Press, 2005.

the investment scale in this period was small, and mainly in the area of services such as construction engineering, consulting and catering, but less in mechanical processing and other manufacturing. Since only import and export companies with the exclusive rights to foreign trade, or economic and technical cooperation companies from the provinces and cities, were eligible for overseas investment, most of the foreign direct investment was made by professional foreign trade companies and large comprehensive groups. China's export trade mainly began in 1980, and the dominant exports were light industrial products, where POEs did not play an important role. With the rapid economic development of China, especially the boom in township enterprises, small and medium-sized enterprises made themselves distinguished in China's export drive, occupying a handsome market share. At the same time, foreign-funded enterprises were booming on account of their introduction of foreign investment. Those state-owned SMEs, however, seldom-received preferential policies while shouldering the same obligations as the large ones, thus making them lag behind their counterparts.

The second stage was from 1986 to 1990. The State Council authorized the Department of Foreign Trade to formulate and promulgate "Regulations and Approval Procedures on Establishing Non-Trade Overseas Joint Ventures" and it eased, to a certain degree, the control over overseas investment by domestic enterprises. Some approval procedures were simplified if enterprises with stable capital and a certain level of technology wanted to expand overseas investment. Hence, the number and the total investment of overseas enterprises greatly increased during this period. And these enterprises were located in more than 90 countries and regions, most of which were in Asia, along with a few developed countries. Large and medium manufacturing enterprises, business groups, international trusts and investment companies and scientific research institutions gradually expanded their overseas investment. Some of the large-scale enterprises had prepared to compete in the international market. With regard to the investment fields, resource development, manufacturing, transportation and another 20 industries were included.

The third stage was from 1991 to 1996, which was deemed the golden age for rapid growth of China's foreign direct investment, with a tremendous increase in the quantity of enterprises and overseas investment value.

For example, the number of China's overseas enterprises authorized from 1991 to 1993 overtook the total authorized in the 12 years from 1979 to 1990. After the "South Speech" delivered by Deng Xiaoping in 1992, China accelerated the reform of the foreign trade regime and further relaxed the approval procedures for overseas investment enterprises.

It is well-known that large-scaled multinational companies had long been devoted to foreign direct investment, which had driven the globalization of the world economy. While for the small and medium POEs in China, their foreign direct investment was pitifully limited. This situation, however, was improving. In 1997, the United Nations Conference on Trade and Development published a "Manual on FDI for Small and Medium Enterprises: Asian Experience" to specially discuss and analyze the characteristics, functions and countermeasures of FDI for SMEs in Asia in the context of globalization and internationalization in the world economy. There were many reasons why small and medium privately-owned enterprises employed international strategies. One of them was that even with the shortened product life cycle and increasing cost of research, enterprises can still obtain favorable profits through foreign direct investment. According to research by the United Nations Trade Development Organization, the foreign direct investment of these enterprises can transform the pressure into strength by augmenting the competence of both capital-outflow and capital-inflow countries.

China's POEs have enjoyed sound development under the "Going Global" policy. The government has adopted the impartial principles by which government provided POEs with identical treatment to enterprises with other ownership, not only for the approval of establishing enterprises overseas, but also for foreign contract projects as well as market qualifications, so as to make sure they can compete with other market participants equally. Meanwhile, the government encouraged POEs in light industry, textiles, household appliances, telecommunications etc., to employ various methods like sole ownership, joint ventures, mergers and acquisitions (M&As) to setup overseas facilities. Enterprises have also been encouraged to participate actively in resources development, agriculture, forestry and ocean fisheries overseas in order to alleviate trade friction in the world and adapt to domestic industrial structural requirements. Moreover, the government encouraged POEs, either alone or with other enterprises, to commit to foreign project contracting in the form of Engineer, Procure, Construct (EPC), public–private partnership (PPP) and Project Management Contracts (PMC), etc. Such policies were aimed at boosting the export of large engineering equipment and complete sets of equipment through infrastructure projects in high value-added transportation, telecommunication industries. The government actively guided those qualified POEs to do overseas business in trade distribution, banking, insurance, securities, futures, fund management, telecommunications and information, logistics, shipping, tourism, culture, entertainment and intermediary services, thus enhancing international competence. Also, the government encouraged POEs to establish R&D centers in foreign areas. Enterprises can fully use the rich science and technological resources there and then improve their research and innovation, thus finally contributing to the upgrade of the domestic industrial structure as well as the quality of products. Also, the government allowed some eligible enterprises to do business in foreign labor service cooperation and regulate their business behavior so as to improve the enterprises' management and maintain the legitimate rights and interests of personnel. And the government also made full use of its embassies in the following three ways: First, by being a middleman, embassies helped POEs understand foreign markets; second, by being the backup, it strengthened the negotiations with local government, thus protecting Chinese enterprises' legitimate rights and interests; finally, by being the safeguard, it coped with emergencies, thus protecting enterprises' personnel and property in case of an emergency.

3.4   Implementation of the "Going Global" Strategies

Since 1997, a policy that invigorates large enterprises while relaxing control over small ones (Zhua da fang Xiao) has been adopted to speed up the development of SMEs. Also, with the reform of government institutions, the National Economic and Trade Commission manifested its macro-control functions. In 1998, the department that specialized in the reform and development of enterprises was founded, which indicated these enterprises drew unprecedented attention at that time. In order to further meet the needs of China's POEs, in March 1999, when amending the constitution, the Second Session of the 9th National People's Congress proposed that the nation should protect the individual private economy and guide it to be the indispensable component of the national economy through supervision and regulation. Thus, the privately-owned economy embraced its second peak since strongly buttressing the private economy had become the social consensus. In August of the same year, China promulgated the "Law of Sole Proprietorship of the People's Republic of China" to set specific rules for investors, establishments, business management, dissolution, and liquidation for sole proprietorship enterprises. The promulgation and implementation of this law provided necessary legal protection and a good external environment for individual startups. In the report of the 16th National Congress of the CPC, the Party proposed that the private economy with non-public ownership was an indispensable component of a socialist market economy, and unswervingly encouraged the development of the non-public economy that can have a crucial impact on activating production. The report also proposed that domestic POEs should be granted market access in aspects of investment, financing, foreign trade and use of land. The implementation of fair competition as well as strengthened supervision and administration can contribute to the healthy development of a non-public ownership economy. Thus, the above-mentioned policies provided opportunities for the development of POEs.

Meanwhile, the "going global" strategy adopted by the government did create a favorable environment for POEs to go international. Grounded on China's basic conditions, the "going global" strategy helped to fully realize the construction of a better-off society and safeguard the long-term welfare of the Chinese. As early as in 1997, the central government had paid attention to how to implement international economic and technical cooperation by going global, emphasizing that both the "introduction" and "going global" were indispensable to the opening up policy, since they were intimately related. Also, the "Tenth Five-Year Plan" and "development outline" explicitly stated that enterprises with all kinds of ownerships were encouraged to invest overseas, i.e. "going global". All local departments, in line with the Central Party, improved policies and services to support these enterprises. As for the internationalization of China's POEs, their development fell far behind state-owned enterprises and foreign-invested enterprises due to the government's earlier weak support as well as their late internationalization. Under the planned economic regime and transitional economy, the government regulated the multinational business of private enterprises in the same way as that of state-owned enterprises, which constrained their development in international business. For example, private enterprises could hardly acquire the right to operate in foreign trade, with export quotas and the use of foreign exchange. In fact, there were almost no private enterprises making business in the import and export trade at the end of 1998. Having no power to directly engage in imports and exports, POEs had to depend on state-run foreign trade companies to import materials and equipment, and export products. Due to the remarkable contributions the private economy had made to the sustainable development of the national economy, the Ministry of Commerce proposed four times, on January 1, 1999, January 1, 2000, July 20, 2001 and January 1, 2002, respectively, to remove the restriction on foreign trade for private enterprises. Department of Foreign Trade first granted self-supporting export rights to 20 privately-owned enterprises in 1999, indicating that POEs could eventually participate in international business. Afterwards, more and more POEs were granted this qualification. As a result, there were 12,700 qualified privately-owned foreign trade enterprises in 2000, with almost 40,000 by the end of 2002.[6] Some POEs began their internationalization process in the form of imports and exports. With China's entry into the WTO, the People's Republic of China Foreign Trade Law was amended to expand the business scope of foreign trade operators to individuals. It is qualification to trade, but not ownership that mattered. Since then, privately-owned enterprises have become the main force in China's foreign trade development.

In recent years the government has adopted a series of measures to encourage POEs to go global. In the meantime, according to the requirements of the Central Committee of the Party and the State Council, the National Development and Reform Commission drafted a "Long-Term Development Plan for Employing Oil and Gas Resources Overseas" and "Long-Term Development Plan for Employing Mineral

---

[6] China Statistical Yearbook, 2003.

Resources Overseas", and held meetings for deployment and arrangements. In order to adapt to reform of the investment system, the National Development and Reform Commission issued a "Notice on the Policy of Giving Credit Support to State Encouraged Key Overseas Investment Projects" to grant preferential credit support for four categories of overseas investment projects including overseas resources development. The government also made intimate contact with main investment target countries so as to improve mutual cooperation on resources and investment. For example, China has signed an investment memorandum with Australia, a mineral energy memorandum with South Africa and Brazil, a mineral energy, forestry and fisheries memorandum with Gabon. Also, China further developed cooperation with the Russian Federation, Cuba, Venezuela and Sweden based on the original cooperative mechanism. These measures played critical roles in improving the "going global" policy and evinced POEs' prospects of participation in global economic integration. In turn, it urged the government to create a more relaxed, transparent and just domestic and international environment for these enterprises.[7]

Meanwhile, the Chinese government, for industrial structure adjustment and environmental protection, reorganized and closed some small and medium-sized POEs who had laggard technology, caused environmental pollution and wasted resources. Furthermore, the government issued a series of policies like "Provisional Regulations of the Innovation Fund for Technological Small and Medium-Sized Firms by the Ministry of Science, and Finance" and "Proposal on Improving Financial Services for SMEs by The People's Bank of China" to support the privately-owned small and medium-sized enterprises. In recent years, China has successively documented regulations to promote SMEs' development and their international business. For example, in October 2000, the Ministry of Finance and Ministry of Foreign Trade and Economic Cooperation jointly launched "Capital Management of SMEs' International Market (Interim)". In June 2001, the two ministries jointly enacted "Implementing Rules on Capital Management of Small and Medium Enterprises' International

---

[7]Wang Zhongming. Government's Thoughts about Business Orientation for Privately-Owned Firms. Economics Frontier, 2003 (12).

Market (Interim)". The State Administration of Foreign Exchange (SAFE) also issued several policies to buttress enterprises in overseas business from 2001 and it piloted looser control over foreign exchange in Zhejiang, Jiangsu, Shanghai, Shandong and Fujian from October 1, 2002, which has expanded across the nation since May 2005. "The Law of the People's Republic of China on the Promotion of Small and Medium-Sized Enterprises" took effect from January 1, 2003, and it aimed to promote the development of China's enterprises. For one thing, domestic enterprises no longer need to submit feasible research reports to the Ministry of Commerce if they want to setup enterprises overseas. For another, privately-owned enterprises received impartial treatment when they went global. The Ministry of Commerce also issued "Provisions on the Examination and Approval of Investment to Run Enterprises Abroad" which clearly indicated that the government encouraged enterprises with all kinds of ownership to setup enterprises overseas, and the government guaranteed equal treatment for all kinds of enterprises in the process, for it had different requirements in detail for different enterprises. The Chinese government has now stimulated qualified POEs to go global and provided favorable policies for all domestic enterprises, both privately-owned and state-owned. In order to remove the barriers which could impede the sound development of POEs, the Ministry of Commerce abolished discriminatory policies against the POEs. In May 2004, the Ministry of Commerce and the All-China Federation of Industry and Commerce jointly established a standing mechanism to boost POEs internationalization. What is more, four ministries including the Ministry of Commerce issued guidelines of encouragement and support for POEs internationalization, where they again emphasized they would focus more attention on POEs. For example, the assistant minister at the Ministry once attended online interviews on the website of The Central People's Government of the PRC and communicated with netizens on the "going global" strategies.

In terms of macro policy, the 16th National Congress of the Communist Party of China twice mentioned the phrase, "Do Not Waver". Do not waver to consolidate and expand the public ownership economy and do not waver to encourage, support and conduct the development of the non-public ownership economy. Furthermore, the 4th Session of the

16th Central Committee strongly confirmed all policies for developing the non-public ownership economy. In February 2006, the State Council promulgated some proposals to promote the development of the non-public economy and detailed several past policies. Thus, the privately-owned economy has embraced a new opportunity. At the end of 2002, the privately-owned economy contributed about 48.5% of the GDP along with rising tax revenue amounting to almost 37% of the total.[8] Some large-scale private enterprises like Huawei, Lenovo, Wanxiang, etc., had already gone global. Although POEs cannot compete with the state-owned ones on the foreign investment scale, they had their own advantages. They may even become the main force of foreign investment after a period of development. As Professor Zhang Weiyin from Beijing University said, it was impossible for state-owned enterprises to realize China's capital outflow. The "going global" policy was risky and the risk can shift from state-owned enterprises to the government. Thus the POEs rather than the state-owned ones can be the ideal internationalizers.[9] In fact, with the development of China's market economy, POEs had prepared themselves for overseas investment and hence can become the main force. What is more, China's SMEs have been burgeoning since China's entry into the WTO.

The past more than 30 years of rapid development has obviously strengthened China's comprehensive national power. For one, China has some industries and products with comparative advantages; Chinese enterprises have also attained a certain experience of going global. Along with economic internationalization, the internationalization process of POEs also accelerated. The development of economic internationalization can be divided into two parts: One is the increased exports and the other is the boosted investment. Currently, the POEs have done a great job with regard to both aspects.

As for exports, there are some POEs all over China specializing in the production of export products. Since the reform and opening up, the POEs have gradually set foot into foreign trade. During the 1990s, their average

---

[8] China Statistical Yearbook, 2003.
[9] Liu Keyin. Analysis of Multinational Investment of China's Privately Owned Firms. Group Economic Research, 2006 (2).

annual growth rate in foreign trade was more than 30%.[10] China entered the WTO in 2001, and from 2000 to 2003 the exports of privately-owned enterprises occupied 4.0%, 5.4%, 6.9%, and 9.2% of the total exports and the ratio of imports was 5.8%, 7.4%, 10.1%, and 13.7%, respectively.[11] What is more, the growth rate in total value of imports and exports for these years was 40.4%, 101.8%, 52.8% and 89% respectively.[12] There were only 5,669 POEs committed to overseas investment in 1998 while this increased to 43,476 by the end of 2003.[13] In 2002, the All-China Federation of Industry and Commerce made a survey of certain POEs (referring to those with revenue above CNY 120 million from January to December in 2001). The following were the results. Among the 1248 qualified enterprises in 2001, the total exports were USD8.6 billion, accounting for 3.2% of the national total exports. Enterprises with import and export rights took up 57%, nearly 70% of which were manufacturing enterprises. The average export value per enterprise was USD13.81 million with an average annual growth of 18%. Amid the top 100 enterprises, enterprises with self-exporting rights occupied 60%.[14] All these data manifested the POEs increasing emphasis on foreign trade.

At the same time, POEs expanded their overseas investment, and the host countries included not only Europe and the United States, but also the Commonwealth of Independent States, the Middle East and Africa. At the end of 2004, the accumulated foreign direct investment was nearly USD37 billion. The volume of foreign labor cooperation was USD27.1 billion and there were 2.89 million expatriated people, quite a number of whom operated in going-global business.[15] According to a survey launched by the World Political and Economic Research Institute of the Chinese Academy of Social Sciences, of over 112 export-oriented

---

[10] China Statistical Yearbook, 2000.

[11] China Statistical Yearbook, 2004. Available at http://www.cnki.com.cn/Article/CJFD Total-HLJW200411018.htm.

[12] http://www.cnki.com.cn/Article/CJFDTotal-HLJW200411018.htm.

[13] China Statistical Yearbook, 2004. Available at http://www.cnki.com.cn/Article/CJFD Total-HLJW200411018.htm.

[14] China Statistical Yearbook, 2005.

[15] China Statistical Yearbook, 2002.

enterprises in Wenzhou, 84% of the surveyed enterprises were private ones.[16] Another survey, from April to July in 2002, showed that about 22% of the 2.05 million private enterprises in 31 provinces had already cooperated with overseas joint ventures and 30% of them planned to take up such business in the next three to five years. Only 6.2% of the privately-owned enterprises refused to take up overseas operations and 41.9% never thought about this issue. In the POEs that already made foreign investment, the average investment was only USD27,300, 3.1% of their own total capital. The manufacturing enterprises ranked first amid those enterprises with overseas investment, occupying 47.8%.[17] There was a tendency whereby the bigger the enterprises' size, the more overseas cooperation they wanted to participate in. In recent years, some large-scale private enterprises such as Wanxiang Group, Oriental Group, Leap Group, increasingly explored the international market. For example, the Oriental Group had 12 multinational companies in the United States, Japan, the Russian Federation and other countries. The Leap Group owned 18 branches. While Wanxiang Group setup, merged or participated with equity in 25 foreign subsidiaries with annual export exchange earnings of more than USD100 million for four years from 1999. Overseas resources development and agricultural cooperation also gained some good results like establishing overseas research institutions and transnational M&A. China's economic development further ameliorated after its entry into the WTO, since the expanded market access and ease of investment created a favorable external environment for enterprises to open up the international market. Actually, some strong POEs had invested overseas, and became a new power to implement the "going global" strategy.

3.5   The Development in the Post-Financial Crisis Era

Since China began to carry out the strategy of "going global" in 1999, it has witnessed a rapid growth in its outward foreign investment and economic cooperation, and its growth momentum has intensified since 2003. By the end of 2008, according to the Ministry of Commerce, China's outward

---

[16]Lu Tong, Li Chaoyang. The Internationalization of Wenzhou Private Enterprises, working paper of Institute of World Economics and Politics, Chinese Academy of Social Sciences, http://en.iwep.org.cn/.

[17]http://www.people.com.cn/GB/jinji/31/179/20030226/931380.html.

foreign direct investment value had reached USD183.97 billion, contracted foreign projects had reached a turnover of USD263 billion and a contract value of USD434.1 billion; foreign labor cooperation had a turnover of USD55.9 billion, expatriate contracted personnel 4.62 million.[18]

China's economic growth is driven by the development of foreign trade and consequently the global financial crisis would definitely exert some impact on China's economy. Trade protectionism has greatly hampered China's foreign trade development. The financial crisis led to the rise of trade protectionism as all countries tend to take measures to protect their national economies, and thus China has become the biggest victim of global anti-dumping investigations.

Labor-intensive products are the traditional comparative advantage for China's exports, and it is difficult to promote the quality and technological content of the goods due to technology limitations in the short term. During the financial crisis, developed countries, such as the member countries of the European Union, the United States, Japan, tended to impose some restrictions on the import of Chinese goods in the form of product standards, which introduced very adverse effects on China's foreign trade development.

According to the General Administration of Customs of China, in January 2012 the Sino–EU trade value was USD42.68 billion, down 7.1%; over the same period, the Sino–US trade value was USD35.46 billion, down 3.9%; Sino–ASEAN bilateral trade was USD25.89 billion, down 10.6%. In addition, the Sino-Japan trade value was USD22.73 billion, down 18.4%.[19]

The severe world economic recession incurred by the outbreak of the 2008 financial crisis slowed down international capital flows, with a sharp shrinking of global market demand; global foreign direct investment flows decreased by more than 20% in 2008, whereas China's "going global" policy has maintained a strong development momentum.

In 2008, China's flow of outward foreign direct investment reached USD52.15 billion, with a year-on-year growth of 96.7%, being the top of the developing countries for six successive years. Contracted foreign projects completed a turnover of USD56.6 billion, up 39.4%, and attained above a 30% growth rate for seven years. Foreign labor cooperation completed a

---

[18] http://data.mofcom.gov.cn/channel/dwjjhz/dwjjhz.shtml.
[19] http://www.customs.gov.cn/publish/portal0/tab49667/.

turnover of USD8.06 billion, up 19.1%, with 427,000 expatriate personnel, a year-on-year increase of 55,000 people.[20]

In the post-financial crisis era, more and more Chinese enterprises are committed to "going global". Some Chinese enterprises took advantage of the financial crisis to be the participants in international M&A in an effort to be multinational companies. M&A has become the mainstream mode for China's enterprises to undertake OFDI. The 2008 financial crisis provided new opportunities for China's "going global".

First, other countries are more willing to expand investment cooperation with China. Since the outbreak of the financial crisis, the depressed global market and the rapidly shrinking credit market have made many countries face a serious lack of capital, which created demand for foreign investments. These countries have great expectations for investments from China, and they have eased investment restrictions in some areas, which provide increased opportunities for investment or M&A in high-quality assets, as well as advanced technology.

Second, the investment cost is reduced. The prices of international assets, energy and resources have plummeted, and consequently many enterprises in developed countries and some emerging countries are at the risk of bankruptcy or of merger or acquisition, especially some enterprises who have key technologies, research and development personnel, marketing networks. Other strategic assets have been losing their favorable positions for the prices are at record low levels, so Chinese enterprises are in a more favorable investment position.

Third, the Chinese government makes more efforts to encourage enterprises to "go global". In order to encourage enterprises to go global, the Chinese government has continuously improved support policies and related measures like an advisory service and coordination system for investment promotion. The government has developed a support policy system including finance, credit, insurance and tax support, and made full use of various fairs and exhibitions to build platforms for enterprises, and established a safeguard mechanism through bilateral investment agreements for promotion and protection, and avoidance of double taxation.

---

[20] http://data.mofcom.gov.cn/channel/includes/list.shtml?channel=dwjjhz&visit=A.

It cannot be denied that currently China's slogan of "go global" has a favorable external and internal investment environment.

(1) Gradually loosen foreign exchange controls on outward foreign investment.

In July 2006, SAFE completely canceled the capital source review and quota restrictions on outward foreign investment. On October 12, 2009, SAFE announced the "Notice of the SAFE on Promulgating the Provisions on the Management of Centralized Operations of the Foreign Exchange Fund of Internal Members of Domestic Enterprises", and consequently the policy environment for outward foreign investment has been further optimized in the following way: First, to relax the limitation on business participants qualifications; second, to clarify the basic business principles, business structure, audit programs and other related programs concerning domestic foreign currency cash pooling, and stipulate that the entrusted bank (financial company) who is in charge of implementation shall be responsible for the application and related statistical submission; third, to further simplify the administrative examination and approval procedures; the related foreign exchange management operations mentioned in the Provisions are approved by the local Administration of Foreign Exchange; SAFE shall no longer be responsible for the audit work; fourth, to regulate and perfect laws and regulations on centralized operations of the foreign exchange fund, by abolishing the *"Notice of the SAFE on Issues Concerning the Administration of Spot Foreign Exchange Settlement and Sale Business Launched by the Enterprise Group Finance Companies"* which was enacted in 2008 and later integrated into the Provisions, and further promote the revision work on foreign exchange management regulations. Last, further simplify approval procedures of related foreign exchange business, the bank (financial company), without the approval of the administration, can use a qualification approval document to help the enterprise settle related business, account-opening as well as domestic foreign exchange transfer, involve centralized operations of the foreign exchange fund.

(2) The Solid Support of Fiscal and Financial Policy.

(i) Special financial support In October 2007, the Ministry of Commerce, the Ministry of Finance, the People's Bank of China and the National

Association of Industry and Commerce jointly issued the "Instruction on Encouraging and Guiding the Non-Public Enterprises Foreign Investment Cooperation". This instruction pays full attention to the support, including discount loans funds, non-public enterprises can enjoy while conducting the overseas processing trade, small and medium-sized enterprises international market development funds and foreign aid projects funds, contracted foreign projects risk-guarantee special funds, etc. This instruction has played an active role in encouraging Guangdong, Zhejiang and other provinces to promote foreign investment in non-public enterprises. On August 21, 2008, the Ministry of Finance put forward six special funds, small and medium-sized enterprises international market development funds, agricultural science and technology achievements transformation fund, small and medium-sized enterprise service system special subsidy funds, small and medium-sized enterprise development special fund, small and medium-sized enterprise platform service system special subsidy funds.

(ii) Credit support

On October 27, 2004, the National Development and Reform Commission and the Export–Import Bank of China jointly issued the "*Notice of the National Development and Reform Commission, the Export–Import Bank of China on Giving Credit Support to the Key Overseas Investment Projects Encouraged by the State*". Four kinds of key projects stipulated in the Notice have been covered by "special loans for overseas investments", and enjoyed export credit preferential interest rates. On July 30, 2010, the SAFE announced the *Notice of the SAFE on the Administration of External Guarantees Provided by Domestic Institutions*, which makes efforts to promote the convenience of foreign investment for enterprises. To provide the financing of external guarantees, a domestic bank qualified to operate the guarantee business may apply to the local branch/sub-branch or foreign exchange administrative department of the SAFE (hereinafter collectively referred to as the "foreign exchange authorities", with the branches and foreign exchange administrative departments being hereinafter referred to as "SAFE branches") for a balance quota for external guarantees. Within the quota approved by the foreign exchange authority, the bank may provide the financing of external guarantees at its sole discretion, and need not apply to the foreign exchange authority for approval on a case-by-case basis. There is no quota limit on the financing of external guarantees provided by a domestic bank qualified to operate the guarantee business, and the bank need not apply to the foreign exchange authority for approval on a case-by-case basis, provided that the relevant risk management provisions of the regulatory authorities are complied with.

(iii) Preferential tax policies

In 2009, the Ministry of Finance and the State Administration of Taxation issued the *"Notice of the Ministry of Finance and the State Administration of Taxation on Issues Concerning the Foreign Income Tax Credit of Enterprises"*, which aims to perfect the enterprise's overseas income tax credit system, and specify the methods to regulate the indirect credit. On May 7, 2010, the State Council announced *"Several Opinions of the State Council on Encouraging and Guiding the Healthy Development of Private Investment"* to encourage and guide private enterprises actively participating in international competition. (1) Encourage private enterprises "going global", to actively participate in international competition. Support private enterprises launching internationalized operations in the aspects of R&D, manufacturing and marketing, etc., develop strategic resources and establish an international marketing network. Support private enterprises exploring the international market with the utilization of own brand, proprietary intellectual property rights and independent marketing, and accelerate the development of transnational enterprises and world famous brands. Encourage the composition of a commonwealth among private enterprises, between private enterprises and state-owned enterprises, displaying the advantages of each unit to jointly conduct various forms of overseas investment. (2) Perfect the promotion and protection system of overseas investment. Establish a policy consultation mechanism concerning the encouragement and promotion of the international flow of private capital between related countries, launch various forms of dialogue and communication, and develop a cooperative relationship for long-term stabilization, based on reciprocity and mutual benefit. Through signing a bilateral cooperation agreement on private investment, utilize the multilateral agreement system, to strive for a favorable investment and trading environment for the "going global" of private enterprises and more preferential policies. Complete and perfect the policy of encouragement for overseas investment, from the aspects of financial support, insurance, foreign exchange management, quality control, etc. Private enterprises and other enterprises should enjoy equal treatment.

To ensure the interests of the enterprise when going global, China has had much success in reciprocal bilateral tax agreements. From January 1981, when China and Japan signed the first bilateral tax agreement, to the end of February 2012, China has signed more than 90 foreign tax agreements, among which 82 are effective agreements. Furthermore, mainland China has signed avoidance of double taxation arrangements with both Hong Kong (SAR of China) and Macao (SAR of China). The above agreements gradually covered all China's investment destinations outside the mainland, and some of the agreements even provide a more favorable tax rate for dividends, interest, transfer of property income than the domestic rate.

(iv) Special insurance support

In 2005, the Ministry of Commerce and China Export and Credit Insurance Corporation jointly issued a *"Circular of the Ministry of Commerce and China Export & Credit Insurance Corporation on Implementing Export Credit Insurance"*, which provides a risk-guarantee mechanism for non-public enterprises to go global. To further perfect export support policies for individual, private and other non-public enterprises (hereinafter referred to as the "non-public enterprises"), improve the export promotion system for non-public enterprises and boost the active participation of non-public enterprises in "going global" so as to explore the international market, the Ministry of Commerce and China Export & Credit Insurance Corporation grant special preferential supporting measures to non-public enterprises. (1) Competent commercial departments at all levels and various business organizations of China Credit Insurance shall establish an effective work coordination mechanism, help non-public enterprises actively use export credit insurance to open up the international market, improve their abilities at risk management and increase their profits from internationalized business. (2) The Ministry of Commerce and China Credit Insurance shall jointly provide non-public enterprises with training for export trade risk management, give assistance to such enterprises in establishing and improving an export trade risk management mechanism so as to avoid trade hazards and realize sound operation.

(3) The Ministry of Commerce has been playing a crucial role in promoting China's enterprises in going global.

(i) The Ministry of Commerce is about to perfect the management system. It has issued some laws, regulations and normative documents. A joint-administration framework in which the Ministry of Commerce is in charge of macro management, with other departments' coordination, local government management, industrial organizations and overseas Chinese chambers of commerce as well as embassies' supervision, has been formed. The Ministry of Commerce has setup some mechanisms. In 2008, the State Council issued *"Administrative Regulation on Contracting Foreign Projects"*, while in October 2009; *"Measures for the Administration of the Competence for Contracting Foreign Construction Projects"* has been enacted. Consequently, both above-mentioned regulations provide a solid legal support for contracting foreign projects. *"Regulation on the Administration of Foreign Labor Cooperation"* took effect from August 2012, and Foreign Investment Regulations that aim at boosting investment possibilities have created a draft proposal.

(ii) The Ministry of Commerce is committed to providing a full range of public services, including the following:

(a) The information service. The State Council and the Ministry of Commerce attach great importance to the information service, and make efforts to provide timely and accurate information for enterprises. Over the years, the Ministry of Commerce has introduced some information, such as the Foreign Market Environment Report MOFCOM. Released annually since 2003, are the "Guide and Directory to Countries and Industries for China's FDI", and the "Guide and Directory to Countries and Industries for China's contracted foreign projects".

Since 2009, MOFCOM has published a yearly report titled "China's Overseas Investment Cooperation by Country (Region) Guide". In 2009 it released the first batch of country guides to twenty countries, introducing each country's investment environment and business environment with respect to law, local culture and customs. It also established a "foreign investment cooperation information service system", by which the enterprise can find the relevant information on the Internet. The Ministry of Commerce attempts to provide effective information in advance for the enterprises that want to "go global" and are ready to "go global". Each enterprise with various motivations and goals can find suitable countries and areas in which to expand its business from this information.

(b) Personnel training. Since 2007, the Ministry of Commerce has asked research institutions and universities to train multinational management personnel. Since the end of March 2009, the Ministry of Commerce has also published a series on multinational business management personnel training, which laid a solid foundation for training, regulation and long-term training.

(c) To maintain enterprises' overseas legal rights, the Ministry of Commerce has established a bilateral mixed commission on economic and trade mechanisms with more than 100 countries and regions in the world, and signed 127 bilateral investment protection agreements and free trade agreements, and government agreements on mutually beneficial cooperation with more than 20 countries and regions. At present the Ministry of Commerce has established an overseas security network, emergency plans, and has improved overseas disputes and emergency settlement measures, established a national foreign labor services aid agency, and has properly dealt with several overseas emergencies.

MOFCOM has gradually perfected its management. MOFCOM, in cooperation with relevant departments, setup a preliminarily policy promotion system, a service guarantee system and risk control system for "going global" business, to guide and boost enterprises' outward investment and cooperation in a positive and steady manner. It accelerated the processes of the legal system and the convenience of outward investment and cooperation, consecutively issuing and implementing several regulations and policies such as Administrative Measures on Overseas Investment, Regulations on the Administration of Overseas Contracts and Regulations on the Administration of Labor Cooperation Overseas. It has played a guiding role in macroeconomic planning and the leverage role of policies, compiling The Twelfth Five-Year Guideline on Investment and Cooperation Overseas, and various plans for outward development, perfecting all kinds of preferential policies in finance, foreign exchange and insurance etc. It has guided Chinese enterprises to integrate themselves with local culture and the interests of invested countries and do well in management, further standardizing enterprises' outward business activities, issuing "Opinions on Cultural Development of Chinese Outward Enterprises", distributing the "Guide on Staff Management of Chinese-Invested Enterprises (Institutions) Overseas" and the "Guide on Social Responsibilities of Foreign Contracts". It has enhanced public service, regularly releasing the "Guide on Outward Investment in Foreign Countries or Regions", the "Guide on Outward Investment to Industries", "Reports on Investment and Operational Barriers", establishing and improving a foreign investment information service system, and strengthening personnel training for a "going global" strategy. It has reinforced the guarantee of rights and interests overseas, pushing forward the development of a rights and interests protection system, enacting "Administrative Provisions on Safety Overseas of Chinese-Invested Enterprises and Institutions as well as their Staff", releasing warning information according to "Outward Investment Risk Indications", compiling an "Administrative Guide on Safety Overseas of Chinese-Invested Enterprises and Institutions as well as their Staff", helping enterprises to properly deal with risks overseas, enhancing the development of bilateral and multilateral systems, positively creating a fair global environment for enterprises, guaranteeing lawful rights and interests of enterprises overseas.

Chapter 4

A General Introduction to Internationalization
of China's POEs

4.1 Internationalization Process

4.1.1 Development path of China's POEs

Since China's reform and opening up, especially in the 21st century, the sudden emergence and rapid development of the private economy have become a beautiful landscape in China's economic development. The development of indigenous China's POEs mainly went through the following stages: The first stage is from 1978 to 1988. The private economy originated in Fengyang County of Anhui Province where people distributed the commune's land among the households, and the well-known "household contract responsibility system" proliferated around the country under the state policy of reform. As China did not acknowledge the existence of the private economy at that time, most enterprises attached themselves to the local government or some state-owned enterprises, commonly known as "wearing a red hat". The second stage is from 1988 to 1992 when the private economy plummeted owing to the reversals of economic policies. The third stage is from 1992 to 1998. After Deng Xiaoping's Southern Talk, an upsurge in doing business spread all over the country. Many people resigned from offices to join the rush of doing business. "Doing business" and "nationwide business rush" had become the most well-known phrases at that stage. The fourth stage is from 1998 up to now. Along with the Internet boom, the private enterprises with knowledge and capital advantages developed quickly and became the highlights of the market. After more than a decade of development, the private economy has already gained its legal status. A realistic challenge it faces is to maintain sustainable development, which impels many private enterprises to have embarked on a road to go public. Therefore, for a further development, private enterprises have to go through some "growing pains", for instance, whether to seek internationalization and how to carry out international operations.

The China Non-Governmental Enterprise Directors Association, the National Statistical Society of China and the research center for enterprises of the China Academy of Management Science jointly released the country's 2010 top 500 private enterprises list, and showed that the private sector has accounted for more than 50% of China's GDP. According to All-China Federation of Industry and Commerce, in 2010 China's POEs saw a boost in tax revenue, which exceeded CNY 1.1 trillion, with an average annual growth of more than 20%. Meanwhile, its share of job opportunities provided was more than 70%.[1] China's private economy continues with a growth rate higher than the national economic growth rate and becomes an important force in the national economy.

By the end of September 2011, the number of registered private enterprises nationwide had reached more than 9 million, up to 14.9% over the same period in the last year. Total registered capital of private enterprises was about CNY 25 trillion, up 38.6% over the previous period in the last year. In addition, the number of registered self-employed households was 36 million, an increase of 8.5% over the last year, with an overall registered capital of CNY 1.5 trillion. Substantial growth of private economic investment was witnessed in the year 2011.[2] By the end of September 2011, the total fixed investment of the urban non-state-owned and non-state-holding economy — the private economy — had reached CNY 14.2 trillion, up 46.5.7% over 2010, accounting for 58.9% of China's urban fixed asset investment.[3] In 2010, China's POEs had boosted export volume to USD481.266 billion, a growth rate of 223% of that in 2005, an average annual growth of 26.4%.[4] Influenced by the increasingly

---

[1] http://www.acfic.org.cn/Web/c_000000010003000100050005/d_12216.htm.

[2] China Statistical Yearbook, 2012.

[3] China Statistical Yearbook, 2012.

[4] China Statistical Yearbook, 2011.

fierce market competition and unprecedented international financial crisis, China's POEs made full use of the state's incentive policies to commit to "go global", actively participating in the international market. Small and medium-sized enterprises made joint efforts to "go global". In addition, the quality of China's POEs has been improved. The organization and governance structure of the private sector has continuously been optimized. The economic strength of enterprises is increasing while the independent innovation capability has been enhanced, and the number of listed private companies has increased significantly.

4.1.2 Overview of internationalization of China's POEs

Since the private economy is an important part of China's national economy, its rapid development not only makes it grow into a new force in the development of China's internationalization, but also speeds up the process of Chinese enterprises' "going global".

First, private enterprises are becoming increasingly important in China's import and export trade. The export value of the private sector in 2004 accounted for about 1/9 of the total export value, while in the first three quarters of 2011 it accounted for 1/3 of the total amount of USD570 billion.[5] Meanwhile, the private-sector imports value is growing very fast. Its growth rate is much higher than that of China's total imports. The proportion of private-sector imports is increasing as well. In 2011, the top 500 POEs realized a total volume of import and exports of USD251.153 billion, increasing by 46.47% over the last year, with an imports growth rate of 64.04% and export growth rate of 16% respectively.[6]

However, the scale of technology imports in private enterprises is relatively small. In 2010, China imported 11,253 technologies, with the contracts amounting to USD25.64 billion, with the technology royalty fee about USD21.85 billion. Among them, the number of private enterprises' imported technology contracts was 1,638, amounting to USD2.138 billion, and the technology fee was about USD1.96 billion. The amount accounted

---

[5] China Statistical Yearbook, 2012.
[6] http://www.chinachamber.org.cn/Web/c_000000020007/d_15650.htm.

for only 2.03% of the total amount of the contract value in 2004, while it accounted for 8.3% in 2010.[7]

Second, the proportion of OFDI in private enterprises continues to increase. The proportion of state-owned enterprises' investment dropped from 35% to 29% in 2004 while the proportion of non-state enterprises continued to increase. The privately-owned enterprise really has become an important force in the "going global" process of Chinese enterprises. According to the ministry of commerce statistics, the proportion of non-state-owned enterprises (mainly private enterprises) in China's foreign investment flow is rising year by year. In 2011, the OFDI flow of non-state-owned enterprises was about 44.4% of the national total.[8] The private enterprises have also played an important role in the practice of overseas listings of Chinese enterprises. In 2004, 84 of China's domestic companies were listed overseas in the United States, Singapore and other countries, as well as on the Hong Kong (SAR of China) stock market. The total amount of funding was up to USD11.15 billion.[9] Shanda, Baidu, Sohu, Qiao Xing, Suntech, Shanghai Quartet, and a number of private enterprises are successfully listed overseas.

Outward foreign investment has not set a new record for a single transaction in 2011, but overseas M&As operations conducted by POEs will become the highlight of Chinese enterprises' overseas M&As. China's POEs seized the opportunity of international industrial restructuring and domestic industrial transformation to extend their position in the production chain to the high-end, and enhanced their product design, research and development (R&D), marketing and multinational managerial skills through cross-border mergers and acquisitions (M&A). A significantly large number of M&A occur in the chemical, machine manufacturing, automobile, electronics, food, clothing, and electrical home appliances industries.

At present, China's POEs are still at a low level of internationalization, as they mainly depend on the low-cost, low value-added advantages in

---

[7] China Statistical Yearbook, 2012.
[8] China Statistical Yearbook, 2012.
[9] http://finance.sina.com.cn/stock/ychd/20050302/17431397509.shtml.

seeking extensive and quantitative export expansion. They lack techno-logical innovation and world-famous brands, and have no access to high-end manufacturing and high-end services on a large-scale. Of course, there are a few private companies actively seeking cooperation with overseas companies, or directly choosing M&As overseas, so as to acquire technology and other resources, to get rid of the low-end manufacturer role in the value chain, and enhance international competitiveness.

4.1.3 Features of internationalization of China's POEs

For China's POEs, their internationalization is a branch of the inter-nationalization of Chinese enterprises in general, and the result of China's economic reform and opening up, which has experienced about 30 years of development with obvious characteristics of the developing countries.

First, the internationalization of China's POEs started late but the speed of development was fast.

Because the government had adopted a policy of weakening the internationalization of private enterprises for a long time, it started relatively late, later than that of both state-owned enterprises and foreign-invested enterprises in China. The time lag is on account of national policy. In early 1999, the right to operate a foreign trade was gradually granted to private enterprises by the Chinese government, which allowed private enterprises to have the opportunity to make some outward inter-nationalization using the simplest pattern, by exporting. So they could participate in the international market and later become eligible to invest abroad.

In fact, before the end of 1998, none of the enterprises engaged in China's direct foreign trade were private enterprises, not to mention the capacity to introduce foreign capital or foreign investment. Being restricted by the right to import and export directly, POEs were required to employ state-owned professional foreign trade agents to export their products and import raw materials and equipment. For instance, faced with the tough domestic market, Zhejiang Universal turned to the state-owned foreign trade companies for help, asking them to promote the products on the international market. But the agency's shortcomings were obvious: First, most of profits were taken by agents; second, the cost was high, private enterprises had to pay an intermediary fee to foreign trade agents; third, private enterprises were unable to grasp the opportunity to meet the customer's real needs in the international market.

In 1999, the Ministry of Foreign Trade gave the right to export to the first batch of 20 private enterprises. Private enterprises finally had the opportunity to achieve the aspirations of participating in internationalization but gradually. Since then, a growing number of China's POEs became eligible to obtain foreign trade rights. Some private companies started internationalization through exports and imports. With China's entry into the WTO, especially in 2004, the foreign trade operators included individuals following the "Foreign Trade Law" amendment. It means that as long as the basic conditions for engaging in foreign trade are met, ownership is no longer a threshold. Private enterprises have become one of the major participants in China's foreign trade.

After China's POEs become eligible for international operations, in just a few years its international development has achieved a series of gratifying achievements: The rapid growth of imports and exports that makes a greater contribution to China's foreign trade, the small but influential foreign investment and growing international competitiveness of enterprises.

Second, the motivation for private enterprises' international operations is original.

On the whole, the motives for internationalization of China's privately-owned enterprises are diverse, such as avoiding fierce domestic competition, seeking advanced technology and equipment to expand sales markets. Of course, we do not rule out the possibility that a small number of China's POEs want to take the responsibility for establishing cross-border corporations.

Let us look at this from another point of view, which is at an advanced stage from the international mode of operation — foreign direct investment. Dunning, a well-known British scholar on multinational companies, summarizes the enterprises' motives for foreign investment into four: resource-seeking, market-seeking, efficiency-seeking and global strategy. From the practice of internationalization of Chinese enterprises, whether it is foreign investment from the Chinese state-owned enterprises or private enterprises, most of the foreign investment is resource seeking or market-seeking.

By the way of investing in neighboring Myanmar, Yunnan Hongyu Group in China has made excellent use of local natural conditions, land resources and low labor costs to do lemon cultivation. Through the acquisition of Philips' overall core CDMA technology and personnel in the United States, Zhejiang Holley obtained leading foreign R&D technology intellectual property rights, so as to gain the world's most advanced technology and human resources. Through the acquisition, Xinjiang Delong Group obtained international marketing network resources and won an international market share. Through the integration of domestic and foreign resources, it has formed a large-scale operation.

Third, private enterprises depend more on their own efforts in the process of promoting internationalization.

Different from state-owned enterprises in the process of internationalization, private enterprises gained little support from government. What is worse, most of the time after the reform and opening up, private enterprises faced discrimination, limitations and constraints by the government and state-owned enterprises. In recent years, the government's attitude to private enterprise has changed a lot. The government is taking a liberal, open attitude towards the internationalization of private enterprises. Thus, in the process of internationalization, private enterprises show a spirit of no fear of difficulties and no flinching when faced with competition. With no right policy offered, they looked for loopholes in the existing policy; with little support from the government, they found a way out by creating their own opportunities.

In the transition period, the government had an inherent requirement to make up for the resource gaps and carry out a national strategic opening up policy. To implement the above strategy in the international market, it should have used enterprises rather than the government. As private enterprises have been connected with weakness, and with the government's long-standing prejudice and discrimination against private enterprises, state-owned enterprises were still the major implementation tools of government strategy and policy in the transition period.

Fourth, China's POEs have risen in the Chinese business world rapidly. "Chinese Business" is a widely used concept, generally referring to business groups who are active on the world economic stage that have Chinese national or ethnic origins, including Hong Kong (SAR of China) and Macau (SAR of China) businessmen and Taiwanese businessmen and overseas Chinese around the world engaged as commercial actors, who are collectively referred to as the "World Chinese Entrepreneurs". The Chinese businessmen, who are going out from Mainland China and are active in the international economic arena, are also included.

With the acceleration of China's "going global", the rapid development of internationalization of private enterprises becomes a major feature and highlight of Chinese entrepreneurs. In recent years, China's net OFDI has grown rapidly. China's OFDI flow amounted to only USD2.9 billion in 2003, while in 2011 it was USD74.65 billion.[10] China's OFDI amounted to USD424.78 billion at the end of 2011, ranking 13th in the world. By the end of 2011, more than 13,500 domestic Chinese investors had established 18,000 foreign direct investment enterprises in 177 countries (regions).[11] The variety of industries invested in is balanced and complete. Business services, mining, financial services, wholesale and retail trade, manufacturing and transportation consist of the major industrial choices for China's OFDI. From 2003 to 2005, the annual growth rate of China's foreign direct investment was 110%, 78%, and 80% respectively, while it declined to 1.1%, 21.7%, 8.5% in 2009, 2010 and 2011.[12] A large number of competitive Chinese companies like Lenovo Group, Haier Group, Huawei Group, ZTE Group, have started international operations, with distribution operations around the world, and have made great progress. A large number of Chinese entrepreneurs go global, becoming a huge new Chinese business power.

China's POEs built a "China mall" around the world, which is also a reason for the significant rise in new mainland Chinese business performance. In 1998, Wenzhou businessmen established the first "China

---

[10] http://www.usc.cuhk.edu.hk/PaperCollection/Details.aspx?id=6538.
[11] http://fec.mofcom.gov.cn/article/tjzl/jwtz/201208/1693366_1.html.
[12] China Statistical Yearbook, 2012.

mall" in Sao Paulo, Brazil. Up to now, the Wenzhou businessmen have established a dozen "China malls" in Cameroon, Russia, the Netherlands, United Arab Emirates, the united States, Mongolia, Britain, Chile and Finland. In March 2007, led by the Cornell Group in Wenzhou, Zhejiang, the Russian Ussuriysk Economic and Trade Cooperation Zone, which cost 2 billion yuan, was established in the far eastern city of Ussuriysk. There are Chinese businessmen building similar Chinese malls in Rome, Italy, Milan and other places, which are engaged in wholesale and retail selling of Chinese products.

4.2 Regional Features

From 2002 to 2011, the total import and export volume of the eastern region (Beijing, Tianjin, Hebei, Liaoning, Shanghai, Jiangsu, Zhejiang, Fujian, Shandong, and Guangdong) went from USD572.19 billion to USD3.22 trillion, increasing 4.6 times, and an average annual growth rate of 21.2%; its share of the national total has stayed at about 90%.[13] In 2011, the import and export value of POEs reached USD772.66 billion, increasing 35.3 times compared with 2002, of which Guangdong, Zhejiang, Jiangsu accounted for 55% of the total national exports from POEs.[14]

By the end of 2011, 13 out of 16 China's overseas economic and trading areas that were in operation had been contracted with enterprises from the eastern provinces. In 2011, OFDI (the non-financial sector) of the ten provinces in the east has amounted to USD62.05 billion, increasing 9.7 times compared with 2004, in which the east accounted for 73.1% of the total amount of all provinces. In 2011, the east had accomplished a foreign projects turnover of USD43.58 billion, 6.2 times that of 2002.[15]

According to the Ministry of Commerce, in 2011, China's non-financial sector domestic investors have made outward direct investment in 3,391 overseas businesses in 132 countries and regions, with a total investment value of USD60.07 billion, in which the equity investment and

---

[13] China Statistical Yearbook, 2012.
[14] China Statistical Yearbook, 2012.
[15] http://www.mofcom.gov.cn/aarticle/ae/ai/201211/20121108414144.html.

other investment reached USD45.67 billion and accounted for 76%; and reinvestment of the profits reached USD14.4 billion and accounted for 24%.[16]

According to the 2010 China's Statistical Bulletin of OFDI, in terms of investors, investors from Zhejiang, Guangdong, Jiangsu, Fujian, Shandong, Shanghai, Beijing, Liaoning, Henan, Heilongjiang accounted for 67% of the total number of investors; Zhejiang Province has the largest number of investors, with a share of 16.3%; 70% of the private enterprise investors are from Zhejiang and Fujian provinces. By the end of October 2011, Zhejiang had 5,031 businesses that have been approved and examined by the authorities, and occupies first place in China.[17]

From 2003 to 2009, Beijing, Shanghai, and Guangdong alternated with each other to occupy the first place for outward FDI in the non-finance sector. But since 2010, Zhejiang has been ranked first.[18]

The share that state-owned enterprises contributed to China's OFDI stock dropped gradually in the past five years, and has decreased from 81% at the end of 2006 to 66% at the end of 2010.[19] According to statistics, in 2010, 137 of the top 500 private enterprises committed to foreign investment; with 592 investment projects, an investment value of USD6.18 billion, and a 174% increase over 2009.[20]

The unbalanced development of China's POEs has led to significant regional features in the internationalization of China's POEs. Zhejiang is known as the cradle of China's private economy, and hence goes ahead in the internationalization of China's POEs, and has a higher internationalization level. In 2011, Zhejiang's POEs occupied first place in terms of OFDI of POEs. In 2011, Zhejiang's POEs conducted 45 overseas M&A investment projects. According to the Department of Commerce of Zhejiang, Zhejiang's POEs have become increasingly active in overseas

---

[16] http://fec.mofcom.gov.cn/article/tjzl/jwtz/201208/1693366_1.html.
[17] http://fec.mofcom.gov.cn/article/tjzl/jwtz/201109/1250630_1.html.
[18] http://fec.mofcom.gov.cn/article/tjzl/jwtz/201109/1250630_1.html.
[19] http://hzs.mofcom.gov.cn/aarticle/date/201201/20120107934068.html.
[20] http://hzs.mofcom.gov.cn/aarticle/date/201201/20120107934068.html.

Table 4.1. China's outward FDI flows by provinces in 2011 (non-finance part) (million USD).

Rank	Province/City	Amount
1	Zhejiang	2113.97
	Ningbo	859.65
2	Shandong	2077.04
	Qingdao	191.27
3	Jiangsu	2001.29
4	Guangdong	1902.69
	Shenzhen	624.08
5	Shanghai	1513.16
6	Hainan	1201.44
7	Liaoning	1149.50
	Dalian	674.84
8	Hunan	804.83
9	Beijing	745.34
10	Hubei	690.09
11	Gansu	634.97
12	Tianjin	572.47
13	Yunnan	570.80
14	Sichuan	533.43
15	Anhui	508.75
16	Shaanxi	441.54
17	Chongqing	418.57
18	Hebei	354.37
19	Fujian	343.42
	Xiamen	127.10
20	Xinjiang	325.57
21	Henan	301.71
22	Jiangxi	280.90
23	Jilin	197.16
24	Helongjiang	158.03
25	Shanxi	149.73
26	Guangxi	122.37
27	Inner Mongolia	104.03
28	Xinjiang	49.71
29	Guizhou	19.50
30	Ningxia	12.49
31	Tibet	2.16
32	Qinghai	1.73

Source: http://hzs.mofcom.gov.cn/aarticle/date/201201/
20120107934068.html.

M&A and improved the benefit steadily. OFDI have been conducted in multiple ways and M&A rather than the simple form of Greenfield have gradually improved investment, which implies that the POEs internationalization management ability.

4.2.1   Zhejiang Province

With the implementation of the "going global" strategy and the rapid development of foreign trade, overseas investment in Zhejiang has boomed.

The development of foreign trade promotes the rise of its foreign investment. With the continuous development of foreign trade, Zhejiang is very active in imports and exports, and its demand for outward foreign investment increases. In 1982, Zhejiang established a company in Hong Kong (SAR of China) called Fuchun Company that was its first outside the mainland China investment project. At the same time, the Zhejiang government got actively involved in promoting foreign investment.

The "going global" strategy facilitated the development of Zhejiang's foreign investment further. In 1999, Zhejiang had proposed the development strategy of promoting foreign investment — a "two push" strategy: to promote the province's manufacturing industry to go global and develop the overseas processing trade; to promote the professional commodity markets in foreign countries and develop transnational business, thus boosting Zhejiang's products, equipment and labor exports. After the implementation of the "going global" strategy by the central government in 2000, in 2001 Zhejiang issued a "Speed up for the Implementation of the 'Going Global' Strategy Advice", and clearly put forward the strategic goals for "going global", promoting enterprises to go global. Meanwhile, the introduction and implementation of policies created a good environment for Zhejiang enterprises to go global.

An increasing number of Zhejiang enterprises have started the implementation of their "Going Global" strategy, which expands the scale of overseas investment. Especially at the beginning of the 21st century, Zhejiang's foreign direct investment developed rapidly. The value of total foreign investment and Chinese investment is growing rapidly. From 2003 to 2006, Zhejiang's total overseas investment grew 51.8%, 108.8%, 176.1% and 99% while China's investment grew 65.9%, 97.1%, 150.7%, and 79%

Table 4.2. 2000–2010 development of Zhejiang's OFDI.

Year	Projects	Total investment (million USD)	Investment by Zhejiang (million USD)	Average investment per capita project (million USD)	Average investment by Zhejiang per capita project (million USD)
2000	107	17.06	15.14	0.159	0.141
2001	144	38.56	33.50	0.268	0.233
2002	226	63.64	51.32	0.282	0.227
2003	301	96.58	85.13	0.321	0.283
2004	378	167.60	151.75	0.443	0.401
2005	435	195.98	167.76	0.451	0.386
2006	425	391.17	300.44	0.92	0.707
2007	420	661.77	606.06	1.576	1.443
2008	427	920.43	860.88	2.156	2.016
2009	475	1340.75	1234.91	2.823	2.60
2010	630	4020.49	3360.08	6.382	5.333

Note: Data collected by Zhejiang Foreign Trade and Economic Cooperation Bureau.

respectively.[21] By the end of 2011, Zhejiang Province had had a total foreign direct investment value of USD211 billion, where the investments cover 16 industries such as business services, manufacturing, wholesale and retail business etc. Hong Kong (SAR of China), Sweden, the US, Germany, and Vietnam are top investment destinations.[22] The development of Zhejiang's foreign investment from 2000 to 2010 is shown in Table 4.2.

Zhejiang's foreign investment has the following characteristics:

4.2.1.1 *A progressive yearly expansion of investment scale*

With the development of Zhejiang enterprises' overseas investment, the scale of foreign investment has increased annually. At the same time, the number of large-scale investment projects has gradually increased. From the aspect of total overseas investment, as shown in Table 3.1, the total overseas investment of Zhejiang expands every year and grows rapidly. From the aspect of the scale of individual projects, large-scale investment

---

[21] China Statistical Yearbook, 2007, http://www.zj.stats.gov.cn/zjtj2012/indexch.htm.
[22] http://www.zj.stats.gov.cn/zjtj2012/indexch.htm.

projects increase year by year. The average total investment and the Chinese investment have increased from USD0.159 and USD0.141 million in 2000 to USD6.382 and USD5.333 million in 2010 respectively, increased by 39.1 and 36.8 times, and their average annual growth rates were 44.7% and 43.8% respectively.[23] In the first 10 months of 2011, Zhejiang's overseas investment projects had an average total investment value of USD7.659 million, USD1.045 million more than the same period in the previous year,[24] an increase of 15.8%; and an average Chinese investment value of USD7.258 million, increased by 27.8% from the same period in the previous year. A big project provides impetus for internationalization obviously, such as Zhejiang FULIDA Co., Ltd. with investment of USD250 million to setup FULIDA Luxembourg holding company; Ningbo JOYSON Holding has made an investment of USD230 million to merge and acquire the German PURY limited liability company; GEELY Group spent USD1.388 billion to conduct the merger and acquisition of Volvo,[25] etc. By the first 10 months of 2011, there had been 34 projects whose investment value had exceeded USD10 million in which 8 projects of more than USD50 million investment have been included.[26]

4.2.1.2 A continuous expansion of investment range

From the aspect of geographical distribution, Zhejiang enterprises' overseas investment is showing a trend of gradual expansion. However, the Asia region, especially East and Southeast Asia remained the focus of Zhejiang enterprises' foreign investment. In the 1980s, Zhejiang enterprises' overseas investment mainly concentrated on Europe, the United States, Japan and other developed countries, and Hong Kong (SAR of China) and Macao (SAR of China). The investment range was relatively small. After decades of development, with the increasing number of enterprises engaged in overseas investment, Zhejiang's foreign investment range is expanding. More than 100 countries and regions become the destinations of foreign investment for Zhejiang.

---

[23] http://www.zj.stats.gov.cn/art/2011/12/22/art_281_48583.html.
[24] http://www.zj.stats.gov.cn/art/2011/12/22/art_281_48583.html.
[25] http://www.zj.stats.gov.cn/art/2011/12/22/art_281_48583.html.
[26] http://www.zj.stats.gov.cn/art/2011/12/22/art_281_48583.html.

According to the geographical distribution of enterprises' foreign investment in 2006, Asia, Europe, and North America were still the hot spots, with respectively, 190, 99 and 74 enterprises. The number in Asia accounted for 37.3% of the total, followed by Europe and North America, accounting for 27.1% and 14%.[27] In 2010 Zhejiang witnessed some changes in geographical distribution and Europe, with a percentage of 40.7%, has overtaken Asia to be the top destination for Zhejiang's outward direct investment, while Asia has undergone a drop in its share to become the second destination.[28] However, Asia is still the key area for Zhejiang OFDI in terms of number of investment projects and investment amount. In 2010, with a total number of 324 projects, Asia accounted for 51.4% of Zhejiang's OFDI, in which Vietnam, Thailand, Mongolia and Hong Kong (SAR of China) were the top host countries and regions. Sweden, the United States, Vietnam, Russia and Hong Kong (SAR of China) were the top five host countries and regions for Zhejiang's OFDI in 2010.[29] Table 4.3 shows the geographical distribution of Zhejiang's foreign investment in 2010.

4.2.1.3 *POEs are major participants*

Zhejiang's foreign investment has its own characteristics — diversified investors with the domination of private enterprises. Foreign investment

Table 4.3. Geographical distribution of Zhejiang's OFDI in 2010.

Region	Percentage
Europe	40.7
Asia	33.9
North America	13
South America	7.0
Africa	4.0
Oceania	1.4

Note: Data collected by Zhejiang Foreign Trade and Economic Cooperation Bureau.

---

[27] http://www.zj.stats.gov.cn/art/2011/12/22/art_281_48583.html.
[28] http://www.zj.stats.gov.cn/art/2011/12/22/art_281_48583.html.
[29] http://www.zj.stats.gov.cn/art/2011/12/22/art_281_48583.html.

in Zhejiang started first from state-owned enterprises, then some of the collective, foreign-funded and private enterprises have gradually joined the overseas investment. Investors became diverse. Along with the rapid growth in the private economy, Zhejiang private enterprises became the main investors overseas. In 2001, Zhejiang private enterprises' overseas investment projects accounted for more than half of the total number of Zhejiang's foreign investment projects. In 2004, among 378 overseas investment projects of Zhejiang, investment projects of private enterprises were about 362, about 95.8% of the total, while the proportion of the investment value reached 90.1%. In 2005, foreign investment projects of private enterprises were 435, accounting for 98% of the total 426 projects of the province.[30]

Some competitive private enterprises in Zhejiang Province have made significant contributions to achieving higher growth in foreign investment. Private enterprises such as Universal Group, Holley Group, Cornell Group, FeiYue and Haitian have begun a global optimal allocation of resources to carry out specialized, intensive, large-scale cross-border production and management, and gradually develop in the direction of multinational corporations. Zhejiang private enterprises have accelerated the pace of foreign investment significantly, greatly contributed to the development of the province's foreign trade and economy and accelerated the internationalization of Zhejiang enterprises.

4.2.1.4   *Increasingly diversified investment forms and areas*

Zhejiang's foreign investment is of various forms, and the investment in trade organizations and a marketing network used to be the focus of OFDI in Zhejiang. Zhejiang's enterprises usually conducted their foreign investment in the form of overseas trade organizations, plant, R&D centers, etc. However, trade organizations used to be the major form of Zhejiang's foreign investment in terms of quantity. By the end of 2004, the approved establishment of foreign trade organizations had accounted for 75% of the total foreign investment projects of Zhejiang Province.[31] These organizations were generally trade companies, offices, chain stores, trade

---

[30] http://www.zj.stats.gov.cn/art/2011/12/22/art_281_48583.html.

[31] http://www.people.com.cn/GB/paper53/15701/1388548.html.

centers, professional commodity markets and so on. For example, Wenzhou HAZAN Shoe Co., Ltd. established 7 sales companies in the US, Italy and Russia and other regions. There are 11 Zhejiang professional commodity markets in Brazil, the United Arab Emirates, Russia and other countries.[32]

Till now Zhejiang overseas investment has gradually changed from an early marketing network to relatively high levels of R&D centers, production base and so on. During the "11th Five-Year Plan" (2006–2010) period, Zhejiang has authorized 132 overseas R&D institutions, with a total investment value of USD1.09 billion.[33] R&D internationalization is the trend for Zhejiang enterprises' "going global", and at present it mainly involves electronics, medicine, machinery, new energy sources, computers and other high technology industries. Overseas M&As have witnessed a rapid growth. The overseas merger and acquisition projects occupied 75% of Zhejiang's OFDI in 2010.[34] Zhejiang occupies first place all over the country in terms of overseas M&As quantity and scale.[35] POEs are the major participants of overseas M&A projects in Zhejiang, and the traditional manufacturing industry is the major overseas industrial choice for M&A projects where the upstream suppliers or downstream importers are the main targets for overseas M&As.

4.2.2 Other eastern regions

4.2.2.1 *Jiangsu*

According to Ministry of Commerce, International Cooperation Department, in 2011 the non-financial OFDI in Jiangsu Province were valued at more than USD2 billion. It accounted for 9.85% of total national non-financial foreign direct investment, and occupied the third place nationally.[36] By the end of 2011, 505 outward foreign investment projects had been approved by Jiangsu Province. The Chinese investment was USD3.6 billion. The average investment was USD8.1 million.[37]

---

[32] http://www.xinhuanet.com/chinanews/2005-06/03/content_4371014.htm.
[33] http://www.gov.cn/test/2006-02/07/content_181020.htm.
[34] http://www.zj.stats.gov.cn/zjtj2012/indexch.htm.
[35] China Statistical Yearbook, 2011.
[36] http://fec.mofcom.gov.cn/article/tjzl/jwtz/201208/1693366_1.html.
[37] http://fec.mofcom.gov.cn/article/tjzl/jwtz/201208/1693366_1.html.

According to the department of commerce of Jiangsu Province, the outward direct investment of Jiangsu Province in 2012 had the following characteristics: One was the extended project scale. 71 Chinese investment projects above USD10 million had been approved; the total Chinese investment was USD3.12 billion; the average project investment was USD9.85 million.[38] The second is the agricultural sector that enjoyed the fastest growth in foreign investment. In the first nine months of 2012, 13 foreign investment projects were approved in that industry, with Chinese investment of USD220 million.[39] Foreign investment involved manufacturing, business services, wholesale business, mining, agriculture and the PC industry. The third is that North America and Oceania have become increasingly important to Jiangsu. Although Asia is still the first choice for Jiangsu's outward foreign investment, with a share of about half of the total in both investment project numbers and Chinese investment, North America and Oceania investment witnessed a rapid growth, a yearly growth of 89.0% and 97.0% respectively.[40] The fourth characteristic is that POEs took the leading role. In the first nine months of 2012, 293 foreign investment projects were approved from POEs, and the Chinese investment was USD2.66 billion, accounting for 67.3% and 65.2% of the province's total over the same period.[41]

4.2.2.2 *Shandong*

In 2011, Shandong Province accomplished non-financial OFDI of USD2.07 billion, a 30.8% increase compared with 2010, ranking the second place in terms of outward FDI flow.[42] Qingdao has played a leading role with USD191.72 million of outward FDI. In 2011, it had 48,840 new expatriate personnel and its total expatriate personnel reached 108,666, ranking the first. Foreign contracted projects had completed a turnover of USD7.47 billion, and occupied the second place nationally.[43]

---

[38] http://www.jsdoftec.gov.cn/NewsDetail.asp?NewsID=51234.
[39] http://www.jsdoftec.gov.cn/NewsDetail.asp?NewsID=51234.
[40] http://www.jsdoftec.gov.cn/NewsDetail.asp?NewsID=51234.
[41] http://www.jsdoftec.gov.cn/NewsDetail.asp?NewsID=51234.
[42] http://hzs.mofcom.gov.cn/aarticle/date/201201/20120107934068.html.
[43] http://hzs.mofcom.gov.cn/aarticle/date/201201/20120107934068.html.

Before the 10th Five-Year Plan, limited by the scale of the enterprise, information, capital, technology, talent and management, etc., major participants in Shandong's OFDI were the small and medium-sized enterprises. Since the 10th Five-Year Plan, in order to adapt to the new situation of economic globalization, Shandong has encouraged large-scale enterprises to commit to internationalization on the basis of resources development, export-oriented business, industrial transfer etc. Thus the main participants of Shandong's foreign direct investment have changed gradually from small enterprises to large enterprises.

During 2001–2009, Shandong Province approved 1,319 overseas enterprises, a total investment value of USD3.559 billion, in which the Chinese investment was USD2.62 billion (73% of the total amount of investment).[44] In 2010 Shandong had 1,099 newly approved outward foreign investment enterprises, totaling 3,125; the total amount of agreed investment was USD59 billion, a 36.3% growth compared with 2009.[45] At present, some powerful state-owned shareholding big investors such as Haier Co., Ltd., Hisense Co., Ltd., China Yankuang Group Co., Ltd., Shandong Gold Group Co., Ltd., Shengli Oilfield are the major outward foreign direct investors in Shandong province.

While the OFDI by POEs have witnessed a rapid growth, and the POEs outward investment involves industries like textiles, garments, light industry, machinery and resource development, etc. Outward foreign direct investors concentrated in Qingdao, Jinan and eastern coastal areas where, by the end of 2009, Qingdao with 635 enterprises and Jinan with 277 enterprises and other eastern coastal areas (Weihai, Yantai, and Rizhao) with 355 enterprises accounted for more than 75% of the whole investment amount.[46]

4.2.2.3 *Guangdong*

By the end of 2010, Guangdong had still occupied the first place in terms of outward FDI.[47] Its export-oriented economy had shown

---

[44] http://www.shandongbusiness.gov.cn/public/html/news/201004/98490.html.

[45] http://www.shandongbusiness.gov.cn/public/html/news/201102/300134.html.

[46] http://www.shandongbusiness.gov.cn/public/html/news/201001/88109.html.

[47] http://hzs.mofcom.gov.cn/article/date/201101/20110107370196.shtml.

remarkable achievements and its imports and exports had occupied first place consecutively for 18 years. Private enterprises (collective, private and individual businesses) in Guangdong Province had become the main force of its exports. As China's most dynamic, flourishing and attractive regions for investors, its foreign investment accounted for one quarter of the national total. In 2011, Guangdong's non-financial OFDI amounted to USD1.90 billion, a 59.1% growth rate compared to the previous year, and occupied fourth place, where Shenzhen has taken a leading role with USD624.08 million. Expatriate personnel were numbered at 42.638, in fourth place. It has completed contracted foreign projects with a turnover of USD11.34 billion and occupied first place.[48]

In 2011, Shenzhen's non-financial OFDI flow amounted to USD1.13 billion, accounting for 31% of Guangdong Province; and its value of USD8.32 billion accounted for 46% of Guangdong province.[49] By 2011, 7 enterprises from Shenzhen had been included in the top 100 enterprises by OFDI value in the non-financial sector, in which Huawei Technologies Co., Ltd. ranked 27th in the list and ZTE Co., Ltd. 44th and Konka Group Co., Ltd. 95th, are POEs. Hong Kong (SAR of China) has become the main destination for Shenzhen's outward FDI.[50] Private enterprises have a "going global" aim that is increasing in momentum. In the first nine months of 2012, more than 80% of the new investors were POEs.

4.2.3   The Mid-western regions

According to China's ministry of commerce, during the period of the 11th Five-Year Plan (2006–2010), the growth rate of imports and exports in the Mid-west was significantly higher than that of Eastern region and the national average level, and the proportion of its imports and exports in the national total increased from 8.3% to 9.9%.[51] Due to the incentives provided to encourage the development of the mid-west, the mid-west

---

[48] http://hzs.mofcom.gov.cn/article/date/201101/20110107370196.shtml.

[49] http://hzs.mofcom.gov.cn/article/date/201201/20120107934191.shtml.

[50] http://www.gddoftec.gov.cn/dept_detail.asp?deptid=1049&channalid=1342&contentid=13224.

[51] http://www.gov.cn/gzdt/2012-11/02/content_2256036.htm.

further improved the trade and investment environment and strengthened its industrial transfer ability, which provided the conditions for faster development of imports and exports. According to China's ministry of commerce, in the first quarter of 2012 the growth rates of exports in the central and western regions reached 23.7% and 30.1% respectively, far higher than the 5.6% of the eastern region. Chongqing in western China has accomplished exports of USD5.84 billion; Henan had exports of USD7.01 billion. The growth rates of exports in Guangxi, Sichuan and Hunan are 41.2%, 31.9% and 18.7% respectively, compared with the same period in 2011.[52]

Encouraged by all kinds of incentive policies, provinces have been active in engaging in OFDI. In 2011, the OFDI flow by provinces in the non-financial category was USD23.56 billion, far higher than the national average rate, of which the growth rate of the Midwest was at a record high level of 110%, with Hunan, Hubei, and Anhui being the top three.[53]

According to The China Council for the Promotion of International Trade, the 2010 survey of the current situation and intention of outbound investment by Chinese enterprises show that most of the enterprises that have committed to OFDI are from the eastern region. Among all the enterprises that have committed to OFDI, the eastern region with 76% ranks first, with the central region at 14% and the western region 10% respectively.[54]

The enterprises that committed to OFDI in the manufacturing industry accounted for over 40% of all investment for every region. Specifically, the western region's investment enjoys a higher proportion focused on agriculture and the service industry, and the eastern region has a higher proportion of investment in the manufacturing industry. From the aspect of regional distribution, the eastern region's outward foreign investment is dispersed, and because of its diverse investment destination it has a certain proportion of investment in all continents. The outward investments of the western region are mainly located in Asia and Europe, and its investments in other regions are much less.

---

[52] http://fec.mofcom.gov.cn/article/tjzl/jwtz/201309/1775847_1.html.

[53] http://fec.mofcom.gov.cn/article/tjzl/jwtz/201201/1276097_1.html.

[54] http://fec.mofcom.gov.cn/article/tjzl/jwtz/201101/1186066_1.html.

4.3 Outward Foreign Direct Investment (OFDI) Mode

Johanson and Wiedersheim-Paul identified four different stages in the internationalization process, the sporadic export stage, exports via independent representatives (agents), establishment of one or more sales subsidiaries and establishment of production facilities abroad. Dunning argued that the international operation of the enterprise includes the four stages stated below: indirectly and passively participate in international trade, directly and actively participate in international trade, non-equity investment stage and foreign direct investment stage. Since the 1980s, OFDI has enjoyed a significantly rapid development and overtaken international trade to become the dominant way for enterprises internationalization.

Since China adopted the policy of reform and opening up, enterprises' internationalization level in terms of exports has enjoyed remarkably great growth, see Fig. 4.1. Consequently, by the end of 2011, China's exports had amounted to USD1.89 trillion in which the exports of general trade have increased from USD20.8 billion in 1981 to USD917.1 billion in 2011. In 2011, China's total value of imports and exports amounted to USD3.6421 trillion, which consequently renders China as the second largest economy in world trade, and China has been for three years the largest exporter and second largest importer in the world in terms of goods traded.[55]

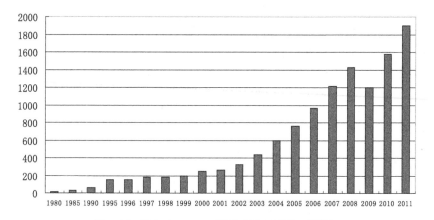

Fig. 4.1. China's exports 1981–2011 (billion USD).

---

[55] China Statistical Yearbook, 2012.

Privately and collectively owned enterprises saw their foreign trade expand faster than that of state-owned enterprises and foreign-funded companies from January to November in 2012. According to data released by the National Development and Reform Commission, in the first 11 months, foreign trade at private and collectively-owned enterprises totaled USD1.09 trillion, up to 18.1% year on year. The total figure included USD687.32 billion in exports, up to 19.4%, and USD402.75 billion in imports, up 15.9%. In contrast, foreign-funded firms saw foreign trade rise 1.9% year on year to reach USD1.72 trillion in the first 11 months of 2012. Meanwhile, trade for state-owned enterprises dropped 1.1% from a year earlier to USD685.9 billion in the first 11 months, as exports declined 4% in the period while imports posted a slight increase of 0.9%.

The General Administration of Customs previously released disappointing trade data for November due to slackened external demand. China's exports grew just 2.9% year on year in November, while the growth of imports remained unchanged from a year earlier.[56]

The global market turmoil and the appreciation of CNY as well as the explosion of trade barriers have rendered exporting no longer the optimum choice for China's enterprise internationalization. Once facing higher technical barriers to trade with the export destination country, a lot of enterprises will have to commit to international operations. After the global financial crisis, along with growing export barriers, many domestic enterprises begin to acquire such related resources as brand names, technology and marketing channels etc., through overseas M&As.

According to the World Investment Report 2011 of the United Nations Conference on Trade and Development (UNTCAD), in 2010 FDI outflow from South Asia, East Asia and Southeast Asia amounted to about USD230 billion, among which mainland China with its record high level of USD76 billion outflow ranks as the first largest home country for OFDI.[57] China overtook Japan in terms of OFDI flow, its share outflow of the global total is 5.2% which ranks the fifth in the world's major countries or

---

[56] http://www.customs.gov.cn/publish/portal0/tab400/info412937.htm.
[57] http://www.chinanews.com/cj/2011/07-27/3211617.shtml.

regions. China's enterprises will enhance their OFDI process in the next few years.[58]

From the perspective of the OFDI amount, the state-owned enterprises are the major participants; conversely, POEs are the major participants in terms of OFDI projects. In addition, China's overseas investment mainly focuses on business services, mining and manufacturing industries. In 2010, business services occupied 47% of the Chinese non-financial OFDI amount.[59] Both export enterprises and domestic processing enterprises setup overseas sales outlets. A large number of POEs conduct their foreign investments in the form of sales outlets or online stores, rather than production abroad. About 20% of OFDI is focused on the mining industry, 10% of OFDI is focused on the manufacturing industry, which is not consistent with China's status as a world factory.

In addition, China's OFDI is mainly concentrated in geopolitically close places such as Asia and Latin America. In 2010, China's non-financial investment in Asia accounted for 65% of its whole investment. In addition, investment in Latin America was about 19%, Oceania 5%, Europe 5%, North America 4% and Africa 2%.[60]

Global non-equity investment is witnessing a rapid growth. In 2010, the cross-border non-equity activities yielded a total sales return of more than $2 trillion in which contract manufacturing and service outsourcing amounted to USD1.1–1.3 trillion, franchising $330 to $350 billion, licensing USD340 to USD360 billion, management contracts to about USD100 billion.[61] Multinational corporations have accomplished most of the non-equity investment. In 2010, global multinational corporations created, both at home and abroad, added value of about 16 trillion dollars — about a quarter of global GDP.[62] China has made tremendous progress in outward FDI, but it is just going to initiate its non-equity investment. Owing to its independence and flexibility, non-equity investment will be an

---

[58] http://www.chinanews.com/cj/2011/07-27/3211617.shtml.

[59] http://www.chinanews.com/cj/2011/07-27/3211617.shtml.

[60] http://www.chinanews.com/cj/2011/07-27/3211617.shtml.

[61] http://www.chinanews.com/cj/2011/07-27/3211617.shtml.

[62] http://www.chinanews.com/cj/2011/07-27/3211617.shtml.

increasingly important choice for China's enterprise internationalization in the future. With the aid of the equity arrangement, China's enterprises are able to take part in the international division of labor system and accumulate the related technology and experience.

A statistical bulletin of China's OFDI includes statistics in two categories: the financial sector and non-financial sector, in which financial OFDI refers to investment in overseas financial institutions by Chinese domestic investing entities, and non-financial OFDI is the investment in overseas non-financial sectors by Chinese domestic investing entities.

According to the China Council for the Promotion of International Trade, a 2010 survey on the current situation and intention of outbound investment by Chinese enterprises shows that Chinese enterprises' outward FDI involves a good variety of industries. The manufacturing industry is the top priority, followed by the wholesale and retail industry, agriculture, forestry, husbandry, fishing and construction, investment in transportation, while the number of enterprises that commit to investment in the real estate industry, lodging and catering services and the software industry is comparatively less. According to the changes in the foreign investment industry structure from 2008 to 2010, the proportion of manufacturing was reduced, the proportion of agriculture, mining and energy has grown greatly, which reflects the increasing importance of raw materials and natural resource development in China's outward FDI.

4.3.1 OFDI pattern choices of China's POEs

From 2001 to 2010, the net flow of China's OFDI has enjoyed an average growth rate of 25.82%. At the end of 2010, China ranked the fifth in the world in terms of OFDI flow. In addition, more than 13,000 China's domestic investors have undertaken foreign direct investment by 16,000 foreign enterprises in 178 countries and regions all over the world.[63]

(1) Acquisition versus Greenfield Investment

The pattern that the private enterprise has selected to conduct outward direct investment is determined by its business condition and its investment

---

[63] http://www.chinanews.com/cj/2011/07-27/3211617.shtml.

motivation, investment performance and the change of market environment at home and abroad. Brouthers *et al.* (2000) identified two entry models of outward direct investment: Acquisition and Greenfield Start-up. Bell (1996) examined the important differences between transnational M&A and Greenfield investment (either solely-owned or joint venture), and he argued that transnational merger and acquisition would shorten the initial construction period of the Greenfield investment, by which it is to be a low-risk entry mode. In addition, compared to Greenfield start-up, multinational acquisition does not increase the stock scale of target industry in the host country. For the new market participant, rising industry has greater market space than a saturated or declining industry. Zhang Shuming and Xu Li (2008) presented an empirical analysis on the investment performance of the entry model of Chinese enterprise's OFDI, and it shows that market entry mode does place a significant influence on the operating performance of foreign direct investment by Chinese enterprises.

Chinese enterprises adopting the entry mode of Greenfield start-up will enjoy a relatively better business performance compared to the merger and acquisition mode. Chinese enterprises adopting the entry mode of merger and acquisition will enjoy a better market performance and especially the investors' recognition, compared to Greenfield start-up mode. Chinese enterprises should consider their main investment motivation and then choose a suitable entry mode. Other scholars examine the entry mode choice from transaction cost and cultural differences. They believe that China's enterprise should setup selection criteria to assess whether it helps to implement the strategic goals of overseas assets development, and avoid investment risk.

(2) Going global by OEM versus by OBM

Brand competition is the advanced stage of market competition. Brand competition is based on product technology and quality, but is also more than technology and quality. In the multinational business, brand competition has two forms: One is to use Original Equipment Manufacturer (OEM) form; the other is to use Original Brand Manufacture (OBM) form. The former is a transitional form, and inevitably evolves to the independent brands, and thus finally the mature international business and multinational companies. From the perspectives of multinational business experiences of

China's private-owned enterprise, Ouyang Yao (2006) argued that China's private-owned enterprises generally follow the laws of gradual development by the sequence "price competition, technological competition, brand competition". Obviously, some enterprises and products with the strong technique power and high market reputation in the domestic market can implement brand strategy and launch brand competition even when they just initiate to develop the international market.

China's private-owned enterprises should form their own core technology and R&D ability through continuous learning and innovation in an effort to cultivate a global brand and surpass the advanced enterprise. Specifically, processing enterprise must first setup the brand consciousness and accumulate manufacturing experience through learning-by-doing while they conduct OEM businesses with developed countries' enterprises. Efforts are made to study, imitate and improve the introduced equipment and technology, which is also a process of introduction, digestion, and assimilation and innovation. After China's POE develops its design and preliminary R&D ability, it should gradually transit to ODM and extend to the upstream of industrial chain. If the enterprise grows up to be strong enough, it can extend to OBM because proprietary intellectual property rights developed from the ODM provide necessary support for the development of independent brand.

(3) Solely-built overseas marketing network versus cluster's overseas investment

Domestic consumer goods producers who possess sales channels of large scale, high efficiency, and low-cost can conquer the market and effectively defeat their rivals. Overseas marketing network, as an important part of the core competitiveness, can make the enterprise gradually setup own brand reputation and market influence at the oversea market, and lay a good foundation for overseas production and a better globalization strategy. This model has the following three main features: It is a famous domestic brand, some even have a long history; it is to establish overseas sales networks but not that necessary to establish R&D or production center; it aims to expand the international market, and improve from a famous domestic brand to a famous international brand. Enterprise can directly sell products to overseas markets through the overseas sales channels and network. It will reduce the intermediate links so that the cost is much lower, but the enterprise can still gain in-depth understanding of the market demand to accumulate valuable experience. At present, overseas marketing channel is one of the main modes by which China's POEs will utilize while undertaking overseas investment.

Different from the model individual enterprise relies on their own strength to develop an overseas market; cluster overseas investment will greatly improve the success rate of transnational investment for enterprises in the cluster. Industry cluster cannot only pool the specialized resources of information, technology, and service and so on, but also can effectively overcome the market failure and internal organization failure. Therefore it is a good choice for private enterprises that lack core competitive ability, ability to resist risk, internal scale economy. Taking cluster mode of overseas industrial park as an example, its main specific advantages include: First, industrial park provides a public investment information and operation service platform for Chinese POE cluster into the host country; second, the establishment of industrial park in host countries generally need to be approved by the host country's government, so good communication between the local government and enterprises in the park will help the enterprise to get a more preferential policy and resource support; third, overseas industrial park cluster model can effectively change China's private enterprise foreign direct investment loose condition, greatly enhance the enterprises' ability to resist overseas business risk.

4.3.2   Typical OFDI modes of China's POEs

The POEs have created various effective modes since they initiated internationalization decades ago. Here are some typical modes.

(1) TCL Group — the transnational merger and acquisition model

M&A has become one of the main means by which the international capital flows, and correspondingly will be main means for China's privately-owned enterprises to enter the US and EU market. POEs consequently obtain qualified local staff, management, market, customers, and government relations by acquisition. Aiming at reducing the entry barriers and risks, accelerating the entry process, replenishing the shortage of resources as soon as possible, some financially and technically strong POEs should make full use of sophisticated and liberal capital market in developed countries to choose the form of acquisition, thus either to expand the overseas market share of the enterprise's products through the horizontal merger, or to achieve their diversification strategy through the vertical merger.

POEs undertake M&A to obtain overseas sales channels or realize local production, and eventually realize the strategic target of developing the international market. Firstly, due to differences of market structure and consumption habits and culture, the enterprise is sometimes very difficult to rapidly integrate into the mature markets by self-built sales network, and M&A can quickly acquire the channel, even if it should undergo the test of the integration of enterprises. Secondly, when the private-owned enterprise does face certain necessity of offshore production (such as direct exports have been imposed trade barriers or restrictions, local production does cost less and can adapt to the local market better), while the cost of greenfield investments is higher than acquisition, M&A will become the first choice for enterprises conducting overseas investments.

M&A's main features include the following three: first, the enterprise who takes this model has a comparative advantage in the domestic market, and even is the leader in this line; second, famous international corporation is usually the M&A object; third, it aims to obtain technology, brand, channel, human resources, global resources integration, and develop the global market especially European and American developed countries.

TCL Group is a typical representative of this model. TCL Group Co., Ltd. founded in 1981, is one of China's largest consumer electronic goods producer with global management. In 1999, the company initiated international business, developed independent brands in the emerging market, merged and acquired European and American mature brands, and thus becoming the pioneer of internationalization process of Chinese enterprises. In September 2002, TCL International holdings Co., Ltd., a subsidiary of China TCL Group, acquired the main assets of a 113-year old, so-called "German national brand" established SCHNEIDER electric Co., Ltd. including the trademark rights of famous brand "SCHNEIDER" and

"DUAL". In July 2003, TCL Group purchased a 100% stake of famous home appliance American manufacturer Govedio. In 2004, TCL Group acquired the French Thomson home appliance business, Alcatel mobile business and Japanese Toshiba white electric business. Developing overseas market by foreign brand has become unique internationalization mode for the TCL group. TCL acquired the brands and channels, and quickly extended its overseas interest through the transnational merger and reorganization.

An important reason for TCL to undertake cross-border M&As is to obtain brands and channels, and expand the overseas market and the scale of the enterprise. Some famous consumer electronics brands possess a very stable market position in the mature market of European and American developed countries. Thus consumers but also in a position to control the local sales channels do not only easily accept it. Therefore, the acquisition is an important mode for Chinese enterprises to extend their interests in these countries. In addition, the business restructuring launched by some multinational corporations because of business strategic transformation may also provide opportunities for Chinese enterprises transnational M&A. The global financial crisis incurred by the US sub-prime mortgage crisis is a huge challenge and an important opportunity for many Chinese POEs. Since 2009, some Zhejiang enterprises have undertaken some M&A deals, such as the world's largest seamless underwear M&A deal launched by Zhejiang Meibang Textile Co., Ltd., Geely acquired the world's second largest independent manufacturer of automatic transmissions. This happened at a time when scholars argued that enterprises should follow the law of selling assets in a bullish market, and buy assets in a bear market.

(2) Huawei Technologies Co., Ltd. — the R&D internationalization model

Overseas R&D investment refers to the investment conducted by some high-tech Chinese POEs to obtain the proprietary intellectual property rights through the higher internationalization degree of R&D in the form of establishment of overseas R&D institutions, the use of overseas R&D resources. Owing to the weak overall strength, China's high-tech private enterprises cannot afford the large-scale "going global". For most of the high-tech enterprises, the feasible way to "go global" is to establish the overseas R&D base, rather than the large-scale investment or M&As. R&D

institutions can be either small or large, and it aims to track the cutting edge theories and technologies in developed countries; to introduce talents or foreign advanced technology. Lenovo and Huawei are typical examples of this category of "going global" practice.

Shenzhen Huawei Technologies Co., Ltd. founded in 1988, is a high-tech private enterprise that adopts the Employee Stock Ownership Plan. Its main business scope covers telecom products like exchange, transmission, and wireless and data communication. It provides network equipment, services and solutions in the telecommunications field for customers around the world. Huawei initiated its internationalization by implementing direct sales model that domestic sales team was expatriated directly to negotiate with telecom operators, and by doing so it has achieved success in the Middle East and other developing countries. Thereafter, Huawei began to extend interest into the developed countries market. In 2001, Huawei's 10 GSDH optical network products entered into the German market; in 2003, Huawei won the bid in France LDCOM's DWDM national trunk network project and British telecom VOIP card commercial toll network project, successfully entering European and American mainstream operators market. Huawei adheres to improve the ability to independently develop, and correspondingly make use of independently developed core technology to explore the overseas market, but the company is also willing to cooperate with others, constantly promote its internationalization of product R&D and consequently establish a global R&D network.

By far Huawei has setup R&D institutions in Stockholm Sweden, Dallas and Silicon Valley the United States, Bangalore, India, Moscow, Russia, and China's Shenzhen, Shanghai, Beijing, Nanjing, Xi'an, Chengdu and Wuhan, etc. It has adopted various incentive policies to attract domestic and foreign outstanding scientific and technological personnel to commit to R&D, and thus timely grasp the latest trends of the industry. It has insisted for a long time on spending not less than 10% of its sales income on R&D investment in which 10% will be reserved for advanced research, tracking the new technology and new field. According to Huawei's official website data, Huawei has ranked No. 1 among Chinese enterprises in terms of patent application for 8 consecutive years. At the end of 2011, Huawei had 36,344 accumulated application for patents in China, 10,650 international Patent Cooperation Treatys (PCT), 10,978 foreign patents, and 23,522 obtained patent licenses in which more than 90% belong to patent for invention. Huawei has more than 62,000 personnel who are devoted to R&D of products and solutions, which accounts for 44% of the total number. Huawei has setup R&D institutions in 23 countries like Germany, Sweden, Britain, France, Italy, Russia, India and China, etc., and consequently make full use of its R&D institutions all over the world and its global technology development network to provide better products and services, faster response speed and better price–quality ratio, and help the global operators to establish sustainable profitable operation mode. In 2007, Huawei in Europe, the United States and Japan and other developed markets achieve growth of more than 150%. By the end of 2008, Huawei's products and solutions had covered more than 100 countries and regions in the international market, and 45 out of 50 telecom operators used Huawei products and services. At present, Huawei's products and solutions has been used in more than 150 countries, covering 45 of the top 50 global service operators and a third of the global population. With the tremendous development of its core technology, Huawei has already been a top multinational corporation in the world telecom market.

(3) Beifa Group — the OEM internationalization mode

Beifa Group was founded in 1994; it is a large stationery group with capabilities in R&D, manufacturing, sale and international trade service. Beifa started from a thirty-people pen mill, and initiated its internationalization by an Arab guest order at the Canton fair. Currently, Beifa has six branches in the domestic market like Beijing, Shanghai, and six oversea branches in the US, Russian, UAE, Panama, France, and Spain. It has more than 2,000 employees, including 242 R&D staff. The total assets of Beifa are over CNY 700 million with annual sales of over 1 billion and over 1.5 billion export. The production and sale ranked No. 1 for 10 consecutive years in China and top 8 in the world in the stationery industry.

Beifa has obtained 1,065 patents, including 10 patents of invention and 13 patents for Utility Models, 529 international patents. Beifa is the well-known trademark in China, the products of Beifa are popular around the world, above 70% products are from Beifa' own brands.

The products of Beifa are exported to more than 150 countries and regions in the world, with 70% of the products entering the international mainstream and the professional market. Beifa group will setup nine distribution centers worldwide, including Pakistan, Frankfurt, Dubai, Ningbo, Guangzhou, Tokyo, Sao Paulo, Bombay, and Shanghai. It is planning to setup 30 global distribution centers worldwide in three years, becoming a network with wide coverage, full products range and multi-functional product.

Beifa Group Co., Ltd. is taking all-in-one service as its main competitive strategy, and OEM service consequently accounted for a very important position in the export business of the company, which is decided by the company's industry background, industry characteristics and the enterprise's business condition. Beifa possessed the following main advantages and opportunity while developing the EU market: scale economy (scale of pen-production: the world's third, European first, China's first); advanced equipment; high-quality service and relatively lower prices than the internal European Union market. The main weaknesses and challenges while undertaking international operation are: lack of price advantage compared with competitors; procurement search ability is insufficient, some products can't meet personalized custom demand; the production cycle is long and 45 days or so is needed from order-acceptance to delivery; the language barrier and purchasing quantity problem and so on. Owing to the above-mentioned factors, Beifa began to establish its overseas sales representative office, and actively integrate into the multinational purchasing system. At present, Beifa has established strategic trade relations with the one of the world's top 500 enterprise, MYRON, and more than 20 world-class vendors such as OFFICE DEPOT, STAPLE'S, WALMART, and TESCO. In addition, it was awarded as the Global product innovator by American company STAPLE'S, OFFICE DEPOT, the world's best supplier by TESCO, and the top supplier by SOURCES.

Beifa Group has constructed a vast variety of product system with independent intellectual property rights. By the end of 2012, Beifa has obtained 1,167 patents, including 10 patents of invention and 13 patents for Utility Models, 545 international patents in which 265 American patents and 280 EU patents. Beifa is the well-known trademark in China, the products of Beifa are popular around the world, above 70% products are from Beifa' own brands. In 2004 Sanford Corporation used "337 Clause" to bring charges against 12 enterprises globally, four of them from Mainland China, among which Beifa Group's is the biggest exporter. Beifa Group President Qiu Zhiming stated that Beifa's pen, from the perspective of quality and technology level, is identical to that of Sanford's, but Beifa enjoyed the price advantage. At the beginning of 2004, Beifa pen sales were seven times that of Sanford's in the 2 months after its debut in the Wal-Mart supermarket. Sanford aims not only to protect their own "business appearance right", but also two deep purposes: One is to use the "337 Clause" investigation to obstruct the expansion of low-cost products; the second is to earn a patent royalty through the litigation and thus weaken the opponent's price advantage. Beifa group gave detailed replies to hundreds of questions put forward by the United States government, and provided enough evidences and samples. At the same time, Beifa made full use of the sued company's rights in "337 Clause" to put forward hundreds of questions stemming from Sanford's charges. Beifa ultimately forced Sanford to actively request peace talks.

China's POEs take OEM as the way to enter the developed market for at least three benefits: One is to integrate into the multinational corporations' global production system by making use of the low-cost advantage of domestic enterprise. The second is to acquire technical improvement through cooperation with multinational corporations. The third is to standardize production mode and improve the management level of enterprises by the collaboration with the multinational company. For China's private-owned enterprise, internationalization is a gradual progress in which it is undoubtedly a feasible path to create its independent brands through the OEM production, obtain its marketing channel by taking advantage of others, and then finally achieve the "going global" purpose.

(4) Zhejiang Tiger Lighter Co., Ltd. — the independent brand internationalization mode

Zhejiang Tiger Lighter Co., Ltd. was founded in 1992, it has become the top enterprise of metal shell lighter manufacture in China under more than two decades development. The Tiger brand was registered at the same time when the company was registered. The company has been attaching a lot of importance to brand development, which makes it one of the top ten famous lighter's in China and its brand "tiger" appraised as China top brand, famous export enterprise with key fostering and developing by Commerce Department of China.

In recent years, the company still insists on improving quality, creating brand name, adopting new techniques, new craftwork and new materials, and introduce advanced equipment and technique, and its several patents have filled the techniques gap in China, and gained national patent. The company successfully developed the lighters that work at high altitude regions, and has successfully entered into the Mexico and Colombia market already. Thus, it has become the knocking brick for the high altitude countries and regions. The high-altitude lighters fill China's technology gap, and gained national patent, and its exports in second half of 2008 reached over 2 million.

In 1987, Wenzhou produced the first hand-made lighter called the "cat's eye". Wenzhou lighter producers initiated their lighters production by imitating the producers of Japan and R.O. Korea, and consequently the quality was inferior to the above-mentioned leading lighter producers. With only a USD1 unit price, Wenzhou producers have price advantages because the price of leading lighter producers is USD30–40, and therefore Wenzhou producers attracted large quantities of orders. In 1992, more than 3,000 lighter "family workshop" appeared in Wenzhou, each with yearly production of about 3,000 to 5,000 lighters. And more than 10 million imitated and Wenzhou producers have exported assembled lighters in 1992. At this time, a growing number of foreign enterprises asked "Tiger" to do OEM production for them, but their request have been declined by "Tiger" lighter's founder Mr. Zhou Dahu. Meanwhile, "Tiger" began to introduce advanced equipment and technology at home and abroad, and hired technical personnel to design, produce lighters and improve product quality in an effort to cultivate its independent brand. In 1998, the relevant inspection authority that it is similar in quality with counterpart Japanese products identified "Tiger" brand lighter. With the help of industrial cluster, specialized division of labor, low-cost labor advantage, "Tiger" constantly strives for its innovation, and its independent brand internationalization mode has made great success.

In September 2001, the European Union started to implement CR regulation on the Wenzhou lighter just like the United States. In May 2002, the European Union adopted the CR regulations. On June 27 2002, the EU formally initiated an anti-dumping investigation on China's export lighter. The purpose of the action is to expel Chinese lighter enterprises out of the European market by collecting high anti-dumping duties on them. Wenzhou is one of world's largest metal shell lighter production bases, in which yearly lighter exports have reached 500 million. Of this number, nearly 30% have been exported to the European market. When the crisis came, Mr. Zhou Dahu as the president of Wenzhou Smoking Set Industry Association, collaborated with other lighter enterprises to jointly respond to the appeal, and finally in September 2003 the European Union put a termination to anti-dumping investigation on China's lighters. It marked the first time China's private-owned enterprises responded successfully to anti-dumping litigation since China's accession to WTO. This is also a monstrous free advertising for "Tiger" brand.

In recent years, through technological innovation and improving the quality and the grade, the "Tiger" brand won a place in the competition with the internationally renowned brand lighters, and takes the lead in foreign products to enter the market. Tiger lighters are selling to more than 70 countries and territories, such as United States, Japan Canada, Mexico and Western European countries; Tiger brand has been registered as a trademark in more than 50 countries worldwide, and in European and American markets, there are many stores that sell Tiger products exclusively.

(5) Kangnai Group — the Self-built overseas marketing network model

Kangnai Group, founded in 1980, is a private-owned enterprise specialized in the production of leather shoes. As China's leading manufacturer of footwear, under the development guidance of "superior quality, stronger brand", Kangnai in the past more than 30 years has enjoyed rapid development, especially its outstanding achievements in the implementation of brand strategy. China is a world factory of shoes, but neither has brand power, nor an international brand. Mr. Zheng Xiukang, President of Kangnai group, argued "Chinese enterprises who started their business much later than their counterparts can choose downstream as a starting point, but we cannot always stay in the downstream". And hence Kangnai has made the issue of planning the production globally early, conquering the upstream market. In 2001, when the OEM mode was very popular with other enterprises for its low risk and profit stability, conversely, Kangnai stores with "Kangnai" mark opened in France Paris 19 area. From 2001 to 2007, Kangnai opened more than 200 exclusive shops in more than 20 countries, including the world's greatest landmark locations like Paris, New York, Milan, Venice, Barcelona, Berlin, etc. Thanks to ERP software managing the global supply chain, Kangnai Group can demonstrate proudly that its exclusive store in Paris has its incoming just like its China's counterpart.

Kangnai Group directly establishes its overseas marketing network for its following two advantages: First, it is to dump the domestic and foreign middlemen, avoid the intermediate forms, sell the product directly to foreign retailers at a favorable price of cost plus necessary export fee, which is beneficial to form price advantage in foreign retail market so as to facilitate sales; second, it is directly build Kangnai brand exclusive shop, which is beneficial to establish brand image rapidly in foreign countries.

Kangnai's success proved the fact that, in addition to low-cost manufacturing advantage, China's private-owned enterprises can also enjoy advantages in raw materials, R&D, design, management, brand management. Kangnai's success lies in integration with international technical standards, and then participating in standard formulating. By participating in SATRA, the world's top level of authentication footwear, Kangnai not only integrates with international standards in safety, comfort level, restricted chemical standards, and makes use of its instruments and standards to develop multiple technologies which provide some help for the development of Chinese characteristic shoes comfort index. And hence Kangnai become the pioneer to break the technical barriers to trade. Kangnai creatively develops an internationalization strategy of product outflow, brand outflow and capital outflow, and integrates its internationalization achievements, which will help it continuously, upgrade toward the upstream of the international industry value chain.

(6) Cathay Capital Private Equity — the overseas industrial park model

Overseas industrial park is an attempt for China's small and medium-sized POEs to make the outward direct investment, because it can depend on the strength of industrial clusters to make industrial investment. As a Yiwu businessman who produces various kinds of trousers said, "It is very difficult for small and medium-sized enterprises to make overseas investment; specifically, the key point is how to build a complete overseas industrial chain. In Yiwu, the trousers industry has a complete production chain, but if we choose to go abroad, the lack of the producers of zipper and buttons will increase the production cost. We temporarily will not consider overseas investment, unless the complete industry chain in the park will be extended to foreign countries." Cathay Capital Private Equity is a typical model where China's POEs undertakes OFDI by relying on overseas industrial park.

Cathay Capital Private Equity is the first French–Chinese private firm focusing on France–China growth capital. Cathay Capital Private Equity aims to support the international growth, and be a long-term partner for mid-size French companies faced with a booming Asian economy, as well as a partner for an increasing number of small and medium-sized Chinese enterprises seeking a European foothold. It is headquartered in Orleans France, and it has branch offices in China: Shanghai, Xiamen, and Quanzhou. Cathay Capital PE industrial park is located in a district which is only an hour's drive away from Paris France, and is the first French park of Cathay Capital PE to accommodate Chinese investment, and also a specialized park of AFII. Cathay Capital PE Industrial Park will incorporate its purchasing and logistics system and provide the best communication platform for Chinese enterprises to successfully enter the European market.

In 2009, Cathay Capital PE setup the first Sino-French industrial park which is located in the core area of Sands park high-tech development zone, Sanming, Fujian. The park occupies 338 acres. It aims to make full use of the local resources of northwestern Fujian, and help the local small and medium-sized enterprises to have trade communication with the European counterpart by introducing European small and medium-sized enterprises. Cathay Capital PE industrial park and it became the Sino-French economic and financial communication platform, helping China enterprises' products to enter the European market better and faster.

The development experience of small and medium-sized enterprise cluster all over the world proved that the following three categories of enterprise clusters could conduct outward direct investment by overseas industrial park: One is "verbal" type of small and medium-sized enterprise clusters, which is usually an agglomerate of a large enterprise as the core enterprise, and many small and medium-sized enterprises. Large enterprises and small and medium-sized enterprise formed between integration to a vertical division of labor system, the "push and pull" effect of core enterprise is the power and source of small and medium-sized enterprise's foreign investment. The second is the "horizontal" small and medium-sized enterprise clusters. The priority is given to related supporting relations and parallel market transaction when it comes to the relations among the internal enterprises in the cluster. Each enterprise completes the production process through the horizontal relation; a single enterprise cannot survive without the support of associated enterprises. Only when the "cluster" moved to the new environment can the foreign investment survive. The third is "market-supported" cluster. "The market-supported" refers to outward direct investment made by private enterprises in the form of a specialized market. Such as in South Africa, Zhonghuamen commercial center in Johannesburg established by Zhejiang Yiwu Huafeng Industrial (Group) Co., Ltd. has developed into the largest-scale Chinese products market in South Africa with an extensive product and service range. And it is also the largest Chinese invested South African shopping mall project in which sales, storage, display, information and service are integrated, as well as all kinds of Chinese famous, excellent, special goods are pooled. Depending on the overseas market, China's POEs establish overseas industrial park and conduct the OFDI, which is both helpful in exerting industry cluster advantage, but also solving the trouble of product sales for enterprises in the industrial park.

Appendix 1. Top 50 private enterprises ranked by import and export value in 2011.

Ranking	Company name/Province	Import and export value (million USD)
1	HuaWei Technologies Co., Ltd. (Guangdong)	10,794.727
2	Jiangsu ShaGang Group Co., Ltd. (Jiangsu)	5,245.625
3	Heilonjiang United Petrochemical Co., Ltd. (Helongjiang)	3,380.896
4	Dongguan Machinery Imp. & Exp. Co., Ltd. (Guangdong)	3,121.273
5	Rizhao Iron & Steel Holdings Ltd. (Shandong)	2,611.228
6	Guangdong Winnerway Holdings Corporation (Guangdong)	1,853.336
7	China-Based Ningbo Foreign Trade Co., Ltd. (Zhejiang)	1,802.476

(To be Continued)

Appendix 1. (*Continued*)

Ranking	Company name/Province	Import and export value (million USD)
8	Ningbo Free Trade Zone Gaoxin Container Co. Ltd. (Zhejiang)	1766.0812
9	Yang Gu Xiang Guang Copper Co., Ltd. (Shandong)	1,441.948
10	Jinhai Heavy Industry Co., Ltd. (Zhejiang)	1,401.979
11	Weiqiao Textile Co., Ltd. (Shandong)	1,353.474
12	Shandong Sunrise Group Co., Ltd. (Shandong)	1,322.279
13	Shandong Huaxin Industry & Trade Co., Ltd. (Shandong)	1,239.661
14	China National Agricultural Means of Production Group Corporation (Beijing)	1,158.159
15	Ningbo Sunha Chem. Products Co., Ltd. (Zhejiang)	1,127.067
16	Jiangsu Tianyuan Mmarine Import & Export Co., Ltd. (Jiangsu)	1,078.334
17	Chaozhou yatai Energy Co., Ltd. (Guangdong)	1,066.225
18	Haier Electric Industrial Co., Ltd. (Shandong)	978.402
19	Suzhou Samsung Electric Appliances Co., Ltd. (Jiangsu)	900.839
20	Huang Jiang Town Capital Introduction Company of Dongguan City (Guangdong)	885.438
21	Shenzhen Guangming Economic Development Co., Ltd. (Guangdong)	841.367
22	Pinggang Iron & Steel Co., Ltd. Ningbo Trading Branch (Zhejiang)	828.974
23	Shenzhen Everich Industrial Development Co., Ltd. (Guangdong)	826.676
24	Shandong Wan Bao Trading Co., Ltd. (Shandong)	808.925
25	Guangzhou PanYu Foreign Trade Co., Ltd. (Guangdong)	802.863
26	Zenith Steel Group Co., Ltd. (Jiangsu)	791.549
27	Guangzhou DaYou Coal Market Co., Ltd. (Guangdong)	739.176
28	Guangzhou ZhiZhiYuan Grease Industry Co., Ltd. (Guangdong)	717.036
29	Shandong TianYuan Copper Industry Co., Ltd. (Shandong)	716.624
30	Sany Heavy Industry Co., Ltd. (Hunan)	706.709
31	Fengli Group Co., Ltd. (Jiangsu)	691.871
32	Sanhe Hope Full Grain Oil Group Feed & Protein Co., Ltd. (Hebei)	686.446
33	Foshan Arts & Crafts Corporation Limited (Guangdong)	681.921
34	Shenzhen YiDaLong Jewellery Co., Ltd. (Guangdong)	663.175
35	Dongguan FuZhiYuan Feed & Protein Development Corporation (Guangdong)	650.858

(*To be Continued*)

Appendix 1. (*Continued*)

Ranking	Company name/Province	Import and export value (million USD)
36	Shicheng Electronics (Shengzhen) Co., Ltd. (Guangdong)	624.093
37	Shandong TaiShan Steel Group Co., Ltd. (Shandong)	619.928
38	Yunnan HuiJia Imp. & Exp. Co., Ltd. (Yunnan)	617.154
39	Zhuhai QinFa Trading Co., Ltd. (Guangdong)	614.738
40	Zhejiang OuHua Shipbuilding Co., Ltd. (Zhejiang)	613.805
41	Wuxi JiaCheng Solar Energy Technology Co., Ltd. (Jiangsu)	599.733
42	Xiamen JiaSheng Foreign Trade Co., Ltd. (Fujian)	596.437
43	Chimbusco Petroleum (Zhuhai) Co., Ltd. (Guangdong)	584.285
44	Dongguan Dingxin Internation Trading Co., Ltd. (Guangdong)	584.167
45	Shenzhen An Sheng Hua Clock Co., Ltd. (Guangdong)	581.267
46	Dongguan Lingnan Imp. & Exp. Co., Ltd. (Guangdong)	577.413
47	BaoKuang International Trade Co., Ltd. (Shanghai)	574.003
48	Ningbo HaiTian International Co., Ltd. (Zhejiang)	571.505
49	Shenzhen ZhaoChi Holding Limited. (Guangdong)	571.326
50	Subaru (Tianjin) Auto Sales Co., Ltd. (Tianjin)	568.149

Source: http://tjxh.mofcom.gov.cn/aarticle/n/201209/20120908354774.html.

Chapter 5

Evidence from Firm-Level Survey Data

Internationalization is the only way for a company to grow into an international enterprise. The development history of most Fortune 500 Companies demonstrates a similar growing path, which started from the domestic market, continued to move toward the world, and eventually ended up in the global market. Internationalization enables a company to acquire various resources from other countries, while the global market provides the company with an incomparable stage for further development. During the past 30 years with rapid economic growth, China has accumulated substantial wealth. Meanwhile, Chinese enterprises correspondingly have achieved rapid internationalization development. The 2008 financial crisis provided an extraordinary opportunity for Chinese firms to accelerate the internationalization process. More than 15,000 Chinese businesses setup overseas subsidiaries, which aggregately owned total assets of more than USD1 trillion. Nowadays, foreign investment of Chinese enterprises has gradually expanded from general exporting, catering, simple processing, to other advanced fields such as marketing network, resource development, shipping and logistics, manufacturing and R&D. The investment destinations include Europe, the United States, Hong Kong (SAR of China) and Macao (SAR of China), Asia, Africa, Latin America and other regions.

The internationalizing activities of enterprises from developing countries are becoming one of the major forces of global capital flows. Among them, Chinese enterprises become a key market participant. Although such activities become more and more important in the real world, the corresponding theoretical research is still creeping at a very elementary stage. It can be partly explained by the unique features of each developing country. Reliable micro-data are also required for building internationalization theory for such enterprises. Previous international management experience can help them better carry out international management, and consequently promote their international competitiveness. The internationalization is not "start from scratch", but based on the experience and lessons learned on during the international stage. Therefore, it is necessary to construct a theoretical framework of internationalization consistent with the features of Chinese enterprises, so as to explain the internationalization process of Chinese enterprises in terms of influencing factors and behavioral patterns.

The recent research on enterprise internationalization turns its attention to the determinants of internationalization at the micro-firm level. In terms of multinational investment decisions, the literature survey mainly includes the following aspects:

Individual advantage is one of the key determinants of outward direct investment (ODI). The ODI theory developed by Hymer and Kindleherger is seeking and stating such a complementary advantage. When a company enters into the foreign market, it should have company advantages, which can be transplanted and complement the market disadvantage in a distance compared with companies of host countries. Caves (1971) claimed that these complementary advantages could be obtained by research and development (R&D) for achieving a heterogeneous production advantage. Production heterogeneity can be represented through physical features, brands, advertisements, and after-sales service. These exotic characteristics were more attractive to foreign consumers so that the company can digest the high cost by outward investment in foreign market. Buckley and Casson (1976) found that when the production heterogeneous advantage exists, the companies would prefer sole proprietorship to control and protect these competitive advantages, which can be considered as a "natural monopoly". Ding's (1997) empirical analysis demonstrated that the ratio of R&D to enterprises' sales had a significant and positive correlation with the preference of sole proprietorship mode. Cui (2001) claimed that the risk of losing advantages impels the foreign investors to choose the sole proprietorship mode.

The scale of an enterprise is an indicator of how much resource it could properly have, and such resource provides a solid foundation for its multinational investment. In spite of such correlation, small and medium size enterprises are also willing to do multinational production and to invest more resources in foreign markets. However, they are inclined to enter foreign markets in the form of joint ventures and cooperative firms (Cui, 2001).

Internationalization experience is further correlated with the extent of multinational operation, as the companies will accumulate such experiences when they operate in other countries. Buckley and Casson (1985) indicated that experience would alleviate the uncertainty and high cost of outward investment so that it would increase the possibility of investing more resources. Anderson and Gotignon (1986) believed that the more international operating experiences a company has, the larger scale it would operate to in foreign countries.

In addition, strategy is one of the factors affecting enterprises' selection of an ODI mode. To choose one mode from the others, an entrepreneur would not only compare each mode's adaptability to foreign product market, but also take its correlation with the long-term strategy of the enterprise into consideration. Product is the first step to penetrate the foreign market. Kim and Hwang (1992) concluded that the leverage effect of one product on other products while in achieving its global strategy would also have some impact on the investment mode.

5.1 Firm-Level Survey of China's OFDI

Although we can get general characteristics from case studies, we cannot explore a company's specific performance in the process of internationalization based on such information. We cooperated with China Council for the Promotion of International Trade (CCPIT) to launch the analysis of "current conditions of outward investment by Chinese enterprises". In April 2010, CCPIT published "Survey on Current Conditions and Intention of Outbound Investment by Chinese Enterprises 2010" which used the database of the national survey dating from December 2009 to March 2010. This database was carried out by CCPIT in collaboration with the European Commission's Directorate-General for Trade and UNCTAD.[1]

---

[1] The copyright of the data and all written reports of this survey are jointly owned by CCPIT, the European Commission and UNCTAD. CCPIT, the European Commission and UNCTAD shall authorize the use thereof by any institutions or individuals.

Altogether 3,000 questionnaires were distributed in the survey and 1,378 valid questionnaires[2] were filled out and collected, with a response rate of 46%. The survey found that 1,020 companies had overseas activities, accounting for 74.0% of the total samples, among which about 320 had made overseas investments, accounting for 23.2% of the total samples.

5.1.1 Firm scale: A threshold of OFDI for Chinese enterprises

On further observation of companies with overseas activities, we found that only 843 companies have reported sales record validly,[3] which accounted for 82.6% of the samples with overseas activities. In terms of scale distribution of the companies,[4] the scale of overseas activities of Chinese companies concentrates on annual sales between CNY 1 million to 1 billion, accounting for 82.2% of all the respondents. The number of companies whose sales are between CNY 10 million and CNY 0.1 billion is 342, accounting for 40.7% of all the respondents. In terms of business revenue, among all the respondents, 709 companies have achieved annual revenue exceeding CNY 500 million. Therefore, according to the general statistical caliber, the ratio of firms above the designated size reaches 84.1%. From the above statistics, the threshold of Chinese internationalization is relatively high, and it is difficult for companies below the designated size to seek international development. In some provinces like Zhejiang and Jiangsu, most private companies' sales are below CNY 5 million so that the scale requirement will hinder the internationalization of private companies in China. Meanwhile, we find that 203 companies with sales lower than CNY 5 million have outward investment activities, accounting for 20% of the samples with overseas activities. For companies with sales higher than CNY 0.1 billion, the ratio of companies with overseas activities to all designated samples has reached 71.9%, much more than its counterpart to the total samples. We can conclude that scale is a very important threshold for the companies having outward investment.

---

[2] The report from CCPIT shows that they have 1,377 valid questionnaires, which is a slight different as our project because of the different rules to count valid samples.

[3] In selection of valid samples, we omit firms with zero and negative sales. In the analysis, we all adopts this principle to screen the valid samples.

[4] We take sales as the indicator.

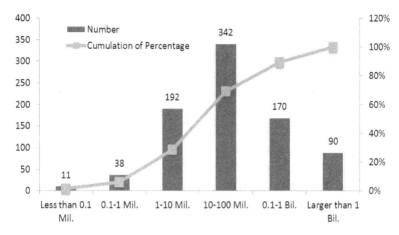

Fig. 5.1. Distribution of business revenue of companies with overseas activities.

The detailed distribution of business revenue of the can be seen in Fig. 5.1.

In terms of the number of employees, 108 respondents had less than 50 employees, accounting for 11.2% of the total samples. Therefore, scale of number of employees is also a very important threshold for a firm having outward investment. Meanwhile, we find that the number of respondents with more than 10,000 employees is only 20, accounting for 2.0% of valid samples. This means that within companies having overseas activities, the number of gigantic multinational players is relatively small.

5.1.2 Non-SOEs: Active players in overseas activities

The "national league" has been playing an important role in overseas activities for a long time. With the progress of China's opening up, and the relaxing of government regulation of Enterprises' oversea activities,[5] privately-owned firms become the new "main force" in overseas activities. This survey reflects that private companies take the biggest share,

---

[5] In 2004, China's Ministry of Commerce released "the registration regulation of foreign traders", and unlashed foreign trade operating right. In 2009, China's Ministry of Commerce released "the management method of investment abroad", and let the approval right of outward investment of firms under the authority of local government.

accounting for 67.7%. Comparatively, the share of state-owned companies is 11.9% and the shares of other forms of firms (listed corporations, joint ventures, and foreign-owned firms) are all below 10%. We find that the numbers exaggerate the private companies' advantages. The average scale of private companies is much smaller than other companies. Particularly, we can tell from Table 5.1 that the average scale of state-owned companies ranks the largest, reaching CNY 4.47 billion. Although private companies are very active in overseas activities, their scales are much smaller than the state-owned and foreign-funded competitors. Therefore, it is further confirmed that scale is an important threshold for overseas activities of Chinese enterprises. Private companies, compared with the state-owned and foreign-funded competitors, are in a disadvantaged position within the competition. As implied by the above analysis, if a company wants to develop overseas activities, it should first realize economies of scale in the domestic market, from which it will gain comparative advantages in production. When such advantages lead to competitive prices in the international market, the company could then expand into the international market and enjoy the returns from the exploitation of economies of scale.

Table 5.1. Average scales of different ownerships' internationalizing activities.

Ownership	Average scale (0.1 billion)	Sample No.
Private	6.0	570
State-owned	44.7	92
Listed	14.9	31
Joint venture	7.2	88
Foreign-owned	29.1	56
Overall	12.5	843*

*denotes in the database, six firms do not report their nature of ownership.

5.1.3 Labor-intensive industries: Internationalization's focus

According to the traditional theory of enterprises internationalization, companies need competitive advantages of OIL (Ownership advantages, Internalization advantages, Location advantages) to commit to international business. From the industrial comparison of enterprises internationalization, we can find competitive advantages from a particular industry. This survey demonstrates that the overseas activities of most companies concentrate on the manufacturing industry, accounting for 81.1% of all respondent samples. The wholesale and retail industry ranks second, accounting for 9.4% of all respondent samples. Comparatively, the internationalization of modern service industry (especially the productive service industry) takes a relatively small share, where transportation, storage, postal and telecommunication services industry and financial intermediary industry take 1% and 1.4% respectively. The data indicates that Chinese service industry has a disadvantage in this international competition. Further study on the manufacturing sub-sectors shows that internationalization mainly concentrates on the textile industry and machine and equipment industry, respectively accounting for 19.5% and 18.2% of all manufacturing industries (see Table 5.2). The above data indicates that

Table 5.2. Industrial sector distribution of overseas investments (detailed classification).

Industry	Number of companies	Ratio (%)
Food products, beverages, and tobacco	48	7.09
Textiles and textile products	132	19.50
Leather and leather products	26	3.84
Wood and wood products	12	1.77
Pulp, paper, and paper products; publishing and printing	16	2.36
Coal, refined petroleum products and nuclear fuel	0	0.00
Chemicals, chemical products and synthetic fibers	58	8.57
Rubber and plastic products	38	5.61
Other non-metallic mineral products	30	4.43
Basic metals and fabricated metal products	56	8.27
Machinery and equipment n.e.c.	123	18.17
Electrical and optical equipment	56	8.27
Manufacture of transport equipment	24	3.55
Manufacture n.e.c.	58	8.57
Sum	677	100.00
Unidentified industries	136*	—
Total	810	—

Note: The unidentified industries refer to firms which report as belonging manufacturing industry, but do not report detailed classification.

internationalization of Chinese enterprises still concentrates on low value added and labor intensive industries. Thus we attribute the major advantage of Chinese enterprises in international operation to low cost and domestic economies of scale, both of which are not there in the traditional OIL theory.

5.1.4 Regional distribution of internationalization

Location selection of Internationalization is one of the most important issues of internationalizing strategy. The distribution of Chinese companies' international operation indicates their competitive advantage and international strategy. This survey shows that Asia, Europe and America are main destinations attracting Chinese companies. About 47.6% of all the respondents invest in Asian Market, while 33% choose EU Market. Only 6% of the respondents choose Africa and Oceania as their internationalization destination.

When industrial distribution is combined with regional distribution, we find those Chinese enterprises' international operation concentrates mainly on machine and equipment industry and textile industry in developed countries. Part of the reasons may be that Chinese companies have comparative advantages in production technology and thus can better utilize their own production and organization experience to do international operation in these domains. As to developing countries, investment from

Table 5.3. Main destination of overseas activity of Chinese enterprises.

Countries and regions	Number of companies	Ratio (%)
USA	110	18.00
Japan	101	16.40
France	75	12.30
Hong Kong (SAR of China)	72	11.80
Germany	64	10.50
R.O. Korea	50	8.10
Vietnam	37	6.00
Italy	27	4.40
The United Arab Emirates	19	3.10
Australia	17	2.70

China concentrates on textile industry, metal industry and chemistry industry. Interestingly, we find that the international operation in developing countries is mainly located in Vietnam, India, and Russia. According to a 2009 survey, Vietnam always ranks among the top 10 investment destinations for Chinese companies and it becomes an important host country for Chinese outward investment, especially investment on textile industry. Among 37 companies that have trade relations with Vietnam, 22 companies choose to invest in Vietnam, and about 18 companies belong to the textile industry. We conclude from such data that south-east Asian countries including Vietnam have become important destinations for international textile industry transfer.

5.1.5 Investment methods and strategies

As data shows, among the newest overseas subsidiaries established by the enterprises surveyed, 69.6% of the subsidiaries are independent Greenfield projects, 20.3% are new joint-ventures, and only 10.1% are merged and acquired subsidiaries. It is observed that the ODI methods and strategies of Chinese enterprises are still dominated by Greenfield investment.

In addition, Fig. 5.2 shows the proportions of difference investment modes to establish overseas subsidiaries in Europe, North America and Africa: A large proportion of the enterprises surveyed chose independent Greenfield investments (over 70%) to establish subsidiaries in Europe, North America and Africa. Another distinct feature is that more investment

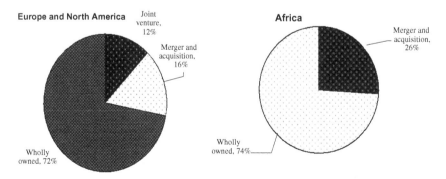

Fig. 5.2. Investment methods to establish new overseas subsidiaries.

in Africa is achieved through joint venture; however, mergers and acquisitions (M&A) is not a choice on that continent.

5.1.6 Self-evaluation of overseas operation

Although in recent years more and more domestic enterprises are taking steps to go global, not all of their overseas operations are optimistic. For example, the success rate of their overseas merger attempts remains quite low.

As Fig. 5.3 shows, more than half of the surveyed enterprises are satisfied with their overseas sales (growth rate), while over half of the same respondents are not satisfied with their overseas sales margin (growth rate) and overseas market shares. It should be noted that the enterprises' satisfaction with the growth of their overseas sales is lower than their satisfaction with their overseas sales, and their satisfaction with the growth of their overseas sales margin is lower than their satisfaction with their overseas sales margin.

5.2 Impacts on OFDI Mode of China's Enterprises

When companies engage in overseas activities, as rational decision makers, they will evaluate various extrinsic and intrinsic factors. However, results of the case studies show that investors do adopt similar strategies (Xiao and Chen, 2008). The internationalization process of Chinese enterprises testifies the "Herd Effect". Although case studies could represent typical

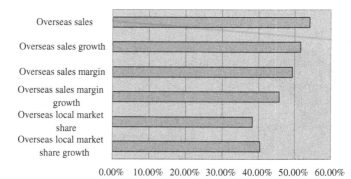

Fig. 5.3. Domestic enterprises' satisfaction with operational indicators of overseas subsidiaries.

decision making process of the companies' internationalization behavior, the factors that have impacts on the internationalization process still need to be explored on the basis of reliable survey. Therefore, this chapter aims to build a regression model to explain those factors for Chinese enterprises. We will look into the influential factors for the ODI mode first, and then analyze the factors for the internalization performance of Chinese enterprises.

There are four major ways of ODI including Greenfield investment, Brownfield investment, M&A, and joint venture. Foreign market entry modes have always been a research interest for international investment studies. However, most researches are confined to international management and marketing. For entry modes, there are only a few qualitative and case studies. According to current research, each of the four entry modes has its own advantages and disadvantages:

The advantages of Greenfield investment are as follows: First, the investors can control the whole process of the investment; particularly they could better control the capital operation by independently selecting geographical location and operational scale. Second, the investors can use patent, technology, material, and equipment as capital input to compensate the lack of foreign exchange finance. In addition, there is no institutional cost with Greenfield mode, while such cost is inevitable in M&A. Finally, the Greenfield investment is low risk, thus it will help the companies to achieve effective management. However, Greenfield investment will grab a market share of other companies, so the competition will be more intensive. Therefore, if taking Greenfield's mode, it's very difficult for newly established subsidiaries to survive at the early stages. According to our survey, 7.9% of the respondents chose Greenfield investment to enter the targeted market.

Unlike the Greenfield investment, the advantage of M&A lies in the fact that firms obtain assets quickly and enter the market easily. M&A avoids building workshop and offices in host countries, which lowers the production cost greatly. Even the reconstruction work can be shortened to a limited time, which accelerates the entering process to the host countries. Meanwhile, M&A facilitates large-scale operation, realizing diversification. In recent years, multinational corporations expand their business ranges by purchasing firms in host countries to compensate technology and experience for the new production. However, the M&A

requires large investment, and the culture difference between firms is too large. Meanwhile, the strong limitation by host countries makes M&A not the uppermost means of outward investment. According to the survey, we found that there were only 2.7% of firms[6] choosing M&A as the modes to enter the targeted market.

In addition to the above two ways, Chinese enterprises also invest through sole investment and joint venture. Sole proprietorship allows foreign investors to manage independently. Wholly owned enterprises can adopt advanced technology and management. Furthermore, the wholly-owned enterprises maintain the interests of the mother company. However, sole investment requires a large sum of cash, thus the operational risk is relatively high for such investment. By contrast, joint venture mode can reduce cash input, and lower the operational risk accordingly. Taking joint venture mode, investors with advanced technology will be at a disadvantaged position when intellectual property protection is inadequate. According to the survey, 6.4% of companies[7] enter the targeted market in the form of joint venture.

As demonstrated by the above analysis, an outward enterprise will choose an investment mode on the basis of its own advantages and understanding of the targeted market. However, the factors that have impacts on the company's investment mode selection are still unclear according to previous academic studies. Considering the limitation of available data, we aim to primarily explore the impacts of company scale, ownership, market potentials of host countries, and domestic incentives on the investment mode selection. It should be noted that Greenfield investment, cooperative investment (joint ventures), M&A, and sole investment are four major investment modes studied in this survey.

The dependent variable is a categorical variable, so that we cannot directly use OLS regression. Alternatively, this chapter adopts logistic regression to do econometric analysis. Logistic regression can be used when dependent variables are binary or are multivariate numbers. The variables used in the paper include four categories without order; therefore, this paper uses regression for disordered categories. The model will first

---

[6] It accounts for 13.2% of firms with outward investment.
[7] It accounts for 31.6% of firms with outward investment.

define a certain level of response variable as reference group (SPSS defaults setting the reference group as the largest level of response variable, the selection of the reference level does not affect the significance of regression coefficients), and then build a general logit model for "level-1" compared with other levels. In our survey, there are four categories (four levels), the values response variable are 1, 2, 3, and 4, which represent Greenfield investment (newly-build investment), Brownfield investment (upgrading available investment), M&A, and joint ventures respectively. The possibilities of each level are π_1, π_2, π_3, π_4. We suppose that there are p variables affecting investment mode so that we can derive three general logit models.

$$\log it\left(\frac{\pi_1}{\pi_4}\right) = \alpha_1 + \beta_{11}x_1 + \cdots + \beta_{1p}x_p,$$

$$\log it\left(\frac{\pi_2}{\pi_4}\right) = \alpha_2 + \beta_{21}x_1 + \cdots + \beta_{2p}x_p,$$

$$\log it\left(\frac{\pi_3}{\pi_4}\right) = \alpha_3 + \beta_{31}x_1 + \cdots + \beta_{3p}x_p.$$

Obviously, it also requires the following equation:

$$\pi_1 + \pi_2 + \pi_3 + \pi_4 = 1.$$

The detailed factors that are crucial for outward investment modes selection by Chinese Enterprises are as follows: (1) Company Scale. According to our survey, there are three approaches to measure company scale: company assets (Ass), employment (Emp), and sales revenue (Rev). (2) Internationalization Experience. We take the number of years since a company's first outward investment as an indicator of its internationalization experiences (Exp). (3) Domestic Incentives. The survey contains several variables representing incentives from domestic policy, and is designed to find out the correlation of these variables. This chapter chooses "Going Global" policies of Chinese Government (Pol_d) and domestic labor cost pressure (Cos) as the domestic incentives. (4) Host Countries' Incentives. There are several variables representing incentives from host countries. Considering the representativeness and independence, this chapter chooses market potentials of host countries (Mar), R&D

capability of host countries (RD), brands availability of host countries (Bra), favoring policies from host countries (Pol_h) and elusion of TB as variables representing incentives from host countries. (5) Other Factors. The survey was sponsored by CCPIT, thus the membership of CCPIT may have an effect on the investment modes of enterprises given that CCPIT will provide related help to the members. In addition, whether the investor is a recipient of FDI or not will also affect its investment mode selection. The regression results were shown in Table 5.4.

Table 5.4. Logistic regression results of determinants of ODI of Chinese firms.

Variable	Greenfield investment (a)	Brownfield ventures	M&A
Intercept	−2.394	−9.199	3.110
Expr	0.372***	0.004*	0.114*
Ass	0.013	−0.109***	0.035**
Rev	0.010	0.009*	0.041**
Emp	0.003	0.062	0.017
[pol_d = 0.00]	0(b)	2.939	−0.938
[pol_d = 1.00]	0.328	−1.791	1.545
[pol_d = 2.00]	4.982**	3.134**	6.861
[pol_d = 3.00]	1.180	1.387	6.928
[pol_d = 4.00]	0.001	0(b)	0(b)
[cos = 0.00]	0.012	0(b)	0(b)
[cos = 1.00]	5.241	−1.896	−5.051
[cos = 2.00]	6.253	4.037	−5.479
[cos = 3.00]	−2.573	8.727	7.544
[cos = 4.00]	0.000	0(b)	0(b)
[mar = 0.00]	1.993	−8.679	2.199
[mar = 1.00]	3.538***	4.054**	0.968**
[mar = 2.00]	0(b)	0(b)	2.714**
[mar = 3.00]	0(b)	0(b)	0(b)
[rd = 0.00]	4.603	6.965*	0.966
[rd = 1.00]	0.793	0.431**	−1.198
[rd = 2.00]	1.3401*	1.147*	1.188
[rd = 3.00]	6.964	1.709*	−7.502
[rd = 4.00]	0(b)	0(b)	0(b)
[bar = 0.00]	0(b)	0(b)	0(b)
[bar = 1.00]	8.030**	3.972*	3.633**
[bar = 2.00]	2.278	1.813*	1.069*
[bar = 3.00]	−1.345	−0.183	−0.921*
[bar = 4.00]	0(b)	0(b)	0(b)

(To be Continued)

Table 5.4. (*Continued*)

Variable	Greenfield investment (a)	Brownfield ventures	M&A
[pol_h = 0.00]	0(b)	0(b)	0(b)
[pol_h = 1.00]	0.849	1.009*	1.592
[pol_h = 2.00]	1.942	3.838	−1.692
[pol_h = 3.00]	0(b)	0(b)	0(b)
[pol_h = 4.00]	0(b)	0(b)	0(b)
[tb = 0.00]	0(b)	0(b)	0(b)
[tb = 1.00]	0.259**	2.137	6.825
[tb = 2.00]	4.009***	1.280	3.107
[tb = 3.00]	0(b)	0(b)	0(b)
[tb = 4.00]	0.012	0.011	0.111
[fdi = 0.00]	1.205	6.002	0(b)
[fdi = 1.00]	1.807	0.251	0.300*
[mem = 0.00]	1.033	0.057	0.009
[mem = 1.00]	0(b)	0(b)	0(b)
Pseudo *R*-Square		0.781	
−2 Log Likelihood		84.901***	

Notes: (a) Logistic regression for disordered categories requires a reference group as the largest level of response variable. We choose joint ventures as our reference. (b) To ensure the maximum likelihood in the recursion process, it sets 0 automatically. (c) *stands for 10% significant level; **stands for 5% significant level; and ***stands for 1% significant level (We use Wald statistics to do the significant test).

From the regression results, the fitness of the model is comparatively good; the likelihood ratio passes the test of 5% significant level. From the regression coefficients, the determinants of firms' outward investment include not only internal factors like firm scale, but also external factors like domestic and foreign incentives.

First, factors that have impacts on Greenfield investment mode include: internationalization experiences, Chinese "Going Global" policies, market potentials of host countries, R&D capability of host countries, value of brand, and elusion of trade barriers (TBs). The regression coefficients reported in Table 5.4 are not standardized estimators so that we cannot compare these coefficients directly. Still, we can get relations by looking at the significance of the variable. The results show that internationalization experiences, market potentials of host countries, and elusion of TBs have a much more significant impact on the investment mode selection.

By contrast, Chinese "Going Global" policies, and R&D capability of host countries have a relatively small impact. Interestingly, company scale, employment, domestic labor cost pressure, membership of CCPIT, and recipient of FDI do not have impact on the ODI mode selection. The direct investment, compared with other investment modes, is more sensitive to the market potential of host countries, but not to R&D capability and incentive policies of host countries. The most interesting finding is that the internationalization experiences have a significantly positive impact on selection of Greenfield mode. This confirms that the past investment experience is practically valuable for Greenfield investment.

Second, factors that have impacts on Brownfield investment mode include: company assets, market potentials of host countries, R&D capability of host countries, internationalization experiences, company sales, Chinese "Going Global" policies, value of proprietary brand, and the incentive policies of host countries. We find that company asset has a significant and negative impact on the selection of cooperative investment mode. The possibility of adopting mode of joint ventures gets lower when the company scale becomes larger. By contrast, internationalization experiences have a positive effect on the selection of joint venture mode though the effect is relatively small. Interestingly, the R&D capability of host countries also has a significant impact. This suggests that the aim of a joint venture is to do cooperative R&D and to obtain advanced technology. The market potentials of host countries are also an important factor, suggesting that the investment and export motive are still an important development strategy after technology cooperation. Unlike the slight effect on Greenfield mode, the incentive policies of host countries do exert a positive influence on the cooperative mode.

Finally, factors that have impacts on M&A mode include: company assets, company sales, market potentials of host countries, value of proprietary brand and recipients of FDI. It is indicated that the risk of M&A is between direct investment and joint ventures, and the company scale is a prominent factor for M&A mode. Compared with three regressions, company assets only have a positive impact on M&A mode. Meanwhile, sales revenue also has a positive impact on the M&A mode. Furthermore, the empirical results show that an investor's domestic status as a FDI recipient will also increase its possibility to choose M&A mode when entering a foreign market.

5.3 Determinants of OFDI Performance

In discussing operation performance of ODI, most of the recent studies focus on the internal factors of the investors. However, the development of ODI also includes external factors such as institutions and markets. This chapter tries to use data collected by CCPIT to investigate the factors behind the operational performance of ODI by Chinese enterprises. The detailed factors that are crucial for their operational performance are as follows:

(1) **Domestic Incentives.** The development of Chinese enterprises' ODI is not only a result of marketization, but also a result of government's support. The domestic incentives certainly have impacts on the ODI performance of firms. Thus we choose "Going Global" policies of Chinese government (Pol_d) and domestic labor cost pressure (Cos) as two variables representing domestic incentives.

(2) **Host Countries' Incentives.** There are several variables representing incentives from host countries. Considering the representativeness and independence, this chapter chooses market potentials of host countries (Mar), brands availability of host countries (Bra), incentives policies from host countries (Pol_h) and elusion of TBs in measuring incentives from host countries.

(3) **Other Factors.** The survey was sponsored by CCPIT, so that the membership of CCPIT may have an effect on the investment modes of firms. Whether the investor is a recipient of FDI or not will also affect the investment mode selection. In addition, internationalization experiences are selected to capture the cumulative effects on the firm's ODI performance.

In terms of firms ODI performance, this paper adopts the TNI indicator released by UNCTAD as a proxy. This index is arithmetic mean of shares of overseas sales, employees and assets to total sales, employees, and assets. Most of variables we use are qualitative indicators because of data limitation. Instead of OLS regression, we follow the treatment of Xiao and Chen (2008), which adopts the categorical regression.

Linear regression requires numeric independent variables, and the regression coefficient of same variable is constant. For example, if independent variable X moves from 1 to 2 or from 100 to 101, the impacts of X on Y are the same for the two cases. This implicitly confines the equidistant measurement of independent variables. However, most of our variables are categorical ones. For example, firms' judgments on the importance of

"Going Global" policies (Pol_d) are collected 0–4... If we simply put this variable into OLS regression, we correspondingly assume different categories are in the equal length, which is a too simple assumption that will lead to wrong conclusions. On the other hand, disordered categorical variables such as membership of CCPIT (0–1 variable), only indicates the membership state' of the firm. We can use dummy variable in the standardized analysis. However, it is difficult to do that when other variables are also categorical variables.

Therefore, this chapter uses optimal scaling transformation to process related variables. The idea behind optimal scaling is to assign numerical quantifications to the categories of each variable, thus allowing standard procedures to be used to obtain a solution on the quantified variables.

The optimal scale values are assigned to categories of each variable based on the optimizing criterion of the procedure in use. Unlike the original labels of the nominal or ordinal variables in the analysis, these scale values have metric properties. In most categories procedures, the optimal quantification for each scaled variable is obtained through an iterative method called alternating least squares in which, after the current quantifications are used to find a solution, the quantifications are updated using that solution. The updated quantifications are then used to find a new solution, which is used to update the quantifications, and so on, until some criterion is reached that signals the process stops. Therefore, we use optimal scaling to run the categorical regression. The regression results can be shown in Table 5.5.

From Table 5.5, model 1, we can see that domestic labor cost pressure and incentive policies from host countries generally do not have significant impacts on ODI performance of Chinese enterprises. Therefore, the economic motive of most companies to invest abroad is not accelerated by the rising domestic labor cost. In other words, the outward investment will not be influenced by the change of domestic production cost. However, we find that for companies investing in the developing countries, especially in African countries, the positive effect of cost pressure cannot be ignored. Meanwhile, membership of CCPIT and whether a firm is a recipient of FDI or not do not have significant impacts on ODI performance of Chinese firms.

Through the coefficients of model 2, we find that internationalization experiences and "Going Global" policies of Chinese government have

Table 5.5. Impacts on operational performance of
ODI of Chinese firms.

Variables	Model 1	Model 2
Expr	0.339***	0.517***
Pol_d	0.021***	0.021***
Cos	0.159	
Mar	0.234**	0.109*
Bra	0.009*	0.045*
Pol_h	0.191	
TB	0.481*	0.401*
Mem	0.035	
FDI	0.519	
R-Square	0.622	0.610

Notes: *stands for 10% significant level; **stands
for 5% significant level; and ***stands for 1%
significant level.

the strongest impacts among all explanatory variables. The categorical
regression coefficients are standardized estimators so that we can compare
the importance of these coefficients of variables. This confirms the
strongest incentive of internationalization experiences. Internationalization
experiences, both successes and failures, will have an enduring impact
on the companies' development. On one side, entrepreneurs will become
more sophisticated in handling risk arising from internationalization. On
the other side, government and the professional agencies will also gain
experience from such success or failure, which may raise the possibility of
success for other investors. In addition, market potentials of host countries,
elusion of trade barriers, and brands availability of host countries also have
positive impacts on ODI performance of Chinese enterprises. Among these
variables, elusion of trade barriers has the biggest impact, indicating that
it is the endogenous motive for Chinese enterprises to enhance their ODI
performance.

5.4 Summary

The poor availability and reliability of micro data appears to be an
obstacle for scholars to study enterprises internationalization in developing

countries. This chapter uses micro data provided by CCPIT to explore the factors behind Chinese enterprises internationalization. Through descriptive and regression analysis, we examine the factors that have impacts on the ODI mode selection and operational performance of Chinese companies. Among the factors that have impacts on ODI mode, Chinese market potentials of host countries, R&D capability of host countries, and internationalization experiences are important factors. Such finding confirms that the internationalization of Chinese companies is greatly affected by extrinsic factors. Meanwhile, "Go Global" policies of Chinese government attract more outward investment, while promoting Greenfield and M&A modes as preferred choices for the investors.

About Impacts on internationalization performance, we follow Xiao and Chen (2008), and further confirm the prominent role of internationalization experiences. The accumulation of internationalization experiences will increase the possibility of successful performance during the development of internationalization.

From comparison of other factors, we also find that the policy of host countries and the increasing production cost do not impose much effective impact on the companies' operational performance during their internationalization process. This evidence further confirms that the institutional barriers may confine the investment of Chinese enterprises. Once the regulation has been loosened, the ODI performance of Chinese firm will gradually reduce their correlation with their cost in domestic market.

Chapter 6

Bound Entrepreneurship and Internationalization

This chapter aims to determine the dependent variable and independent variables influencing the internationalization of indigenous Chinese privately-owned enterprises (POEs), through literature review and a comparative case study. Optimal scaling regression has been employed to test the model developed in the survey conducted.

The theory of enterprise internationalization presents explanations and summarizations of an enterprise's operations abroad. Various theories have been proposed by scholars in different countries to explain how enterprises go global from the confined domestic market. And a wide range of factors has been identified for explaining enterprise internationalization. Anderson (2004) suggests various factors may affect the internationalization process. These include factory conditions, demand conditions, technological development, industrial structure, domestic competition, company strategy, market imperfections or transaction costs, psychological distance, organizational learning, business networks, market potential, geographical priority, managerial decisions, the founder or entrepreneur's experiences of internationalization, age at international entry and risk management. All these relevant influences present to us the answers to questions as follows: What impels an enterprise to go global? How does a domestic enterprise grow up to be an international company or multinational corporation? Why can some enterprises manage to realize their internationalization strategy as expected, but some others cannot?

Meanwhile, scholars who explore various factors that affect internationalization have applied empirical studies like case- or survey-based studies. These include organizational learning (Anderson and Skinner, 1999), social or business networks (Anderson, 2002; Chetty and Holm, 2000; Chetty and Wilson, 2003; Coviello, 2006) or social capital (Yli-Renko *et al.*, 2002), entrepreneurship (Anderson, 2000), international entrepreneurial/ marketing orientation (Knight and Cavusgil, 2004), resource-based views (Dhanaraj and Beamish, 2003; Westhead and Wright, 2001), clustering (Maitland *et al.*, 2005) and localized capabilities (Mariotti and Piscitello, 2001). Anderson (2004) suggested that whether any of the above factors was important depends on the enterprise's degree of internationalization and whether the industry is mature or growing.

Among all the theories in the domain of enterprise internationalization, PTI and theory of INV are the two overwhelmingly significant ones. From the literature review, we can see that most of the theories in this domain are upheld by the theories of PTI and INV. While reviewing or improving PTI and INV, scholars evaluate or conduct comparative studies on these influences. We have made great efforts to sort out all internationalization theories upheld by PTI and INV, and we include the following influences on enterprise internationalization in our research: external conditions for early internationalization, entrepreneurial cognition of international business opportunities, resource requirements when internationalization is initiated, psychic distance and selection of foreign markets and entry modes, competitive strategies of enterprises, and the relationship between the timing of internationalization and enterprise performance.

Whether theoretical or empirical, the research on the internationalization process is overwhelmingly focused on enterprises from developed countries. All the studies quoted in the preceding paragraphs are on either European, North American, Australian or New Zealand enterprises. Attention has been focused on qualitative research, and there is much less quantitative research on enterprise internationalization in China. Econometric methods have hardly been employed to estimate the model and fit the data on enterprise internationalization in China. The research on influences on internationalization of indigenous Chinese POEs is almost nil, both at home and abroad.

Being the largest developing country in the world, China's economy has gained tremendous growth since its adoption of the policy of economic reform and opening up in late 1978, and its impact on the world economy has been increasingly felt. Correspondingly, under the "Going Global" strategy, more and more Chinese enterprises choose to devote to outward FDI, and the issue of internationalization of Chinese enterprises has attracted much attention. For instance, recently a large number of media focused on high-profile international acquisitions and take-over bids by Chinese companies. These include Lenovo–IBM, TCL–Thomson, as well as the aborted CNOOC–Unocal and Haier–Maytag deals (Economist, September 3, 2005 and June 17, 2006; Wu, 2005). In addition, Haier as a single case has been extensively studied (e.g. Du, 2003; Liu and Li, 2002; Palepu *et al.*, 2005). The international expansion of these Chinese enterprises seems to "have dramatically shifted media attention from spotlighting China as a 'giant sucking vacuum cleaner' for global inward FDI to characterizing the country as a cash-rich 'predator' embarking on a global buying binge" (Wu, 2005).

Compared with the so-called "elite enterprises", the position of Chinese POEs in the domestic economy has been rapidly expanding, as well as its role in China's entry to foreign markets. The share of value-added production by the non-farm business contributed by the private sector has overtaken SOEs. Statistics from the *2010 China's Industrial Development Report* show that by the end of 2009, the private sector had accounted for over 65% of China's GDP and contributed about 55% of total fiscal revenue. Meanwhile, its share of created job opportunities has exceeded 75%. China's POEs have been the new force in exports and outward foreign direct investment. Exports by domestic private enterprises nearly doubled, while the share of exports produced by SOEs fell. China's entry into the WTO provides opportunities for Chinese enterprises to further integrate in globalization, especially for the POEs who have gained improved social status and competitiveness. Meanwhile, it is acknowledged that enterprise competitiveness embodies the competitiveness at the national and industrial level. Internationalization is not only a significant approach for the enterprise to acquire competitiveness but also a foundation for the nation and the industry to improve the competitiveness. Endowed with the characteristics of clear property rights and flexible mechanisms, China's POEs have been keen to participate in the world market competition, especially enterprises from coastal regions like Zhejiang, Guangdong and Jiangsu, etc. The decision-making process in China's POEs has been much more influenced by market forces than that in SOEs, where there is still government intervention. Since private enterprises as a sector may be a more appropriate candidate than SOEs, it is of vital importance to explore the influences on internationalization of China's POEs, and hence we need to figure out why and how China's POEs go international.

This chapter will conduct some empirical studies on the influence of China's POEs' internationalization to test relevant western theories of enterprise internationalization and discuss various factors influencing private enterprises' internationalization choices in the context of China. We conducted a comparative case study of 16 indigenous Chinese POEs, as a multiple-case design is more compelling and the overall study is more robust than a single-case design (Herriott and Firestone, 1983; Yin, 2003). Multiple cases are considered as multiple experiments. This design follows a "replication" logic, and is different from a "sampling" logic (Yin, 2003, pp. 46–47). Consistent with Eisenhardt (1989), we chose multiple cases, i.e. samples within roughly each category in terms of their industry, geographic location, years of business and degree of internationalization to allow findings to be replicated within categories. Thus, if common patterns of internationalization emerge from different types of enterprises within this private section of the Chinese economy, then our findings would be more generalizable.

Table 6.1 illustrates the basic characteristics of the 16 enterprises. These enterprises cover a good variety of industries such as machinery, electrical and electronics, automobile, chemical, agricultural, telecommunications and textiles and garments. While it is difficult to judge whether an industry as a whole is knowledge intensive or not, if an enterprise is assigned a "Y" in column 3, it means that this enterprise has been awarded the title of "high and new technology enterprise" at least at the provincial level. This means that the enterprise is engaged in businesses in a high-tech section of the industry by Chinese standards. In terms of the year of official launch, enterprises vary. Significant differences exist in the degree of internationalization: It varies from 1 to more than 100. The final column shows that the majority of interviewees are enterprise founders, and the remainders are those who are very close to the founders.

Table 6.1. Basic profiles of the 16 cases.

Enter-prise code	Main products	Knowledge intensive	Location	Year of registra-tion	Degree of internatio-nalization	Interviewee
F1	Special machinery	Y	Zhejiang	1997	4	Founder, President
F2	Electrical appliances	N	Zhejiang	1996	6	Founder, General Manager
F3	Industrial valves	Y	Zhejiang	1995	9	Founder, President
F4	Bearings	Y	Zhejiang	1994	1	Founder
F5	Auto components	Y	Zhejiang	1969	>50	Assistant General Manager
F6	Chemicals, agricultural products	Y	Zhejiang	1986	3	Assistant to President/ Founder
F7	Semiconductors	Y	Zhejiang	2000	9	General Manager
F8	Communications equipment	Y	Zhejiang	1987	3	Assistant to President, Founder
F9	Electronics	N	Zhejiang	2000	1	Founder, President
F10	Metrological instruments, medicine, telecoms	Y	Zhejiang	1994	>20	Manager foreign trade
F11	Textiles	N	Jiangsu	1994	7	Deputy General Manager
F12	Textiles	N	Jiangsu	1992	6	Founder, President
F13	Textiles	N	Jiangsu	2000	5	Founder, President
F14	Textiles and garments	N	Zhejiang	1979	>100	Deputy Manager — enterprise management
F15	Textiles	N	Zhejiang	1998	5	Deputy Manager
F16	Special machinery	Y	Zhejiang	1975	>50	Chief Engineer

We collected data mainly from in-depth interviews supplemented with archives to "provide stronger substantiation of constructs and hypotheses" (Eisenhardt, 1989). The archives were obtained from company reports, the press as well as company websites. The time length for an interview was between 1.5 and 2.5 h.

As suggested by Eisenhardt (1989), we also made use of multiple investigators in the majority of our interviews to increase the likelihood of capitalizing on any novel insights that may be in the data and enhance the creative potential of the study. All interviews were conducted during June, July and August 2006.

Interviews were tape-recorded unless the interviewees objected. To ensure the accuracy of the interview data, we not only checked the factual information and opinions provided by the interviewees against the archives, but also asked some important questions in alternative ways to see whether the answers were consistent. Following the idea of pattern matching, we constantly compared the main propositions from the existing theories of enterprise internationalization as highlighted in the previous section with our multiple cases to "confirm, challenge or extend the theory" (Yin, 2003). While the interviews were conducted in line with a pre-designed protocol based largely on existing theories and particularly on the six pairs of propositions, open questions were often asked to allow for possible theoretical modification. As the existing theories have grown from experiences of enterprises from developed countries, they may well be challenged by the experience of enterprise internationalization in a developing country setting.

6.1   External Conditions and the Timing of Internationalization

An enterprise's external environment includes its political, social, technological, economic and business conditions, both at home and abroad. The PTI holds the assumption that the domestic and foreign business environments vary greatly in terms of language, culture, business traditions and industrial development, among others. The PTI treats the lack of such knowledge as an important obstacle to the development of international operations (Johanson and Vahlne, 1977). Johanson and Vahlne (1977) argued that, at the beginning, enterprises lacked the basic internationalization experiences that could be acquired continually during the internationalization operation. Therefore, it is hard for an enterprise to conduct international business shortly after its official launch.

Oviatt and McDougall (1994, 1997) argued that changing economic, technological and social conditions had reduced the transaction costs of multinational interchange, and increased the homogenization of many markets in distant countries. As a result, the conduct of international business becomes much easier for everyone to understand. Put another way, lessons learned in the domestic business environment can be easily leveraged for expansion in another country's environment (Autio, 2005). Thus, it is possible for an entrepreneur to treat both the domestic and foreign markets as a single market and start internationalization upon inception.

Thus, we can conclude the following propositions: The more closely linked and homogenized the domestic and international business environments are, the earlier the entrepreneur will initiate enterprise internationalization. Correspondingly, if the domestic market and international market are highly integrated and homogenized, the performance of markets both at home and abroad will be identical.

We used a seven-point Likert scale to examine the relationship between early internationalization and degree of integration/homogeneity of the domestic and foreign markets. We asked whether the founder agreed that the domestic and foreign markets were treated as a single integrated market for the enterprise. (1) indicates "strongly agree" and 7 means "strongly disagree". As the final column of Table 6.2 shows, 6 out of 16 enterprises strongly agreed but the same number of enterprises strongly disagreed. The remaining four enterprises mostly agreed.

If we examine columns 3, 6, and 10 of Table 6.2 respectively, we cannot confirm a relationship between the perceived market integration and the time of internationalization or determine whether it is a pre-formal enterprise launch or post-formal enterprise launch. Some enterprises, agreeing that the domestic and foreign markets were integrated into one, did not initiate their internationalization early, while other enterprises, disagreeing with the statement, started their internationalization relatively early. These enterprises felt that although market integration in general promotes early internationalization, many other external factors influenced the founders' market selection decisions.

Table 6.2. Initiation of Enterprise Internationalization.

Enterprise code	F1	F2	F3	F4	F5	F6	F7	F8
Founder starts relevant business	1985	1989	1993	1987	1969	1986	1956	1987
First int'l activities	2004 (Exp.)	1992 (Exp.)	1997 (Exp.)	1995 (Exp.)	1984 (Exp.)	1994 (imp.)	1989 (Exp.)	1993 (Tec. license)
Proactive or passive	Passive	Passive	Combine	Passive	Proactive	Combine	Passive	Combine
Official Enterprise launch	1997	1996	1995	1994	1969	1986	2000	1987
First int'l activities after launch	2004 (Exp.)	1996 (Exp.)	1997 (Exp.)	1995 (Exp.)	1984 (Exp.)	2000 (Exp.)	2001 (Exp.)	1999
Proactive or passive	Combine	Proactive	Combine	Passive	Proactive	Combine	Proactive	Passive
Founder educat'l backgrd. at official launch	Sec. Sch.	Sec. Sch.	Sec. Sch.	Sec. Sch.	Sec. Sch.	Illiterate	Univ.	Sec. Sch.
Founder int'l experi. at official launch	No	Yes	No	No	No	No	Yes	No
Market integration	7	1	7	7	1	7	1	3

(To be Continued)

Table 6.2. (*Continued*)

Enterprise code	F9	F10	F11	F12	F13	F14	F15	F16
Founder starts relevant business	1968	1970	1994	1992	1986	1979	1998	1966
First int'l activities	1992 (Process)	1998	1996 (imp.)	1993 (imp.)	1998 (F'Trade Office)	1990 (JV)	2000 (Tecco.)	1980 (Exp.)
Proactive or passive	Combine	Proactive	Proactive	Proactive	Proactive	Proactive	Proactive	Proactive
Official Enterprise launch	2000	1994	1994	1992	2000	1990	1999	1975
First int'l activities after launch	2002 (Exp.)	1998 (Exp.)	1998 (Exp.)	1994 (Exp.)	2001 (Exp.)	1991 (Exp.)	2003 (Exp.)	1985 (Exp.)
Proactive or passive	Proactive	Proactive	Passive	Passive	Passive	Proactive	Proactive	Proactive
Founder educat'l backgrd. at official launch	Sec. Sch.	Sec. Sch.	Sec. Sch.	Sec. Sch.	Sec. Sch.	Sec. Sch.	College	Primary
Founder int'l experi. at official launch	Yes	No	Yes	Yes	Yes	No	Yes	No
Market integration	3	2	2	7	7	1	1	1

For instance, under the state export trading monopoly before the late 1980s, F5 as a private enterprise was not allowed to exhibit its products at the Guangzhou Trade Fair, which was the most important means for state-owned enterprises to directly export their products. Instead, the enterprise displayed its products just outside the exhibition hall. Eventually, F5 found its business partners successfully and exported its products for the first time in 1984. The domestic institutional barriers hampered F5's early internationalization although it treated the whole world as a single market for itself.

Take F12 as another example. It seems that the enterprise could not be treated as an INV (in terms of age), because it disagreed that the domestic and foreign markets were integrated as one. It proactively imported advanced machinery to produce high quality products to meet the domestic demand, which had great potential. It then passively exported the products to Asia and Europe and "accidentally" continued its internationalization process. "Whatever internationalization strategy you use, your ultimate purpose is to earn profits", the founder commented.

Table 6.2 illustrates that 4 out of the 16 enterprises did start their internationalization process by reacting to unsolicited export orders. For example, F2 started a family business in small electrical appliances with three workers in 1989. This was only one of many small enterprises specializing in the industry in a small town, a well-known production base for the appliances. In 1992, a friend introduced an Indonesian businessman to F2, and the enterprise started exporting in the same year. Quickly, it became an enterprise exporting all its products. F4 and F7 also passively internationalized in similar ways.

Four enterprises were driven into international markets for the first time by a combination of both passive and proactive methods. For instance, F3 was approached by a state trading company for a possible export opportunity in Southeast Asia. Following this, F3 quickly prepared leaflets and distributed them by stealth at the Guangzhou Trade Fair, where only approved state-owned enterprises were allowed to display their samples. In the same year, F3 started exports. The remaining eight enterprises also proactively pursued their internationalization processes. As mentioned earlier, F5 was a typical example of a proactive internationalization.

Hence, the Chinese evidence does not seem to confirm the above theories. However, we do not think the theory is incorrect. We believe that the result is related to the bounded entrepreneurship. Their bounded education, experience and institutional barriers made the founders unable to correctly recognize the exact degree of market integration. Even if they were able to do so, they may not be able or willing to act accordingly due to various other considerations.

6.2 Entrepreneurial Cognition of International Business Opportunities

Given that business opportunities may exist in markets both at home and abroad (Zahra and Dess, 2001; Zahra *et al.*, 2005), why do some new ventures opt to go international from inception whereas many others decide to focus on their domestic markets? Is the decision to go international made at the enterprise or individual entrepreneur level? In the PTI, there is only a little role for an entrepreneur to play as the model is interested in the decision-making system rather than the individual decision maker.

INV theory holds that entrepreneurs play a very important role in enterprise internationalization, as "internationalization must be wanted and triggered by someone (Boddewyn, 1988). Dunning (1988) and Oviatt and McDougall (1994) argue that enterprises are international because they find advantage in transferring some moveable resources (e.g. raw materials, knowledge, and intermediate products) across a national border to be combined with an immobile, or less mobile, resource or opportunity (e.g. raw material, a market). This foreign location advantage distinguishes international from domestic business.

However, Oviatt and McDougall (1994) also realize that a firm conducting transactions in a foreign country has certain disadvantages if compared with indigenous enterprises, such as trade barriers and an incomplete understanding of laws, language and business practices in foreign countries. With the advantages and disadvantages of going international relative to focusing on the domestic market, an entrepreneur has to decide whether, when and how to enter foreign markets. Some authors assume that entrepreneurs and managers are rational and well informed. Following this logic, entrepreneurs can compare the cost and benefits and identify opportunities for leveraging their strategic assets in foreign markets. Others maintain that managerial cognition is rationally bounded and influenced by the business environment. Cognitive biases influence entrepreneurs' decisions. The entrepreneur's education, functional expertise and past track records of success and failure can significantly influence risk calculations and hence might determine how entrepreneurs define and evaluate opportunities in international markets (see Table 6.3).

The above discussion leads to the following result: The choice between focusing on domestic and international business is determined by entrepreneurial cognition of relative advantages and disadvantages of internationalization, which is in turn influenced by the entrepreneur's education, experience and environmental conditions.

From Table 6.2, we conclude that indigenous Chinese entrepreneurs are not well educated, as their average education is just at a secondary school level. Very few of them had knowledge of foreign languages or international experiences before they initiated internationalization. In addition, they have been constrained by institutional arrangements. The combination of this special business environment and the founders' educational background has led to our key argument of "bounded entrepreneurship" for enterprise internationalization from China, which is consistent with Zahra *et al.* (2005). It argues that entrepreneurs are embedded in a social context and the interaction between entrepreneurs and their environment plays a major role in shaping their cognitive process, and, consequently, behavior.

With the bounded entrepreneurship and facing a relatively large domestic market size, indigenous Chinese entrepreneurs tend to pay relatively more attention to the domestic market. As Table 6.3 shows, seven entrepreneurs agreed that there were only limited channels for information on foreign business opportunities, and another two entrepreneurs did not even bother to actively seek foreign opportunities. Five of them did not have any strategic plan for internationalization. They felt that an increase in internal resources would eventually lead to internationalization. Their typical argument for focusing on the domestic market was that "so long as we work harder to become No. 1 in China, there is no problem for us to go international". They did not realize that internationalization could also enhance their firms' internal resources.

The remaining firms said that they could find sufficient information on foreign business opportunities. Most of them also felt that there was a

Table 6.3. Internal resources and internationalization.

Firm code	Limited information of foreign opportunity	Internal resources leading to internationalization	Strategic plans; resource commitment to internationalization
F1	Pay little attention to foreign opportunity	Internal resource — internationalization	No plan; focus on domestic market & amp; go international in future
F2	Yes	Internationalization — internal resources	Plan, and R&D commitment
F3	No	Internal resources — internationalization	Plan; HR commitment
F4	Pay little attention to foreign opportunity	Internationalization — internal resources	No plan; focus on domestic market
F5	Obtaining information from various sources	Internal resources — internationalization	Detailed plan
F6	Yes	Internal resources — internationalization	Rough plan; product features demand us to focus on domestic market
F7	Obtaining information from various sources	Internal resources — internationalization	Plan
F8	Obtaining information from various sources	Internal resources — internationalization	Initially no, now detailed plan; HR commitment
F9	Yes	Internationalization — internal resources	No plan; only some slogans
F10	Yes	Internal resources — internationalization	Detained plan
F11	No	Internal resources — internationalization	Plan, HR commitment
F12	Obtaining information from various sources	Internal resources — internationalization	No detained plan
F13	Yes	Internal resources — internationalization	No plan; focus on domestic market first
F14	Obtaining information from various sources	Internal resources — internationalization	Detailed plan; sufficient HR and financial commitment
F15	Yes	Internationalization — internal resources	Detailed plan; sufficient HR and financial commitment
F16	Yes	Internal resources — internationalization	Detailed plan; sufficient HR and financial commitment

two-way relationship between internal resources and internationalization, but they learned this gradually in the internationalization processes.

With the bounded education level and international experiences but facing a relatively large domestic market, the entrepreneurs in the private sector were inclined to focus on the domestic market.

6.3   Resource Requirements During Early Internationalization

Johanson and Vahlne (1977) indicated that an international activity involved a decision to commit current resources to a foreign operation. These resources include marketing, organizational, personnel and other resources. The decision to commit resources is made in response to perceived problems and/or opportunities in the foreign market. This perception comes from experiential knowledge. The PTI is a dynamic model in which experiential knowledge as a dimension of human resources and market commitment of current resources affect both commitment decisions and the ways current decisions are performed — and these, in turn, change market knowledge and commitment. This experiential knowledge is confined to certain market environments, and cannot be extended to other people and markets.

As mentioned earlier, networks have in recent years been increasingly regarded as an important type of resource required for internationalization. Johanson and Vahlne (1990) had extended their original PTI by explicitly incorporating industrial networks. They assume that network knowledge is part of market knowledge that is based on experience from current business activities, or current business interaction. The relationships of a firm can be used as bridges to other networks. These relationships can help the firm in getting inside networks in foreign countries. In some cases, business relationships can even force the firm to enter foreign networks (Johanson and Sharma, 1987). This is the case when a customer demands that the supplier follows him abroad. Johanson and Vahlne (1990) assumed that direct or indirect bridges exist between firms and different country networks. Such bridges can be important both in the initial steps abroad and in the subsequent entry into new markets.

More importantly, Johanson and Vahlne (1990) were already aware from the existing literature that personal relationships and net-works are especially important in turbulent, high-technology industries

(Laage-Hellman, 1989). They notice that some small high-tech enterprises go directly to more distant markets and setup their own subsidiaries more rapidly (rather than follow the traditional pattern of internationalization) partly because the entrepreneurs behind these companies have networks of colleagues dealing with the new technology (Lindqvist, 1988). Interestingly, it is this type of small firm that Oviatt and McDougall (1994) focus on and make use of to challenge the original PTI of Johanson and Vahlne (1977).

The above discussion leads to the proposition of the PTI model with respect to the resources required when internationalization is initiated: Firms need experiential knowledge to identify foreign opportunities and other resources to commit to foreign markets when they initiate internationalization. In addition, for small high-tech firms, networks are important in the initial steps abroad, the subsequent entry into new markets and the shortening or skipping of stages of internationalization.

By definition, an INV is "a business organization that, from inception, seeks to derive significant competitive advantage from the use of resources and the sale of outputs in multiple countries" (Oviatt and McDougall, 1994). Given the common lack of sufficient resources to control many assets through ownership, new ventures tend to internalize, or own, a smaller percentage of the resources essential to their survival than do mature organizations. These new ventures begin with a proactive international strategy. This feature challenges traditional theory that large size is a requirement for multi-nationality. So long as an organization owns some assets or resources to exchange in an economic transaction, firm size is not required for an INV. INV argues that pre-firm experience of entrepreneurs is vital. Founders of INVs are individuals who see opportunities from establishing ventures that operate across national borders. They are "alert" to the possibilities of combining resources from different national markets because of the competencies (networks, knowledge, and background) that they have developed from their earlier activities. Following the logic of the resource-based view of the firm, the INV model argues that only the entrepreneur possessing these competencies is able to combine a particular set of resources across national borders and form a given INV.

Networks, as one of the indicators of a founders' competence, are also regarded as one of the four elements of the INV model. According to Oviatt and McDougall (1994), alternative transaction structures cover both hybrid structures and networks. Entrepreneurs have to depend on hybrid structures to control many vital assets, such as licensing, and franchising. However, they agree with Aldrich and Zimmer (1986) and Larson (1992) that an even more powerful resource-conserving alternative to internationalization for new ventures is the network structure.

Thus, the INV model has the following proposition regarding resource requirement when internationalization is initiated: Only entrepreneurs who have developed competences such as networks, knowledge and background from their earlier activities are able to form INVs. So long as an organization owns some assets to exchange in an economic transaction, firm size is not required for an INV.

From Table 6.4, the sizes of the firms vary in terms of the number of employees and annual sales when they internationalized for the first time, ranging from only 15 employees with sales of CNY 1 million (about USD125,000) to 2,000 employees with sales of CNY 1.8 billion (about USD0.225 billion). This means that size is not an important determinant for a firm to internationalize for the first time.

All the founders except two had no pre-firm internationalization experience when their firms internationalized for the first time. Furthermore, although the majority of the firms understood the importance of innovation for internationalization and allotted resources to R&D, and although some firms regarded their technologies as the leading ones in the domestic market, few claimed that they possessed leading technologies by world standards. In general, their prices were not the lowest in their respective industries. As a result, they had neither differentiation nor cost leadership advantage.

As regards networks, F3 and F8 indicated that local supply chains and firms business relations played important roles in firm internationalization. The founder of F3 said, "if we order a component during the daytime, it can be delivered locally in the night. Thus, we can catch up with shipping dates". Interestingly, both F2 and F6 felt that networks could be both important and unimportant. The founder of F2 conducted his very first export activity via a recommendation by a friend. But he argued, "social networks are not as important as entrepreneurship because an entrepreneur has to exploit this opportunity". F6 expressed a similar view: "The most important determinant was the entrepreneurship, i.e. the spirit of exploration and exploitation. To initiate a project you have to rely on entrepreneurship.

Table 6.4. Firms resources when internationalizing.

Firm code	F1	F2	F3	F4	F5	F6	F7	F8
No. of employees	120	15	25	300	NA	1200	80	200
Experience of founder	No	No	No	No	No	No	No	Yes
Annual sales	3 m	1 m	4.5 m	3 m	NA	1 bm	3.5 m	NA
*Importance of business network	No	Yes (friend's introduction)	Yes (local supply chains)	No	No	No	No	Yes (firm networks)
Leading technology by Chinese standards	2	1	1	6	6	7	7	4
Leading technology by world	1	1	1	2	2	6	2	3
Innovation for int'lization	1	1	1	6	7	7	7	6
Resource allocated to R&D	6	1	1	6	7	7	7	5
Lowest price in industry	1	4	4	4	7	1	1	2

(To be Continued)

Table 6.4. (*Continued*)

Firm code	F9	F10	F11	F12	F13	F14	F15	F16
No. of employees	200	2,000	1,000	550	200	NA	2,000	NA
Experience of founder	No	No	No	No	No	No	Yes	No
Annual sales	10 m	1.8 bm	25 m	50 m	100 m	NA	100 m	NA
*Importance of business network	No	No	Yes (industrial cluster)	(industrial cluster)	Yes and No (industrial cluster)	No	No	No
Leading technology by Chinese standards	5	5	2	1	NA	7	3	7
Leading technology by world	3	3	2	1	NA	7	3	5
Innovation for int'lization	6	6	2	1	NA	7	7	7
Resource allocated to R&D	4	4	2	1	NA	7	7	7
Lowest price in industry	2	4	2	3	NA	1	4	6

Notes: (1) From column 6 "Leading technology at home" to column 8 "Lowest price in industry", the values in the cells are the seven-point Likert scores with 1 being "strongly agree" and 7 being "strongly disagree". (2) NA: means the interviewee was unable or unwilling to provide the information.

Networks are needed to propel company progress, but they do not come out of thin air. Because you are at work, the networks are gradually established". Finally, although F11, F12 and F13 did not think that networks were important for their internationalization, they did not actually realize that they were operating a local industrial cluster which facilitated their acquisition of information about foreign markets. Most of the firms did not think that networks were important for their internationalization.

Thus, the information in Table 6.4 suggests that firms do not have to have pre-firm internationalization experience, sufficient resources or business networks to internationalize. The evidence of China's indigenous privately owned enterprises supports neither the PTI nor the INV theory.

Although bounded by the lack of experiential knowledge or pre-firm internationalization experience and networks, many founders of indigenous Chinese entrepreneurs managed to obtain knowledge about foreign opportunities via other means in their business environment, such as attending exhibitions. Different from the PTI and INV theory, our results show that while they are very helpful, experiential knowledge or pre-firm internationalization experience and networks are not the prerequisite for entrepreneurs to initiate their internationalization process, whether at an early or a late stage.

6.4   Psychic Distance, Selection of Foreign Markets and Entry Modes

Johanson and Vahlne (1977) argued that the psychic distance is the sum of factors preventing the flow of information in the market. Examples are differences in language, education, business practices, culture and industrial development. These differences lead to a difficulty in obtaining adequate market knowledge in international operations, and constitute the main characteristic of international operations, as distinct different from domestic operations.

The PTI assumes that firms enter new international markets as a function of their psychic distance to the firms' prior experience. A firm's internationalization is treated as an incremental, risk-averse and reluctant adjustment to changes in a firm or its environment (Johanson and Vahlne, 1977, 1990). While selecting the entry mode, firms typically "start exporting to a country via an agent, later establish a sales subsidiary and eventually, in some cases, begin production in the host country" (Johanson and Vahlne, 1977). Put another way, this model assumes "sequential progression from low-control modes to high-control modes" (Autio, 2005).

Johanson and Vahlne (1977, 1990) also observed a similar successive establishment of operations in new countries. Specifically, the time order of such establishments was found to be related to the psychic distance between the home and the import/host countries (Hornell *et al.*, 1973; Johanson and Wiedersheim-Paul, 1975). Typically, firms will start by entering neighboring markets and later, as experience grows, more distant markets will be entered (Johanson and Vahlne, 1990).

Thus, from the PTI we can make the following proposition: Given psychic distance, firms develop their international operations in small steps. Typically, firms enter new markets with successively greater psychic distance and use entry modes with successively greater control.

Oviatt and McDougall (1994) had challenged the PTI proposition. They argue that in the past, the slow speed of communication and transportation channels between countries inhibited gathering of information about foreign markets and increased perceived risks of foreign operations. However, in recent years, improved international communication and transportation along with the homogenization of markets in many countries simplify and shorten the process of a firm's internationalization. These changes "minimize the relevance of psychic distance during a firm's internationalization" (Chetty and Campbell-Hunt, 2004). Thus, firms may skip stages of international development that have been observed in the past, or internationalization may not occur in stages at all (Oviatt and McDougall, 1994). Therefore, the proposition of the INV model regarding the psychic distance and the size of internationalization steps is as follows: Technological and economic changes can minimize the psychic distance and shorten, simplify or skip stages of a firm's internationalization.

As Table 6.5 shows, the majority of the firms entered foreign markets more or less with successively greater psychic distance, and used the entry modes more or less with successively greater control, i.e. indirect exports (if any), trading agencies (if any), direct exports or FDI (joint venture or wholly owned subsidiary). This orderly internationalization process of these firms seems to be consistent with the PTI. This also reflects indigenous

Table 6.5. Time order of market and entry mode selections.

Firm code	Founder's first international activities	First international activities after launch	Second international activities after launch	Third international activities after launch	Fourth international activities after launch	Orderly
F1	2004 (Export, Libya, Japan)	2004 (Export, Libya, Japan)	2005 (Export, Romania)	2006 (Export, Romania, HK (SAR of China))	—	No
F2	1992–1995 (Export, Indonesia)	1996 (Export, Egypt)	1997 (Export, Syria)	1998 (Export, Argentina)	1999 (Export, United Arab Emirates)	More or less Yes
F3	1997 (Indirect export, Malaysia)	1997–1998 (Indirect export, Malaysia, Thailand)	1999 (Indirect export, UK)	2001–2004 (Export, USA, Taiwan of China, Italy, Portugal)	2005 (Export, Germany)	Yes
F4	1995 (Indirect export, USA)	1995 (Indirect export, USA)	2000–2001 (Trading office in USA)	Since then, export via the office to USA	—	Yes
F5	1984 (Export, USA)	1984 (Export, USA)	1992–1994, (Subsidiary, USA)	Since then, export worldwide	Since then, JVs, subsidiaries, worldwide	Yes and No
F6	1994 (Import, USA); 1996 (Tech. license in Japan)	2000–2001 (Export, Southeast Asia, Germany)	2002 (JV, Japan)	2004 (processing trade, Japan)	—	More or less Yes

(To be Continued)

Table 6.5. (*Continued*)

Firm code	Founder's first international activities	First international activities after launch	Second international activities after launch	Third international activities after launch	Fourth international activities after launch	Orderly
F7	1989 (Indirect export, Taiwan of China); 1996 (export via agency in USA)	2001 (Export, via agency in USA and Canada)	Since 2005 (Export, Singapore, USA, Japan, R.O. Korea, Malaysia)	Since 2005 (import, raw materials from USA, Japan, Germany)	—	Yes
F8	1993 (Tech. license in); 1998 (JV, Japan)	1999 (Export, USA)	2001 (Export, North America, Japan)	2004 (mergers and acquisitions (M&A), Hong Kong (SAR of China))	—	No
F9	1992 (Processing trade, Japan)	Since 2002 (Export, Japan)	—	—	—	Yes
F10	1998 (Export, Thailand)	1998 (Export, Thailand)	2000 (Subsidiary, Thailand)	2001–2002 (Export, South America)	2003 (Subsidiaries, Argentina, India)	More or less Yes
F11	1996 (Import, machinery from R.O. Korea and Taiwan	Since 1998 (Export, Middle East, Southeast Asia)	2002 (Import, machinery from Japan, Germany)	2005 (Tech. R&D with Japan and Germany)	—	Yes
F12	1993 (Import, machinery from Japan and Europe)	Since 1994 (Export, R.O. Korea)	Since 2005 (Export, USA, R.O. Korea, Japan, Middle East, EU)	—	—	Yes

(*To be Continued*)

Table 6.5. (*Continued*)

Firm code	Founder's first international activities	First international activities after launch	Second international activities after launch	Third international activities after launch	Fourth international activities after launch	Orderly
F13	1998 (Foreign Trade Office); 2000 (import, materials from R.O. Korea, Taiwan of China and Machinery)	Since 2001 (Indirect and direct export, Vietnam, R.O. Korea, Italy, Portugal)	—	—	—	Yes
F14	1990 (JV, Macao (SAR of China))	1991 (Export)	1997 (Business links with HK and Japan for market development)	2004 (JV with Japan)	2005 (Tech. & marketing co-op. with Japan & Italy)	No
F15	2000–01 (Tech. co-op., Japan)	2002 (JV, Japan)	2003 (Export, Japan)	2005 (Export, USA, HK, India)	Considering (subsidiary, Pakistan)	No
F16	1980 (Export, Southeast Asia)	1981 (Import)	2000 (JV with HK SAR of China)	2002 (Tech. co-op. with Germany)	—	More or less Yes

Chinese entrepreneurs' bounded entrepreneurship. However, once these firms initiated the internationalization process, their pace seems to be higher than what the theory may suggest: they quickly expanded into different foreign markets rather than by doing this in small steps. They were able to learn very quickly by doing this.

However, the table also indicates that some firms did not follow this orderly process. For instance, F1 went into Libya 2 years earlier than into Hong Kong (SAR of China) and it is obvious that the psychic distance of mainland China with Hong Kong (SAR of China) is much smaller than that with Libya. F5 established a wholly owned subsidiary before it established joint ventures and it is clear that a subsidiary involves greater control than a joint venture. Similar to F5, some firms such as F8, F14 and F15 formed joint ventures before they started exporting. These are not examples of the shortened or skipped internationalization process as both the PTI and INV theory observe. Rather, they follow an inverse order of internationalization.

We also observe that F6, F9, F11 and F12 started their internationalization by imports. This seems to be consistent with traditional theory as importing is often regarded as a lower order of internationalization. However, what these firms imported included machinery and possibly raw materials, together with technical guidance from suppliers. Like using JVs, they started inward internationalization to learn both about technology and managerial and marketing skills, and then began outward internationalization.

Therefore, we hold that while firms can follow the outward internationalization patterns described by the PTI and INV theory, they can also be engaged in inward-oriented internationalization activities to enhance their knowledge and resources on the home market before initiating their outward internationalization process. This inward part of the internationalization process is particularly useful for those firms with bounded technological and managerial knowledge.

6.5 Competitive Strategies of Internationalizing Enterprises

There is no explicit discussion of what competitive strategy the internationalizing enterprise should follow in the PTI. Johanson and Vahlne (1977) argued that the internationalization process could be seen "as the consequence of a process of incremental adjustments to changing conditions of the enterprise and its environment". Common knowledge and professional market knowledge are required by the enterprise while conducting business in foreign markets. Implicitly, the PTI focuses on the role of knowledge in keeping a fit between enterprise's resource commitments and the characteristics of the foreign market in order to remain effective and earn long-term profits. Hence, in the PTI market knowledge is related to market conditions, competitive conditions, distribution networks, and terms of payment and currency convertibility, both at home and abroad. Clearly, this view is consistent with traditional strategic management theory, which calls for continuous strategic renewal to keep the enterprise in step with shifting opportunities and threats in the environment (De Wit and Meyer, 2004).

The INV model also pays special attention to knowledge as a unique resource for international competitiveness. As mentioned earlier, enterprises conducting international business have certain disadvantages compared to indigenous enterprises. To overcome the advantages of indigenous enterprises in many countries simultaneously, private knowledge may be used to create differentiation or cost advantages for MNEs and INVs (Oviatt and McDougall, 1994). Thus, the INV model considers proprietary knowledge to be the fundamental source of both differentiation and cost leadership strategies, although no explicit discussion is offered.

According to Porter (1985), the logic of the differentiation strategy requires that an enterprise choose attributes in which to differentiate itself that are different from its rival. By doing so, the enterprise can expect a premium price. On the other hand, the sources of cost advantage may include the pursuit of economies of scale, proprietary technology, preferential access to raw materials and other factors. Following such a discussion, we can propose the proposition of INV with respect to enterprise strategy: Knowledge is required in the internationalization process for the enterprise to adopt a differentiation or cost leadership strategy.

From columns 2 and 3 of Table 6.6, most enterprises tended to minimize differences between their existing scope of activities and new market entries and only a few enterprises proactively maximized the size of market potential by selecting the markets with greatest growth potential. The evidence indicates that most Chinese enterprises are risk-averse rather than

Table 6.6. Sources of international competitiveness.

Firm code	Risk averse	Opportunity seeking	Leading technology by Chinese standards	Leading technology by world standards	High-quality products difficult to imitate	Lowest price products	Main reasons for your international success
F1	Yes	No	Yes for some products	Yes for some products	Yes for some products	No	Brand name
F2	No	Yes	No	No	No	No	Reputation; quality and business relations
F3	Yes	No	Yes for some products	Yes for some products	No	No	High ratio of quality/ function to price
F4	No	Yes	No	No	No	No	High ratio of quality/ function to price
F5	No	Yes	Yes for some products	Yes for some products	Yes for some products	No	High ratio of quality/ function to price
F6	Yes	No	No	No	No	No	High ratio of quality/ function to price
F7	Yes	No	Yes	No	No	No	High ratio of quality/ function to price
F8	No	Yes	Yes for some products	No	No	No	High ratio of quality/ function to price

(To be Continued)

Table 6.6. (*Continued*)

Firm code	Risk averse	Opportunity seeking	Leading technology by Chinese standards	Leading technology by world standards	High-quality products difficult to imitate	Lowest price products	Main reasons for your international success
F9	Yes (initially)	Yes (now)	Yes	No	No	No	High ratio of quality/function to price
F10	Yes	No	No	No	No	No	High ratio of quality/function to price
F11	Yes	No	Yes	Yes	Yes	No	Quality
F12	Yes	No	Yes for some products	Yes for some products	No	No	High ratio of quality/function to price
F13	Yes	No	Yes for some products	No	No	No	High ratio of quality/function to price
F14	Yes	No	Yes	Yes for some products	No	No	High ratio of quality/function to price
F15	Yes	No	Yes	No	No	No	High ratio of quality/function to price
F16	No	Yes	Yes	No	No	No	High ratio of quality/function to price

opportunity seeking when internationalizing. This seems to be consistent with the PTI, where knowledge is required in the internationalization process to keep the enterprise in step with the foreign business environment.

To see whether technological knowledge was used to maintain competitiveness by differentiation, we asked the enterprises to assess their technology and quality standards and their answers are summarized in columns 4–6.

The technologies used for at least some of their products in most of the enterprises were advanced by Chinese standards. Their claims are confirmed as these enterprises were awarded the "high-tech new enterprise" title by Chinese authorities mostly at the national level. However, far fewer of them claimed that their technologies were advanced by world standards. Even if they so claimed, they admitted that these technologies were only for a very limited range of products and, more importantly, for those products that developed countries were no longer interested in producing. The latter category includes textiles, garments and plastic machinery.

Cost leadership is another competitive strategy identified by Porter (1985). However, column 7 of Table 6.6 indicates that cheap price alone is not the means for these Chinese enterprises to keep competitive in the world market, as only one enterprise claimed that its price seemed to be the lowest in the industry. Instead, the majority of the enterprises indicated that their fundamental source of international competitiveness lay in a high ratio of quality/function/performance to price. As the interviewee from F5 indicated, "internationally, some enterprises provide better-quality products and others offer lower prices than we do. We can only say that our ratio of quality/function/performance to price is the best". Chinese enterprises relied on a combination of reasonable quality and relatively low price to compete in the world market, rather than pursuing a pure differentiation or cost leadership strategy.

Chinese evidence shows that enterprises can either rely on differentiation or cost leadership, which can be acquired by developing technological knowledge to compete in the world market, or implement other strategies that satisfy the endogenous advantage, disadvantage and market condition. For instance, enterprises that possess limited technological knowledge can pursue a combination of low price and differentiation. Therefore, we argue that enterprises should select a proper strategy that keeps enterprises in step with the changing international business environment and thus enhance their competitiveness in the world market.

6.6 Timing of Internationalization and Enterprise Performance

When commenting on the INV theory, Zahra (2005) argued that international business environments are characterized by dynamism. It is important to investigate the conditions that encourage INVs to change their strategic directions, and to document the consequence of these changes for their survival and financial performance. According to Autio (2005), one important implicit argument for the PTI is that late internationalizers are more likely to survive internationalization moves than early internationalizers. Enterprises' management is normally risk averse, and enterprises typically tend to accumulate resources over time, so that survival chances are more likely to be enhanced if the internationalization process is started late. On the other hand, McDougall *et al.* (1994) argued that early internationalization may be not only an opportunity but also a necessity to ensure chances for growth, because opportunity windows are short in dynamic sectors. The relationship between timing of internationalization and enterprise performance is not argued explicitly in the INV theory, and hence the existing literature regarding this relationship leads to the argument that the timing of internationalization will possibly exert its influence on the enterprise's survival and performance both by the early internationalizer and the late internationalizer.

From Table 6.7 there does not seem to be a clear relationship between the timing of internationalization and enterprise performance. Both early and late internationalizers could perform well or poorly. We asked the interviewees to explain their answers, and none of them related the enterprise performance to the timing of internationalization. The central message from the interviews was that enterprises benefited from their internationalization activities as they were generally happy with their overall performance in foreign markets.

F4 was unhappy with sales of its main products in foreign markets simply because the sales were not as high as the enterprise should have achieved. "We have not put enough energy in. In addition, the condition is

Table 6.7. Timing of internationalization and enterprise performance.

Enter- prise code	Founder starts relevant business	First int'l activities	Time lag for first int'l activities	Satis- factory foreign sales	Satis- factory pre-tax profits	Leant advanced tech. & man skills	Satis- factory overall perfor- mance	Higher returns than at home
F1	1985	2004	19	NA	NA	7	NA	5
F2	1989	1992	3	4	3	6	4	6
F3	1993	1997	4	5	5	6	6	6
F4	1987	1995	8	1	5	2	4	2
F5	1969	1984	15	6	6	7	7	7
F6	1986	1994	8	1	6	2	7	4
F7	1956	1989	33	7	7	7	7	6
F8	1987	1993	6	5	5	6	7	5
F9	1968	1992	24	4	5	6	6	5
F10	1970	1998	28	5	5	6	4	5
F11	1994	1996	2	5	6	6	5	7
F12	1992	1993	1	6	6	3	7	5
F13	1986	1998	12	NA	NA	NA	NA	NA
F14	1979	1990	11	6	4	7	6	6
F15	1998	2000	2	3	3	5	5	4
F16	1966	1980	14	6	6	7	7	7

Notes: (1) From column 5 "Satisfactory foreign sales" to column 9 "Higher returns than at home", the values in the cells are the seven-point Likert scores with 1 being "strongly disagree" and 7 being "strongly agree". (2) NA: the interviewee was unable or unwilling to provide the information.

not mature yet, and we still need time", the founder of F4 commented. Given limited international activities, the founder did not feel that they had learnt a lot from their foreign operations. F6 also felt that its export volume was still small, and hence there were no economies of scale. Although the pre-profit rate was high abroad, returns on total investment in foreign markets were similar to those at home. Both F4 and F6 decided to develop the home market and wanted to be No. 1 in China before they could naturally go international.

We believe that enterprise performance is influenced by various factors, both external and internal. Business environments might exert an influence on enterprise survival and performance by various means, whether an early internationalizer or a late internationalizer. Perhaps the best way for an entrepreneur to achieve good performance is to consistently enact strategic change to remain in harmony with external conditions.

6.7 Model Specification and Empirical Analysis

Model specification and data description:

Based on the above case studies, we conclude the following six hypotheses:

H1: The more closely linked and homogenized the domestic and international business environments are, the earlier the entrepreneur will initiate enterprise internationalization, and the better the internationalizer will perform.

H2: Age, educational background and international experience of the entrepreneur will influence the internationalization performance, while for age, the younger the better; for education background, the higher the better; and for international experiences, the more experienced the better.

H3: Scale of the enterprise, years of business and networks the enterprise possesses will influence the internationalization performance, while for the scale, the larger the better; for years of business, the longer the better, for networks, the more extended the better.

H4: The closer the psychic distance is, the better the internationalization performance.

H5: The competitive strategy will influence the internationalization performance.

H6: Early internationalizers will perform better than late internationalizers.

Based on the above six hypotheses, we used the data obtained from the interviews conducted with 39 Zhejiang private enterprises to carry out empirical analysis on influences on the internationalization of indigenous private enterprises. In addition, we tested how internationalization theories, which overwhelmingly focused on enterprises from developed countries, fit China's evidence with respect to the internationalization of indigenous Chinese POEs, and we consequently tested the results that were concluded from the comparative case study in the preceding part.

From the above six hypotheses we developed the following model:

$$TNi = \beta_0 + \beta_1 X_1 + \beta_2 X_2 + \beta_3 X_3 + \beta_4 X_4 + \beta_5 X_5 + \beta_6 X_6$$
$$+ \beta_7 X_7 + \beta_8 X_8 + \varepsilon,$$

where TNi, as the dependent variable, denotes the performance of internationalization. We used the Multinational Index of UNCTAD to assess internationalization performance, which is the weighted average of the ratios of enterprise sales abroad to total sales, overseas employees to total employees and overseas assets to total assets. The index is rather compact and its data is available.

The formula is:

$$TNi = (FSTS + FETE + FATA)/3,$$

where FSTS (Foreign Share in Total Sales) denotes the ratio of overseas sales to total sales; FETE (Foreign Employment in Total Employment) denotes foreign employees as a percentage of total employees, which is reflected by the ratio of employees devoted to overseas operations to total employees.

FATA (Foreign Assets in Total Assets) denotes the ratio of overseas assets to total assets, which is equal here to assets devoted to overseas operations divided by total assets.

Independent variables are:

X_1: denotes differences in the domestic and international business environments (as psychic distance reflects to a great extent the differences in the domestic and international business environments, it is a good indicator to H1 and H4), and data are collected in the form of the ordinal, categorical variable in which we classify the entrepreneurs according to their knowledge of the degree of integration and homogeneity of the domestic and foreign markets ranging from 1 to 7, with 1 indicating "complete homogeneity" and 7 indicating "complete heterogeneity".

X_2: age of the entrepreneur.

X_3: education background of the entrepreneur; denotes years of full-time education the entrepreneur received.

X_4: previous international experience of founders or entrepreneurs; denotes years of overseas operations before they initiate internationalization.

X_5: scale of the enterprise; denotes the employees the enterprise has when the survey is conducted.

X_6: years of business after the official launch; denotes years of business from the year when the enterprise was officially launched to 2006.

X_7: Competitive strategy of the enterprise, where 1 indicates the pricing strategy; 4 indicates the strategy which attaches importance to the ratio of quality/function/performance to price; 7 indicates the technology strategy; while 2 and 3 indicate the intermediate strategies in the range from 1 to 4; correspondingly 5 and 6 indicate the intermediate strategies in the range from 4 to 7.

X_8: Years of internationalization since initiation; denotes the time from the first initiation to 2007.

Hence, we have the following the econometric model:

$$\text{TN}i = \beta_0 + \beta_1 X_1 + \beta_2 X_2 + \beta_3 X_3 + \beta_4 X_4 + \beta_5 X_5 + \beta_6 X_6$$
$$+ \beta_7 X_7 + \beta_8 X_8 + \varepsilon.$$

Namely:

$$\text{TN}i = \beta_0 + \beta X_j + \varepsilon \ (j = 1, 2, \ldots, 8),$$

where $\text{TN}i$ denotes the internationalization performance of enterprise i, X_j denotes the vector of influences of internationalization performance, ε denoting disturbance is a stochastic variable.

See Appendix 1 for data obtained.

The optimal scale regression & model modification:

The dependent variable is required to be a numerical value in a linear regression model. The regression coefficient of the same independent variable is a constant value, namely the impact of X's variation on Y is B, whether it increases from 1 to 2 or from 100 to 101. And this implies that the independent variable is an isometric. However, there are categorical data in the context, for instance, X_1 denotes differences in the domestic and international business environments, which have been categorized in the survey, ranging from 1 to 7. Given the distance between two classifications is identical, there is a natural ordering (ascending or descending) of the classifications' impact on the independent variable. It is definitely a simple and unrealistic assumption, which can possibly lead to a false conclusion.

Meanwhile, for unordered categorical variables like X_7, the competitive strategy is not a natural ordering (ascending or descending) of the values. It is impossible to estimate the regression coefficient that reflects the changes in the dependent variable caused by a unit change in the independent variable. For unordered categorical variables, it is a common practice to employ a dummy variable to fit the model, and then simplify the result. However, it is a thorny task to employ a dummy variable, especially when most variables in the model, not all, are categorical variables.

Therefore, we apply the optimal scale transformation to process the data of X_1 and X_7. The optimal scale transformation is designed to transform categorical variables into numerical values. Based on the model that needs fitting, we examine the degree of impact of every category on dependable variables. The econometric function hypothesizes that the dependent variable is linearly related to the explanatory variable, i.e. the transformed variables. The nonlinear transformation has been taken to carry out iterations until we figure out the optimal numerical value for every category of the original categorical variables, which will substitute the original variables to develop the successive estimates. By doing so, traditional methods can be extended to all measurements which include the unordered categorical variable, ordered categorical variable, and continuous variable, and eventually to estimate the regression and factor models.

Using SPSS, we obtained the following regression results:

Table 6.8. Model summaries.

Multiple R	R square	Adjusted R square
0.979	0.959	0.901

Dependent Variable: TN
Predictors: X_1 difference, X_2 age, X_3 education, X_4 experience, X_5 scale, X_6 years of business after official launch, X_7 competitive strategy, X_8 years of internationalization.

Table 6.9. ANOVA.

	Sum of squares	df	Mean square	F	Sig.
Regression	17.266	10	1.727	16.458	0.001
Residual	0.734	7	0.105		
Total	18.000	17			

Dependent Variable: TN
Predictors: X_1 difference, X_2 age, X_3 education, X_4 experience, X_5 scale, X_6 years of business after official launch, X_7 competitive strategy, X_8 years of internationalization.

Table 6.10. Coefficients * reformat.

	Standardized coefficients				
	Beta	Std. error	df	F	Sig.
X_1 difference	−0.077	0.090	1	0.734	0.420
X_2 age	−0.082	0.112	1	0.531	0.490
X_3 education	−0.202	0.091	1	4.951	0.061
X_4 experience	1.008	0.130	1	60.164	0.000
X_5 scale	0.153	0.151	1	1.027	0.344
X_6 years of business	−0.524	0.175	1	8.983	0.020
X_7 competitive strategy	0.145	0.086	3	2.827	0.116
X_8 years of internationalization	0.338	0.146	1	5.329	0.054

Dependent Variable: TN.

Table 6.11. Correlations and tolerance.

	Correlations				Tolerance	
					After transfor- mation	Before transfor- mation
	Zero-order	Partial	Part	Importance		
X_1 difference	0.331	−0.308	−0.065	−0.027	0.713	0.714
X_2 age	0.644	−0.265	−0.056	−0.055	0.465	0.451
X_3 education	−0.028	−0.644	−0.170	0.006	0.705	0.587
X_4 experience	0.908	0.946	0.592	0.954	0.345	0.361
X_5 scale	−0.219	0.358	0.077	−0.035	0.256	0.239
X_6 years of business	−0.455	−0.750	−0.229	0.248	0.191	0.182
X_7 competitive strategy	0.035	0.536	0.128	0.005	0.784	0.664
X_8 years of internationalization	−0.274	0.657	0.176	−0.097	0.272	0.327

Dependent Variable: TN.

We can conclude from Tables 6.8 and 6.9, adjusted $R^2 = 0.901$, overall significance testing shows $P = 0.001 < 0.005$, hence the model as a whole has a statistical significance. However, from Table 6.10, we find that three out of the eight independent variables, i.e. X_1 difference, X_2 age and X_5 scale, fail in the significance test, which is consistent with the conclusions we drew from the above case studies. Namely:

(1) Since the data assessing the difference of domestic and international business environments come from the entrepreneur's knowledge regarding this difference, chances are that their limited education and international experience hampered the founders from correctly recognizing the exact degree of market integration. Even if they were able to do so, they may not be able or willing to act accordingly, due to various other considerations.

(2) Age of the entrepreneur cannot be regarded as an influence on internationalization; both the veteran and the recruit can launch a perfect campaign.

(3) Scale is neither the prerequisite for the enterprise to initiate internationalization nor the significant influence on the internationalization performance, which supports the theory of Small Scale Technology, namely comparative advantages, exist universally, even developing countries and small and medium-sized enterprises are possibly embedded with some particular advantages regarding foreign investments and international businesses. These countries and SMEs maximize the utilization of resources and advantages and production in the comparative advantage sectors to acquire comparative benefits.

From Table 6.10, we find that among five variables, X_3 education, X_4 experience, X_6 years of business after official launch, X_7 competitive strategy and X_8 years of internationalization, X_4 experience is the only variable that succeeds in the significance test, whereas the remaining four variables fail. Considering their p values are much lower than those of X_1 difference, X_2 age, X_5 scale, it is possible that variables (X_1 difference, X_2 age, and X_5 scale) cause some negative impact on significance tests of variables (X_3 education, X_6 years of business, X_7 competitive strategy and X_8 years of internationalization).

Therefore, we estimate the regression model again by removing X_1 difference, X_2 age, X_5 scale and then we obtain the following results:

Table 6.12. Model summary.

Multiple R	R square	Adjusted R square
0.977	0.955	0.924

Dependent Variable: TN.
Predictors: X_3 education, X_4 experience, X_6 years of business, X_7 competitive strategy, X_8 years of internationalization.

Table 6.13. ANOVA.

	Sum of squares	df	Mean square	F	Sig.
Regression	17.198	7	2.457	30.623	0.000
Residual	0.802	10	0.080		
Total	18.000	17			

Dependent Variable: TN.
Predictors: X_3 education, X_4 experience, X_6 years of business, X_7 competitive strategy, X_8 years of internationalization.

Table 6.14. Coefficients * reformat.

	Standardized coefficients				
	Beta	Std. error	df	F	Sig.
X_3 education	−0.303	0.072	1	17.528	0.002
X_4 experience	0.827	0.074	1	124.432	0.000
X_6 years of business	−0.396	0.125	1	10.039	0.010
X_7 competitive strategy	0.304	0.076	3	16.166	0.000
X_8 years of internationalization	−0.007	0.118	1	0.004	0.952

Dependent Variable: TN.

Table 6.15. Correlations and tolerance.

	Correlations				Tolerance	
					After transfor-mation	Before transfor-mation
	Zero-order	Partial	Part	Importance		
X_3 education	−0.014	−0.798	−0.280	0.004	0.850	0.641
X_4 experience	0.875	0.962	0.745	0.757	0.811	0.811
X_6 years of business	−0.536	−0.708	−0.212	0.222	0.286	0.341
X_7 competitive strategy	0.041	0.786	0.268	0.013	0.779	0.725
X_8 years of internationalization	−0.463	−0.020	−0.004	0.004	0.323	0.346

Dependent Variable: TN.

Table 6.12 shows that adjusted R^2 of the modified model is higher than that of the original model, namely, $R^2 = 0.924 > 0.901$. Meanwhile, Table 6.13 shows that the modified model with the improved statistical significance can fit the data better.

However, Table 6.14 leads to the following result: X_8 years of internationalization cannot be regarded as a good explanatory variable, which is consistent with case studies in the context, namely years of internationalization is not a significant influence on the performance. As the case study in Chapter 3 reveals, timing of internationalization is not clearly related to the enterprise's performance. Both late internationalizers and early internationalizers can potentially perform either well or badly.

Furthermore, from Table 6.15 we find that variable X_8 captures the feature of inferior indexes, both in importance and tolerance. Importance is measured by a standardized coefficient and correlation coefficient to examine the percentage of importance of the variable to the model. The importance of all variables in the model will attain 100%. The higher the value is, the more important is the variable to the predictors of the dependent variable. Tolerance denotes the ratio of its influence on the dependent variable which cannot be explained by other independent variables, the higher the better. It is a tool to reveal the multicollinearity, and too low a tolerance may lead to an incorrect optimal scale regression result.

X_6 years of business satisfies a property of low importance and tolerance and fails in the significance test. However, we can extend the identical method in the context here, and re-estimate the regression model by removing X_8. We obtain the results as shown in Tables 6.16–6.19.

Table 6.16. Model summary.

Multiple R	R square	Adjusted R square
0.977	0.955	0.931

Dependent Variable: TN.
Predictors: X_3 education, X_4 experience, X_6 years of business, X_7 competitive strategy.

Table 6.17. ANOVA.

	Sum of squares	df	Mean square	F	Sig.
Regression	17.197	6	2.866	39.265	0.000
Residual	0.803	11	0.073		
Total	18.000	17			

Dependent Variable: TN.
Predictors: X_3 education, X_4 experience, X_6 years of business, X_7 competitive strategy.

Table 6.18. Coefficients * reformat.

	Standardized coefficients				
	Beta	Std. error	df	F	Sig.
X_3 education	−0.301	0.067	1	20.232	0.001
X_4 experience	0.831	0.071	1	138.408	0.000
X_6 years of business	−0.394	0.077	1	26.116	0.000
X_7 competitive strategy	0.300	0.070	3	18.566	0.000

Dependent Variable: TN.

Table 6.19. Correlations and tolerance.

	Correlations				Tolerance	
					After transfor- mation	Before transfor- mation
	Zero-order	Partial	Part	Importance		
X_3 education	−0.014	−0.805	−0.286	0.004	0.904	0.672
X_4 experience	0.877	0.962	0.749	0.763	0.812	0.812
X_6 years of business	−0.534	−0.839	−0.325	0.220	0.683	0.740
X_7 competitive strategy	0.039	0.792	0.274	0.012	0.836	0.725

Dependent Variable: TN.

From Table 6.16, we find that adjusted R^2 is higher. Tables 6.16 and 6.17 lead us to the result where the model has been improved econometrically. All four independent variables have succeeded in the significance tests in Table 6.18. The high tolerance values of these four independent variables in Table 6.19 indicate the low multicollinearity in the model. The proportion that cannot be explained by other independent variables plays a dominant role in its entire influence on the dependent variable. Furthermore, Table 6.19 also illustrates the importance of these four independent variables, where X_4 experience ranks the first, 76.3%, X_6 years of business 22%, X_7 competitive strategy 1.2%, and X_3 education 0.4%.

Significant information has been revealed in Table 6.18, the influence of both education and years of business on performance are negative, that is to say the higher the formal education the entrepreneur receives, the worse the internationalizers will perform; the longer the enterprise exists, the worse the internationalizers will perform. This result departs from the traditional theories, but it is feasible.

First, an excellent entrepreneur should be endowed with spirits of innovation and divergent thinking. Exam-oriented education has prevailed when the interviewees were educated at their school ages. They started the business from inception just when China adopted the policy of reform and opening-up. In the era of drastic changes and a land of adventure, the lack of formal education has to some extent been transformed from a disadvantage to an advantage. On the one hand, the limited education rendered them more willing to take risks; on the other hand, the limited education excluded them from a position in the traditional sectors. While they were eager to improve their living standards, the reform and opening up has just provided them with a good opportunity to be involved in the private sector.

Second, they received a low level of formal education, but they survived in the fierce competition in the market economy, and they accumulated plenty of experiences. What is more, they received informal education later, i.e. the administrative training, which prevails in the coastal regions. A large number of entrepreneurs have attended exclusive training courses for managers and presidents organized by various training centers and agencies. The mode of doing-before-learning which has been proved more effective than learning-before-doing, benefits the private entrepreneur a lot.

Finally, there is a departure from traditional theories regarding the relationship between years of business and internationalization performance. The traditional theories, for instance PTI, argue that the longer the enterprise exists, the more abundant the reserve of inner resources the enterprise will hold, and the better the enterprise will perform. Others, for instance INV, argue that the inner resources accumulated in the long history of the enterprise development cannot be regarded as the factors that influence the internationalization performance. Some new enterprises can be the elite in the internationalization circle. They are born global. Our econometric result cannot provide a reasonable explanation for this departure.

Hence, it takes three iterations before we accept the optimal scale regression result. The modified model is:

$$TNi = \beta_0 + \beta X_3 + \beta_4 X + \beta_6 X_6 + \beta_7 X_7 + \varepsilon.$$

Thus, from the above econometric models, we can make the following propositions:

(1) The entrepreneur's knowledge of the differences in domestic and international business environments cannot be regarded as an influence, which is consistent with our case study.

(2) Age cannot be regarded as one of the influences. Both the veteran and the recruit can launch a perfect campaign in the internationalization process.

(3) Education plays a negative role in the influence, whereas we cannot deny the importance of education, especially the administrative training for entrepreneurs and managers.

(4) Experiences play a key role in the process of internationalization. Plentiful internationalization experiences will lead to better performance, and hence entrepreneurs in private sectors should focus on the accumulation of the internationalization experiences either by means of practice in state-owned enterprises or foreign-funded enterprises before starting the business or getting to know some foreign friends to extend the network.

(5) Scale is neither the prerequisite for the enterprise to initiate internationalization, nor the significant influence on internationalization performance, which is consistent with the result of our case study and has supported the theory of small-scale technology.

(6) The influence of years of business on internationalization performance is negative, namely the earlier the enterprise is officially launched, the worse the internationalization will perform. We cannot offer a reasonable explanation for this.

(7) Competitive strategy exerts a huge influence on internationalization performance. If the enterprise embodies the technology strategy, its internationalization performance will be better.

(8) Timing of internationalization, when to initiate the internationalization, cannot be the factor to influence the performance, which is consistent with our case study and the INV theory.

6.8 Summary

In the preceding section, we have found that the Chinese experience is unique. We notice that the most unique phenomenon of the internationalization processes of indigenous China's POEs is that they were closely linked with the special entrepreneurship possessed by the founders of these enterprises. The interviewees were asked to choose the most important influence on their internationalization process among government policy, business networks, company resources, domestic competition, entrepreneurship and others, and their answers are summarized in Table 6.20.

Table 6.20. Most important factors influencing internationalization process.

Firm code	Most important	Second most important	Third most important
F1	Company resources	Domestic competition	—
F2	Entrepreneurship	—	—
F3	Entrepreneurship	Business networks (local supply chain)	Luck
F4	Know the world and obtain opportunities	—	—
F5	Entrepreneurship	—	—
F6	Entrepreneurship	Company resources	Business networks
F7	Entrepreneurship	—	—
F8	Entrepreneurship	—	—
F9	Domestic competition	Government policy	Entrepreneurship
F10	Entrepreneurship	Government policy	Market conditions
F11	Profit seeking	Government policy	—
F12	Government policy	Entrepreneurship	—
F13	Entrepreneurship	—	—
F14	Entrepreneurship	—	—
F15	Government policy	Entrepreneurship	—
F16	Entrepreneurship	International competition	—

As can be seen from the above Table 6.20, 10 out of the 16 enterprises regarded entrepreneurship as the most important, while the other two treated it as the second most important factor influencing their internationalization process. In addition, opportunity or profit seeking as stated by F4 and F11 was also closely related to entrepreneurship. There is no other single influence that was comparable to entrepreneurship in explaining the Chinese experience.

It is not novel to apply entrepreneurship to enterprise internationalization. However, it is equally clear that "normal" entrepreneurship embedded in and prevailing in a developed market economy is unable to provide a satisfactory explanation of the Chinese experience. The entrepreneurship possessed by the founders of indigenous Chinese POEs is very much bounded, and this provides a powerful explanation of the unique characteristics of the internationalization activities of these enterprises. Buckley (2002) called for informing and building on the strengths of existing internationalization theory by importing entrepreneurship theory.

This advice is quite consistent with the Chinese experience. As for other influences like resources and networks as the relevant explanatory variables, Jones and Coviello (2005) suggest developing a different theoretical framework by incorporating various theories. Following this, we expanded the existing theoretical framework by proposing the argument of bounded entrepreneurship is added, aiming at optimizing the framework.

Corresponding to the discussions in the preceding sections, our so-called bounded entrepreneurship can be summarized by the six relationships. We start with R1, i.e. the relationship between external conditions and early internationalization. From the literature review, we understand that the more closely linked and homogenized the domestic and international business environments, the earlier the entrepreneur will initiate enterprise internationalization. Then, the more closely linked and homogenized the domestic and international business environments, the more identical the performances of both at home and abroad will be.

From the previous empirical evidence, we know that the Chinese evidence does not seem to support this relationship. We do not think that the relationship is incorrect. Rather, we feel that the result is caused by bounded entrepreneurship. Because of their limited education, experience and institutional barriers, the founders were unable to correctly recognize the exact degree of market integration. Even if they were able to do so, they may not be able or willing to act accordingly due to various alternatives. For instance, even if there is a high degree of homogeneity between the domestic and foreign markets, the founders may well use their limited resources to concentrate on the domestic market.

From the literature review, we can make the following proposition: The choice between focusing on domestic and international business is determined by entrepreneurial cognition of relative advantages and disadvantages of internationalization, which is in turn influenced by the entrepreneur's education, experience and environmental conditions. Because of limited education and hence limited knowledge about foreign markets and because of the relatively large domestic market, indigenous Chinese entrepreneurs tended to start their businesses in the domestic market. This result is consistent with the sociological view that entrepreneurs' cognitive process and behavior are shaped by their business environment. This sociological view is reflected in Fig. 6.1 as R2.

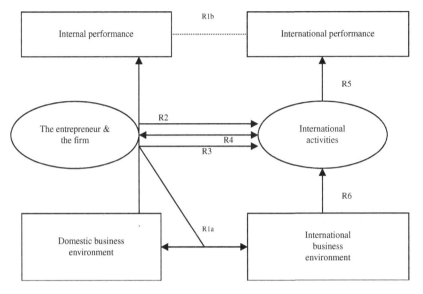

Fig. 6.1. Entrepreneurship and internationalization.

The above literature review leads to the proposition that experiential knowledge or pre-firm internationalization experience is required for initiating internationalization. In addition, networks are important for small high-tech enterprises in their initial steps abroad, the subsequent entry of new markets, and shortening or skipping stages of internationalization.

Although bounded by the lack of experiential knowledge or pre-firm internationalization experience and networks, many early indigenous Chinese entrepreneurs managed to obtain knowledge about foreign opportunities via other means in their business environment, such as attending exhibitions. Different from the PTI and INV theory, our result, R3, shows that while they are very helpful, experiential knowledge or pre-firm internationalization experience and networks are not the prerequisites for entrepreneurs to initiate their internationalization process, whether at an early or a late stage.

R4 in Fig. 6.1 presents a two-way relationship between the enterprise and selection of foreign market entry modes. It is different from the PTI and INV theory, which discuss whether a firm follows an incremental pattern or can shorten or skip stages of one-way (outward-oriented) international business activities given the psychic distance. While enterprises can follow the outward internationalization patterns described by the PTI and INV theory, they can also be engaged in inward-oriented internationalization activities to enhance their knowledge and resources in the home market before initiating their outward internationalization process. This inward part of the internationalization process is particularly useful for those enterprises with bounded technological and managerial knowledge.

From the literature review, PTI suggests that knowledge is required in the internationalization process to keep the firm in step with its business environment. The knowledge here mainly refers to the information about foreign markets and operations. INV suggests that knowledge is required in the internationalization process for the enterprise to adopt a differentiation or cost leadership strategy. The knowledge in the INV theory is mainly technological knowledge. Although focusing on different aspects, the two definitions of knowledge can be complementary to each other. We can develop our technological knowledge to enhance differentiation or cost leadership to position the enterprise favorably in a foreign market. However, enterprises can adopt other competitive strategies according to the enterprise's own strengths and weaknesses and the market conditions. For instance, an enterprise with limited technological knowledge may pursue a combined strategy of cost efficiency and differentiation, as the indigenous Chinese POEs do. From the above review we obtain our R5, i.e. in order to improve competitiveness in the international market, an enterprise has to pursue a proper strategy which can keep the enterprise in step with its changing business environment.

R6 focuses on the relationship between the timing of internationalization and enterprise performance. We believe that the enterprise performance is influenced by both internal and external factors, and it is possibly influenced by international business environments by various means, whether their internationalization process at an early or a later stage, a quick or a gradual speed. And it is possible that there is no influence at all. Business environments are changing. Perhaps the best way for an entrepreneur to achieve good performance is to consistently enact strategic change to remain in step with external conditions.

Based on the econometric analysis of the 39 enterprises interviewed, this chapter presents a comparative case study of the internationalization processes of 16 indigenous Chinese privately owned enterprises. It has developed six major propositions from the existing literature, which have then been compared with the multiple cases. As a result, the argument of bounded entrepreneurship is proposed to explain the unique internationalization patterns and competitive positions of these enterprises.

Embedded in a transitional and emerging country, indigenous Chinese entrepreneurs are bounded by their low education and experience and by unfavorable institutional arrangements. They satisfy the properties of limited technological, managerial and linguistic knowledge. Thus, (1) they have limited capabilities in assessing the degree of integration and homogeneity of the domestic and foreign markets; and (2) they have bounded entrepreneurial cognition of international business opportunities and hence tended to start their businesses in the home market. (3) Given the lack of business networks and experiential knowledge about foreign markets and operations, they either "waited for a windfall" or strove to obtain the information by other means such as attending exhibitions. (4) Given the bounded entrepreneurship, some of them carried out inward-oriented internationalization activities to attain technological and managerial knowledge before they started outward oriented activities. (5) Given the bounded technological knowledge, they pursued a combined strategy of differentiation and cost leadership. (6) Finally, the timing of internationalization alone may not be sufficient to interpret enterprise performance, as the latter may be influenced by many other factors.

We extend our pattern by incorporating the market imperfection and transaction cost approach, the network approach, resource-based views and competitive strategic theories, aiming at explaining the internationalization of indigenous Chinese entrepreneurs.

Appendix 1. Data obtained in the interview.

ID	TN	X_1	X_2	X_3	X_4	X_5	X_6	X_7	X_8
1	0.04	7.00	45.00	16.00	8.00	1,876.00	7.80	4.00	2.00
2	0.36	3.00	50.00	16.00	10.00	60.00	6.70	4.00	5.00
3	0.96	7.00	59.00	12.00	25.00	118.00	1.30	4.00	1.00
4	0.24	4.00	43.00	25.00	10.00	15.00	3.50	6.00	3.00
5	0.04	3.00	49.00	5.00	0.00	71.00	5.30	4.00	1.00

(To be Continued)

Appendix 1. *(Continued)*

ID	TN	X_1	X_2	X_3	X_4	X_5	X_6	X_7	X_8
6	0.06	4.00	45.00	3.00	0.00	650.00	5.30	5.00	1.00
7	0.08	4.00	52.00	9.00	0.00	76.00	6.50	4.00	4.00
8	0.25	1.00	31.00	15.00	3.00	200.00	2.20	4.00	1.00
9	0.01	6.00	52.00	12.00	0.00	285.00	7.20	6.00	1.00
10	0.01	1.00	42.00	16.00	0.00	86.00	5.00	4.00	1.00
11	0.09	4.00	35.00	12.00	0.00	30.00	13.00	6.00	11.00
12	0.13	5.00	38.00	12.00	2.00	400.00	10.00	5.00	6.00
13	0.26	5.00	42.00	15.00	0.00	89.00	5.00	5.00	2.00
14	0.11	2.00	41.00	6.00	1.00	100.00	4.00	3.00	3.00
15	0.37	7.00	39.00	9.00	4.00	100.00	7.00	4.00	7.00
16	0.40	1.00	42.00	12.00	10.00	50.00	4.00	3.00	4.00
17	0.15	3.00	42.00	16.00	1.00	150.00	4.00	4.00	3.00
18	0.14	4.00	35.00	6.00	0.00	250.00	10.00	3.00	6.00
19	0.08	4.00	39.00	12.00	0.00	35.00	12.00	4.00	1.00
20	0.08	2.00	33.00	15.00	0.00	43.00	3.00	2.00	1.00
21	0.09	3.00	35.00	12.00	0.00	25.00	2.00	4.00	1.00
22	0.21	5.00	39.00	16.00	2.00	8.00	6.00	4.00	2.00
23	0.05	4.00	38.00	12.00	0.00	20.00	4.00	3.00	1.00
24	0.05	7.00	41.00	6.00	0.00	150.00	9.00	4.00	2.00
25	0.32	1.00	46.00	9.00	0.00	150.00	10.00	1.00	10.00
26	0.27	7.00	37.00	12.00	0.00	260.00	11.00	7.00	9.00
27	0.02	7.00	43.00	12.00	0.00	2,800.00	12.00	7.00	11.00
28	0.43	1.00	61.00	9.00	0.00	31,800.00	37.00	5.00	22.00
29	0.17	7.00	46.00	12.00	0.00	1,800.00	20.00	6.00	6.00
30	0.32	1.00	42.00	16.00	5.00	500.00	6.00	6.00	5.00
31	0.33	3.00	43.00	9.00	0.00	2,900.00	19.00	4.00	7.00
32	0.10	3.00	49.00	9.00	2.00	2,000.00	6.00	4.00	4.00
33	0.28	2.00	42.00	9.00	2.00	12,000.00	12.00	5.00	8.00
34	0.14	2.00	36.00	9.00	2.00	7,000.00	12.00	5.00	8.00
35	0.03	7.00	43.00	12.00	2.00	8,000.00	14.00	3.00	12.00
36	0.05	7.00	41.00	12.00	3.00	1,000.00	6.00	4.00	5.00
37	0.21	1.00	45.00	6.00	0.00	25,000.00	16.00	4.00	15.00
38	0.12	1.00	45.00	15.00	2.00	1,020.00	7.00	4.00	3.00
39	0.33	1.00	70.00	6.00	0.00	3,500.00	31.00	4.00	21.00

Chapter 7

Case Study for Pattern Selection

7.1 Case Selection Statement

Four private enterprises in Zhejiang Province were selected as cases for comparative analysis in this chapter, including Wanxiang Group, Transfar Group, Holley Group, and Youngor Group. The main reason for choosing these companies is that the various characteristics they demonstrated during their internationalization processes can better illustrate different internationalization patterns of privately-owned enterprises (POEs) as well as factors that influence the internationalization process.

According to Johnson and Vinsent, enterprises should pass through four stages in an orderly way during the process of internationalization: (a) irregular export activities; (b) export through agents; (c) establishment of overseas sales subsidiaries; and (d) overseas production and manufacture. As can be seen from Table 7.1, these companies are at different stages of the internationalization process with different degrees of internationalization. Transfar Group is still in the phase of irregular export activities, while Wanxiang Group and Holley Group have already begun direct overseas production and manufacture and engage in international operations with capital budgeting techniques such as overseas mergers and acquisitions (M&A). They are all relatively large-scale enterprises in Zhejiang Province, adopting different patterns in their internationalization processes that are affected by various characteristics due to their different industry backgrounds and development paths. This chapter explores the internal principles of these firms' internationalization process through an analysis of their strategies and the determinants of the process, and documents the unconventional characteristics by combining the unique characteristics of China's private enterprises.

Table 7.1. Introduction to samples.

	Industry	Rank (Top 100 private enterprises in Zhejiang province in 2005)	Stage of internationalization
Transfar Group	Daily Chemicals Manufacturing	26	Irregular Export Activities
Youngor Group	Textile Clothing Manufacturing	3	Establishment of Overseas Subsidiaries
Holley Group	Other Electronic Equipment Manufacturing	11	Overseas Production and Manufacture
Wanxiang Group	Mechanical Equipment and Parts Manufacturing and Sales	2	Overseas Production and Manufacture

Based on PTI theory and INV theory, this chapter tries to explain the basic development principles with those theories by combining the characteristics of the internationalization development of different enterprises. Of course, the process of these enterprises' internationalization, as mentioned above, will deviate from PTI and INV theories because of the particularities of Chinese entrepreneurship. Buckley (2002) once advocated that entrepreneurship theory should be introduced to endow the existing internationalization theory with more explanatory power. This proposal is consistent with China's experience. Thus, we can better understand the characteristics of the internationalization process of China's privately-owned enterprises by analyzing these four groups.

7.2 Wanxiang Group: A New Technology Generator

Wanxiang Group was founded on July 8 1969. It has been listed as one of the separate-list state plan groups in Zhejiang Province since 1990, one of the 120 pilot enterprise groups by the State Council since 1997, and one of the 520 national key enterprises since 1999. In 2005, its sales revenue was CNY 25.215 billion; and foreign exchange earnings were USD818 million. In 2010, its sales revenue reached over CNY 60 billion, which enrolls it into Forbes Top 100 Chinese Enterprises List. Wanxiang now dominates the auto parts business, including eight major items: universal joints, bearings, constant speed transmission devices, transmission shafts, brakes, shock absorbers, roller and rubber seals, and two complete and major systems for suspension and braking. Wanxiang has gone through development from the supplier of parts, components to systematic module. Wangxiang has founded 32 professional manufacturing enterprises and a manufacturing base with a four square kilometer area was built in mainland China, as well as a national technology center, national laboratory and postdoctoral research station. Since 1969, Wanxiang explored the production specialization and products serialization, and then achieved its goal of going global by the successive internationalization of products, personnel and enterprises, becoming one of the largest Chinese automobile manufacturers. Its major products occupy more than 65% of market share in China with 18 overseas subsidiaries in eight foreign countries and it has integrated the production lines of global automobile companies such as General Motors and Ford, covering more than 60 countries and regions. In 2011, Wanxiang ranked No. 122 in the list of the "Top 500 Chinese Enterprises", No. 50 in the manufacturing sector; No. 60 in the list of "Top 1000 Chinese Industrial Enterprises" in 2010; No. 15 in machinery industry section; No. 8 in automobile industry section; No. 1 in auto parts industry section. It was Lu Guanqiu, the president of Wanxiang Group, who created this miracle.

Wanxiang Group led by Lu Guanqiu has experienced four stages of development process. The first stage (prior to 1980) was the initial period of start-up. The second stage (1980–1989) was the growth period of "specialization of production and modernization of management", in which Lu Guanqiu used his family property as collateral to contract the Hangzhou Wanxiang Joint Factory. In 1988, Lu completed the joint-stock reform of Wanxiang. In the third stage (1990–1999), Wanxiang has entered into the phase of "incorporate into enterprise groups and internationalize its management" by building a modern enterprise system. Starting from being ranked in the top 50 in domestic market, Wanxiang now has occupied more than 50% market share in the industry. It had 18 subsidiaries in eight foreign countries including the United States and it began to cooperate with the world's first-class automobile companies, including General Motors and Ford. In the fourth stage (after 1999), Wanxiang Group adopted the strategy of "Capitalized Business and Internationalize Operations" which led the Wanxiang Group not only to become the largest automobile parts manufacturer in China, but also to gain great achievements in finance, agriculture and other fields.[1]

7.2.1   Internationalization process

Since the late 1970s, Wanxiang has begun to implement the strategy of internationalization and actively explored the international market. In 1984, Wanxiang exported 30,000 sets of universal joints to the US, which made Wanxiang the first Chinese auto parts manufacturer to enter the US market. In 1992, Wanxiang sent staff to develop the US market. In 1994, Wanxiang founded its subsidiary in Chicago. Wanxiang has become the first Chinese parts manufacturer that entered the international production line. Wanxiang has established 18 overseas companies in 8 foreign countries, and building an international marketing network that covered more than 50 countries and regions. It has become the supplier of General Motors and Ford.

At present, Wanxiang's subsidiary in US, a representative of Wanxiang international business, is responsible for its international operations and markets. It registered in Kentucky in 1995. Several years later, Wanxiang acquired the American companies Scheler and UAT. UAT, a NASDAQ listed company specializing in the production and sales of brakes. These two companies enjoyed the largest number of universal joint patents in the world. Wanxiang holds stake more than 30 companies abroad, has an international marketing network covering more than 50 countries and regions, and became a supporting manufacturer for multinational corporations such as General Motors and Ford. Its overseas business has accounted for more than half of the whole industrial sales of the group. In April 2000, Wanxiang acquired a US company Scheler, one of the three major auto parts dealers in America. Interestingly, Scheler was the first American company who bought Wanxiang's products. Wanxiang enlarged its exports to the US and Europe through Scheler's existing channels. In 2001, Wanxiang acquired nine enterprises, including the American listed

---

[1] Chen, L. and Lu, G. (2006) The Blacksmith's international complex, *China Investment*, 2006(6).

company, Universal Automotive Industries Inc. (UAI). By 2002, total assets of Wanxiang's subsidiary in US reached more than USD13 million that made it the largest Chinese-funded company in Midwest America. August 12, 2002 was named "Wanxiang Day" by the state government of Illinois in honor of the contribution to the local economy made by Wanxiang. In October 2003, Wanxiang acquired Rockford, the world's largest supplier of wing-style universal joints and transmission shafts. In 2003, Wanxiang came to headlines again, for the solar silicon chip developed by Wanxiang was used by the Shenzhou V manned spacecraft. Wanxiang also made great achievements in international acquisitions such as General Bearing Corporation (GBC), one of the oldest bearing manufacturers. Thus, Wanxiang received orders worth USD80 million every year, laying a solid foundation for its bearing industry. Currently, Wanxiang's overseas subsidiaries are as follows:

(1) Wanxiang's US subsidiary
(2) Distribution System in the Maintenance Market

    (i) Wanxiang's European subsidiary;
    (ii) Wanxiang Dynamic in Europe;
    (iii) Wanxiang's Australian subsidiary;
    (iv) Wanxiang's South American subsidiary;
    (v) HMS Company;
    (vi) ADI Corporation.

(3) Manufacturing System

    (i) Wanxiang QC Bearing Company;
    (ii) DL Company;
    (iii) Rockford;
    (iv) PS Company.

(4) Other investment companies

    (i) Venture Capital Investment Company;
    (ii) Prairie River Golf Course;
    (iii) Wanxiang Petroleum Technology Development Corporation;
    (iv) Investment Network Corporation;
    (v) Chicago Central Park Golf Course, Inc.;

(vi) Wanxiang-Horton Insurance Group, Inc.;
(vii) Wanxiang Finance Company.

7.2.2   Internationalization strategy

According to the INV theory aforementioned, in order to keep a foothold in overseas markets successfully, enterprises can enhance differentiation or cost advantages by developing technological knowledge or by adopting other competitive strategies on the basis of a company's own strengths and weaknesses, as well as market conditions. First of all, Wanxiang did not act like other companies to take the strategy of "import prior to export" as the first step to go abroad, so as to minimize the risk. Actually, in the early 1980s, China was still in the era of the planned economy, in which township and village enterprises were not listed in the national plan. Wanxiang, an auto parts manufacturer, was facing an extremely tiny domestic market due to such a policy limitation. In order to survive, Wanxiang had to shift its focus to overseas markets. At that time, many restrictions were placed on exports, which led to the result that few township enterprises had awareness of exporting or, even if they did, they dared not export. The entrepreneurs who decided to export had to have great courage and resolution. Lu Guanqiu, the soul of the group, played a significant role in the internationalization of the group and it was his persistence that made the first export business to the US possible. This phenomenon can be explained by the entrepreneur's understanding of international business opportunities as mentioned earlier.

According to INV theory, the entrepreneurs or the decision-makers' understanding about the advantages and disadvantages of internationalization plays a key role in deciding if an enterprise focuses on domestic market or on overseas market. The influential factors are in the following sequence: educational level of entrepreneurs, experience of internationalization, and external environment of enterprises. The main reason for Lu to make exporting the first step in internationalization was that the market and the policy environment forced Wanxiang to shift its focus to overseas markets and the priority to export was the optimal choice for Wanxiang, taking the cost advantages of its own products and the demands of overseas markets into comprehensive consideration.

Secondly, when Wanxiang gradually gained a firm foothold in the overseas markets, its internationalization strategy changed accordingly. It implemented the strategy of "three connections": (a) connected to large multinational corporations by establishing of strategic alliances; (b) connected to international advanced technology by developing new products overseas; (c) connected to international mainstream markets by expanding its share of supporting facilities supplier in international main engine plants. According to INV theory, proprietary technical knowledge and differentiated localization strategies can promote the internationalization process of enterprises. Wanxiang has taken these two factors into account while they implemented the "three connections" strategy. They adopted a business localization strategy and global technology cooperation in overseas markets. On one hand, they increase overseas market share, on the other hand, they strengthen the product competitiveness by improving their technologies. In addition, Wanxiang also targeted the international high-end market, which was consistent with the earlier-mentioned external business environment theory, for it believed that homogeneity of overseas markets is a key factor for the enterprises in expanding the international market. Wanxiang's selection of the international high-end market can, on one hand, increase the technical sophistication of their products; on the other hand, shorten the distance to the high-end market, preparing for the next round of international expansion.

In terms of business localization strategy, Wanxiang took international operation regulations as reference to exert localization strategy that included personnel, capital, management, and technology. Lu Guanqiu holds that globalization is an entity of contradictions between integration and localization. On one hand, globalization is breaking the traditional national barriers, and international norms and principles are increasingly accepted. On the other hand, countries are trying to combine the international norms and domestic traditions in an effort to localize the international norms.[2] In this regard, Wanxiang's overseas companies adopted a strategy of "Internationalize thought, localize action". The localization advocated by Wanxiang included localization of management, localization of marketing, and localization of capital operations.

---

[2]Lu, G. Blacksmith rushes to the world, *China Finance Net.*

Take localization of management as an example, the management of Wanxiang's overseas companies is in accordance with internationally accepted standards with financial accounting and legal affairs in charge of local accounting firms and law firms to win the trust of clients as soon as possible. Wanxiang's domestic manufacturers and overseas companies got QS 9000 system certification as manufacturers and distributors respectively, which is the highest standard in the automobile industry in early 1998. In February, 2001, Wanxiang's subsidiary in the US attempted to reform the property rights and established a manager fund. Under the premise that group input still belonged to the group, if the annual profit growth was over 26.58%, the excess was assigned to the manager fund that was owned by managers. At the same time, the fund could be transferred into no more than 40% of the total capital stock of the company by purchasing new shares. The establishment of the manager fund was not to clarify property rights simply, nor to allocate stock assets. But according to Lu Guanqiu, the operation of the manager fund was totally based on the incremental assets.

As to the localization of technology, Wanxiang introduced technology by introducing the technology of the clients from whom they got orders, and it gradually assimilated foreign technology and built an overseas technological center to keep abreast of the development of advanced technology and international main engine plants. Now, Wanxiang's products are in line with the quality standards of the international automobile industry and new products have been launched to meet the ever-changing demands of the markets.

In terms of localization of the capital operation, Lu Guanqiu believes that the acknowledgment of bank and shareholders serves as the criteria when judging whether the business is successful or not. The operational efficiency and development speed of Wanxiang's overseas companies drew the attention of local banks. These banks offered financial support, increasing the credit from USD5 million to USD80 million, and actively made finance plans for Wangxiang. Currently, the investment of local banks is more than twice that of the parent company. Wanxiang's subsidiary in the US intends to go public to fully localize its capital operation.

In addition, Wanxiang has taken a leading role in personnel internationalization strategy. From October 2001, foreign investors started to gain the access to the domestic job market. Lu Guanqiu believed that the era of internationalization of domestic competition and localization of international competition has arrived. If domestic enterprises do not adopt the internationalization strategy, they will not only have difficulties in recruiting new personnel, but also bear the risk of losing personnel. Starting from localization, overseas companies employ all kinds of personnel with different nationalities and multi-cultural backgrounds through channels like local banks, law firms, accounting firms, media, and so forth. For example, when Wanxiang initiated its subsidiary in the US, many people suggested sending the domestic "army" out. Wanxiang deliberated on the issue and decided that the indirect cost, especially opportunity cost, was high even if the direct cost of sending the domestic "army" was not high. The domestic "army" had to get over many barriers including language, law, daily life, and they needed to get familiar with the environment and new colleagues. It would take one or two years before they could work independently. It is time-consuming and more importantly, many opportunities might be missed. Wanxiang chose to recruit local employees, and there were only six from China, while the rest are all local people among 480 employees in its subsidiary in the US. Relying on overseas companies, Wanxiang created space for international personnel by employment integration internally and externally. A large number of domestic staff was sent abroad for training, Wanxiang's 19 overseas companies made contributions to the flows of international personnel. Wanxiang's domestic staff can apply for overseas positions and after certain procedures relating to job evaluation, they could work abroad. At the same time, overseas staff also receives domestic training to learn Chinese domestic conditions and Wanxiang's culture to become familiar with the group's manufacturing capacity.

In terms of global technological cooperation, Wanxiang actively enhanced its independent innovation capability by re-innovating its introduced products, inviting foreign experts to China, launching cooperation with foreign laboratories, etc. Wanxiang mastered core technology and then was capable of independent research and development (R&D) through product cooperation with foreign manufacturers. Through the introduction of the Delphi wheel hub unit, Wanxiang mastered the core technology of this product and committed to further R&D. So far, Wanxiang has successfully developed the third-generation wheel hub unit and now it is working on developing the fourth-generation wheel hub unit. Wanxiang invited foreign experts to stay in China to develop new products. Wanxiang Electric Motor Company employed famous British automobile experts to assist in the R&D of electric vehicles. In 2007, this project had 56 patents including seven invention patents. Its Electric cars won awards in the 2004 Bibendum International Clean Vehicle Competition and four individual gold medals granted by the International Automobile Association. Besides, having cooperation with overseas laboratories to improve its R&D ability is also a key method of Wanxiang's global technology cooperation. Since the establishment of a state-class laboratory, Wanxiang Group has made full use of external intelligent resources by actively committing to technological cooperation with main factories and laboratory abroad. The test reports issued by Wanxiang's state-class automobile parts laboratory received mutual recognition by 46 countries and regions. In addition, Wanxiang made effort to develop independent innovation capacity to improve the technical level. Wanxiang regards independent innovation as the lifeblood of the enterprises and it insists on independent R&D of core technologies. Wangxiang constantly improved the core competitiveness by independent innovation.

Lu Guanqiu, founder of Wanxiang Group, emphasized that the group has relied its development on independent innovation and intellectual property. In 1998, in order to promote innovation, Wanxiang setup a patent department to centralize patent management in an effort to realize the standardization, process-orientation, systematization and professionalization. In 2000, the group built up a patent management system to effectively connect patent technology with the market. In recent years, based on the strategy of "connected to international advanced technology", Wanxiang gradually explored its technology internationalization by performing the patent competition strategy. For example, it proposed an idea of patent competition with "external patent development, patent introduction, patent purchase and cooperation in patent development" as the main direction. According to statistics, Wanxiang has been involved or independently drafted 11 approved industry standards in addition to 1 national standard. It also has more than 600 patents at home and abroad, more than 600 new projects and technologies, more than 1,000 new products every year. The annual output value of Wanxiang's patented products has reached more than CNY 1 billion. Besides independent innovation, Wanxiang also introduced advanced technology and a scientific research team on a large-scale through acquisitions. On December 11, 2003, Wanxiang's subsidiary in the US successfully acquired Rockford, an established American company. Wanxiang became the largest shareholder with 33.5% of Rockford's equity. And it was the 26th overseas company Wanxiang merged and acquired. Rockford, founded in 1890, was the inventor and world's largest first-class supplier of Cardan shaft, and accounted for 70% of the US market. In addition to heavy-duty drive shafts, Rockford also produced non-highway vehicles, hydraulic clutches, power steering gear, etc. Rockford has constantly relied on its strong R&D capacity and testing methods to improve the products. While its profitability began to decline in 1998, its reputation cannot be shaken.

As to exploring international high-end markets, Wanxiang made full use of international market principles to target main markets, main projects, main competitors through tremendous studies and investigations, and actively get connected with world-known automobile enterprises by joint businesses and projects. It sped up international resources integration and always focused on the development of the international automobile industry to choose the right time for low-risk acquisitions.[3]

As to the criterion for international projects selection, Wanxiang chose to cooperate with the world's first-class factories so as to develop the high-end market. In 1995, Wanxiang targeted General Motor's automobile production line. On August 18, 1997, General Motors placed an order of 1,410 new-type universal joints with Wanxiang's subsidiary in the US, which symbolized that "Made in Wanxiang" was finally acknowledged by a leading company with high standards in the world automobile industry and became the first Chinese automobile parts manufacturer to enter the supply chain of international main factory.

Second, Wanxiang could make use of their distribution channels to sell their products all over the world through cooperation with world famous automobile parts manufacturers. In July 2001, Wanxiang's Qianchao Project began to develop the largest cross-axis cold extrusion products, a 4,000 circular cross-craft groove for Visteon, the world's largest

---

[3] Wanxiang's "three connections" to the international market, *Enterprise Management*, 2007(9).

automobile parts manufacturer. They succeeded in 2002 and its annual output revenues increased from CNY 4 million to CNY 13.7 million in 2003 and more than CNY 39 million in 2005. Through this project, Wanxiang became the supplier of Visteon and sold products to the whole world through its supply chain.

What is more, Wanxiang focused on the world's first-class accessories market and improved its product quality. The products of Dana Corporation represented the quality demand of the world's first-class accessories market. Wangxiang could significantly improve its production capacity, quality-control ability and enhance international competitiveness by processing Dana's product. In 2002, Wanxiang Qianchao Project officially launched the Dana project and the project team completed the submission of more than 40 types of Production Part Approval process (PPAP) samples from Dana, and 36 of them have been approved. Its annual sales in 2005 reached CNY 49 million. Although business and project connections with world famous automobile enterprises enhanced the core competitiveness of the group, striving for these opportunities was not easy and Wanxiang was in a relatively passive position to some extent. Besides the joint projects with the world's high-end market, Wanxiang also actively integrated international resources, strengthened overseas acquisitions and expanded overseas influence. To further strengthen the overseas market control, Wanxiang studied the standards of overseas acquisitions; assessed the industrial structure, market potential and the return on investment of the targets enterprise by using comprehensive market information; examined the cost of different targets; consulted the world's main suppliers, target companies, clients, and other experts. Thus, Wanxiang minimized its risk in overseas acquisitions and at the same time maximized its return from acquisitions.

As to the main reason for acquiring Rockford, Ni Pin, vice-president of Wanxiang Group and manager of Wanxiang's subsidiary in the US, said, "This acquisition is not an isolated action. Actually, it is part of a successful internationalization strategy. Wanxiang's internationalization strategy is to find, integrate and allocate the resources we need." Rockford's technology was the most attractive for Wanxiang, for it has a large amount of patents, an advanced test center, a technology center, a high professional capacity for product authentication, test and development, and an excellent

R&D group. Rockford's technology was always regarded as absolutely advanced in the American market. Wanxiang focuses more on potential growth areas after Wanxiang's resource infusion. Rockford is a mature first-class supplier, while Wanxiang cannot live up to this standard overseas only by its own resources and capacity. Rockford's strong brand effect was very beneficial to Wanxiang's future. There was infinite space for Rockford to develop highway vehicle products. The biggest barrier was the small-scale, dispersed shareholders. The manufacturing foundation of Wanxiang was able to help it get through the bottleneck to expand from the single product to diverse development. Lu Guanqiu believes that, in a world of global economic integration and era of altruistic symbiosis, the competition law is win–win rather than a zero-sum game. The cooperation between Wanxiang and Rockford was to achieve resources complementation and thus to have a better grasp of the market and maintain sustainable competitive advantage.

7.2.3 Determinants of internationalization

According to the psychological distance hypothesis of PTI theory, if there is psychological distance, an enterprise should conduct its international business in small steps. Usually, companies will enter the new markets where psychological distance is expanding and gradually expand their control. It is with such a psychological distance hypothesis that Wanxiang continually expands its overseas market, but the uncertainty of overseas acquisitions increases the difficulties of its internationalization, which has also become a potential concern for Wanxiang's internationalization. According to the theory mentioned in the earlier paragraphs, only when an entrepreneur has relationship networks, experience, knowledge and other resources in different markets can an entrepreneurship be formed by the integration of unique resources from different countries. However, due to the restrictions on limited entrepreneurship, it is not always a smooth expansion.

First, the uncertainty in overseas acquisitions is a potential worry for Wanxiang's internationalization. In 1994, Wanxiang's subsidiary was registered in the US with the approval of the Ministry of Foreign Economic Relations and Trade. Three goals set were: First, to establish the Wanxiang image in the US, bring products to General Motors, Ford, Chrysler and other main engine manufacturers; second, to collect market information and feedback to the group in time to explore new areas; third, to optimize the combination of international resources, especially to make use of available international capital.

The first two goals have already been fulfilled after several years of unremitting efforts, but the fulfillment of the third goal leaves much to be desired. On December 18, 2006, Delphi, which was on the brink of bankruptcy, decided to sell 72% of its equity to an American private investment group. This investment group consists of APA Roosa Asset Management Company, Barron Asset Management, Merrill Lynch, and UBS Securities and it offered 3.4 billion to Delphi in the form of purchasing preferred stock and common stock. Delphi was willing to accept this offer, which dealt a serious blow to domestic enterprises, including many Chinese companies with overseas ambitions — Wanxiang Group, Dongfeng Group, Shangqi Group, Fuyao Glass, and even Weichai Power, who had a newly established relationship with Delphi. Because of the huge loss, on October 1, 2005, Delphi entered bankruptcy protection procedures, actively seeking buyers for reorganization, stripping the business with low-tech and added value, which were sold successively. After separating the electronic control system, mechanical power system, and other Delphi assets, several Indian automobile parts companies also acquired the assets of Delphi's control system. When the disposal of Delphi's bankrupt assets was about to end, many automobile parts companies, including American Johnson Control System Company, began to seek involvement in Delphi's reconstruction. Wanxiang Group was the first applicant in Delphi's reorganization. On December 20, 2005, Lu Guanqiu, the president of Wanxiang Group, told the media that Wanxiang was negotiating with Delphi about the acquisition of its American assets, but Lu Guanqiu knew that it was impossible for Wanxiang to do it alone and it needed alliances. In September 2005, Zhou Jianqun, general manager of Wanxiang Qianchao, stated that the negotiation between Wanxiang and Delphi went smoothly and results would be seen at the end of the year. However, as more and more Chinese enterprises appeared on Delphi's list for reorganization, Wanxiang and Delphi were more and more alienated and finally Wanxiang did not complete the acquisition. On December 18, 2006, Lu Guanqiu told

American "Automobile News" that Wanxiang and Delphi were negotiating the acquisition of the ailing part of the company's assets, but Ford had expressed adequate cautions which was an unexpected coincidence with Delphi's idea of selling its shares. In fact, buying Ford's parts assets was the second best choice for Wanxiang Group.

Wanxiang was once regarded as the most successful Chinese enterprise who had explored North American business. In 1984, Scheler, one of the three biggest parts suppliers in the American automobile maintenance market, ordered 30,000 sets of universal joints and thus Wanxiang entered the North American market by Scheler's channels. In 1998, Scheler suffered a huge loss, but at the same time Wanxiang's sales in America had reached USD30 million. Two years later, Wanxiang cooperated with a US company LSB and bought Scheler's brand, technological patents, and special equipment at a price of USD420,000. After its first overseas acquisition, Wanxiang had become one of the enterprises with the most enormous universal joints patents. In the next few years, Wanxiang acquired two other parts enterprises, UAI and Rockford in the same way.

Currently, Wanxiang has founded 26 branches in America, Britain, Germany, Canada, and other countries in total, including 10 acquired enterprises. Ni Pin, president of the Wanxiang subsidiary in the US repeatedly claimed that Wanxiang's subsidiary had a 100% investment return, though the real situation is unknown to outsiders. With the delay in the acquisition of Delphi's assets, Wanxiang's setbacks on the road to internationalization were increasingly clear. The existing facts proved that the situation was not as optimistic as before. According to "The Wall Street Journal", Wanxiang acquired 21% stake of UAI, the ailing parts enterprise, at a price of USD2.8 million in 2001, but in 2005 UAI did not avoid the fate of bankruptcy and finally collapsed. Similar to its domestic investment, Wanxiang's investment in the US is also diverse, covering various areas, such as golf courses, oil fields, etc. These involvements in industries brought USD500 million revenue to Wanxiang Group in 2005. These successful cases pushed Wanxiang to acquire some shares in Paragon Med Management (PMM), a small company in Chicago. After the struggle in Detroit, Delphi, Visteon, and other American parts enterprises entered bankruptcy protection procedures successively. Lu Guanqiu's involvement in Delphi's reorganization was called the "best opportunity" for Wanxiang

Group.[4] According to the analysts, this "best opportunity" might have two meanings: First, Wanxiang Group could clean up its American business to enhance the efficiency of North American investment; second, Wanxiang Group was eager to expand the automotive parts business and this was a good chance to get through the business bottleneck. There were some rumors that Wanxiang had suffered a huge loss in the North American market, but the specific number was not disclosed.

Second, the decline in profitability was another potential worry for Wanxiang's internationalization. Wanxiang is now is focusing on steering systems, transmission shafts and other chassis fittings. Wanxiang had occupied 70% of the domestic market of universal joints, but Wanxiang's future profitability still remained uncertain. The reorganization of Delphi was aimed to adjust 41 subsidiaries in the US to restore stable profitability by focusing on core products, automobile electronics and other high-tech products, and also those non-core products. But Delphi finally had to choose liquidation, which meant that the global parts industry was less prosperous. Maybe it is because insiders had realized the potential crisis, so that even those companies not in recession began to plan for their future. Some of them began to operate jointly for business complementarities; some of them began to strengthen the development of high added-value products and technology besides the main business; some of them acquired those loss-making companies in the industry to consolidate their own strength and status. Zhou Jianqun, general manager of Wanxiang Qianchao, also identified with this action. In the five years after entering the World Trade Organization (WTO), the car production capacity increased by 5 million, which is 3.5 times more than that before entering the WTO. But Wanxiang Qianchao's main business revenue and net profit decreased rather than increased. Net profit rate declined from 13.61% in 1993, the beginning of going public, to 4.71% in the first three quarters in 2006. The net profit of CNY 14 million, declined by 9.3% in 2004. In fact, Wanxiang Group had already been facing the problem of cost increases, and price decreases. In recent years, prices of upstream raw materials increased, but the product price was only half of that in the past, which was the opposite of

---

[4] Anonymous, Wanxiang's dilemma, New Automobile, 2007(1).

what had been predicted in INV theory on internationalization competition strategy.

Besides, although production capacity expanded, Wanxiang Group faced more intensive international competition, and more products had to be sold in the international market. Thus, it is natural that profitability cannot be compared to the past. Seen throughout the process of internationalization, it is the entrepreneurs' psychological distance that causes the dilemma today. According to traditional opinion, enterprises should first focus on surrounding markets and then gradually expand their range. However, Wanxiang excessively expanded its field regardless of cost and the uncertainty of international acquisitions, which goes against the basic principles of INV theory. In fact, Wanxiang's technology had already reached a certain level and moving into developing countries would have been better than into developed countries.

7.3   Transfar Group: A New Model of Sino-Japanese Joint Venture

Transfar, founded in October 1986, is a group with diversified businesses covering chemicals, logistics, agriculture, Sci-tech city and investment. In 2011, the group realized the total industrial and service revenue of CNY 20.79 billion, and is ranked "Top 500 Chinese Enterprises", "Top 500 Chinese Private Enterprises". The group has more than 10 subsidiaries. It has undergone the historical development as shown in Table 7.2.

Transfar's Chemical Engineering, starting from the business of liquid detergents, now has possessed two listed companies including "Transfar Co., Ltd." (Shenzhen Stock Exchange: 002010) and "Xin'an Chemical Industrial Group Co., Ltd." (Shanghai Stock Exchange: 600596), six national-level high-tech enterprises and one state-class technological center. Its main products include textile chemicals, papermaking chemicals, plastic chemicals, agricultural chemicals, daily chemicals, leather chemicals, and coating. In each field, its technology and market share has ranked at the forefront of national counterparts, even in the world market. For example, organic silicon: Its production capacity and main technical indexes ranks first in China. Textile chemicals: Its market share ranks first in China. Papermaking chemicals: The output of its main product, APC,

Table 7.2.   Development path of transfar group.

Year	Event
1986	Xu Chuanhua founded the enterprise.
1992	Hangzhou Transfar Chemical Co., Ltd. was founded.
1993	Hangzhou Transfar Daily Chemical Co., Ltd. was founded.
1995	Transfar Group was founded.
1998	Hangzhou Transfar Huayang Chemical Co., Ltd. was founded.
2000	In the agricultural field, Zhejiang Transfar Jiangnandali Development Co., Ltd. was founded.
2001	Zhejiang Transfar Co., Ltd. was organized, Hangzhou Transfar Coating Co., Ltd. was founded.
2002	Hangzhou Transfar Logistics Base Co., Ltd. was founded, Hangzhou Transfar Huawang Co., Ltd. was founded.
2005	Taking controlling interest in Xinan Chemical Engineering, investing Suzhou synthetical logistics zone, initiating investment on logistics in other cities.

ranks first in the world. Plastic chemicals: The output of its main product, whitening agent, ranks first in China. Daily chemicals: Washing powder and cleanser are famous-brand products in China. Agricultural chemicals: The product of glyphosate ranks first in Asia and second in the world. By virtue of its sound creativity, Transfar Chemical Engineering got involved in drafting many industrial standards, and some of its products obtained national patents or were listed in the national or provincial "torch projects", and established close cooperation with famous colleges both domestically and abroad.

Transfar's logistics innovated both its technology and its business models. With the collaboration of the following six centers — management service, business information, transportation, warehousing, distribution, and less-than-truckload (LTL) express, and complete supporting functions, Transfar became the innovator and leader of China's logistics platforms. Many third-party logistics companies were introduced by the new logistics platform in which resources were fully integrated within the supply chain, and a labor division system has been formed which resulted in a huge decrease of transaction costs and an increase of the logistics efficiency. As "the base of the Chinese logistics experiment" and the first Chinese "International Trade Center (ITC) international purchase and supply chain management training center", Transfar's logistics sector will continue to pilot industrial practice in the construction of a Chinese logistics base by using information as its core advantage while further exploring the replication of bases and the new model of e-commerce.

Transfar's agricultural sector started from High-tech Demonstration Zone of Zhejiang Province and successfully applied biological technology to field crops and committed to reforming traditional agricultural farming methods, and cultivation techniques. Thus, it became a key enterprise in the horticultural sector, the largest supplier of commodity seedlings and high-quality flowers in East China, and its products are sold to the US, Japan, Spain, and so forth. Transfar's agriculture sector spared no effort to build an international agricultural platform, a biotechnology R&D platform and business platform to promote the strategic concentration of scientific enterprises in Hangzhou Bay and to facilitate Zhejiang Province to take a leading role in the national biotechnology industry so as to become the main production base of Asian agricultural biotechnology. Transfar Group adheres to the corporate spirit of "pioneering, never satisfied" and cultivates the long-term culture of integrity and responsibility, commits to building a sustainable business group.

7.3.1 Internationalization process

In 1996, Xu Guanju, the president of Transfar, went to Japan to attend the (first) Enterprise Management Seminar organized by the National Federation of Industry and Commerce. Transfar and Japan Daikin Company held a signing ceremony in the Golden Horse Hotel. On October 11, 2002, Transfar Group officially signed a joint venture agreement with Kao (China) Investment Co., Ltd., one of Fortune 500 enterprises and a wholly owned subsidiary of Kao Corporation. Transfar & Kao had a successful cooperation. The new joint venture had a total investment of USD38 million. On November 4, the opening ceremony of the joint venture was held in Transfar. This was the biggest joint venture project in China's detergents industry in the 21st Century. In order to bring a new excellence to China's daily commodity market, the newly founded Hangzhou Transfar Kao Co., Ltd. established a scientific management pattern, built an advanced daily commodity production and sales base, and developed the products that can satisfy the demands of customers.

Chinese detergent products market has long been an objective of international giants, but they had encountered some troubles: Although foreign brands already dominated China's hair care products market, yet they did not perform well in the detergent products market. Since 2001, both Procter and Gamble (P&G) and Unilever had ended their joint venture cooperation with Chinese counterparts. However, in November, 2002, Kao Corporation, the largest daily commodity enterprise in Japan, built a joint venture with Transfar Group. Kao Corporation was founded in 1887, and located in the central area of Tokyo. Cleaning products are its primary business, at present, besides the production of detergents, it also has more than 300 kinds of products including hair care products and cosmetics. Kao has sold its commodity products all over the world, providing detergents, shampoos and other cleaning products in Asia; providing mainly skin care products and in Europe and hair care products in North America. Owing to many chemical production bases in Asia, North America and Europe, Kao is mainly committed to exploring businesses in different industries on a global basis.

In fact, since 1999, Xu Guanju, Transfar's president, has initiated the idea of forming a joint venture in the domestic chemical industry. From then on, Kao attracted Transfar's attention gradually after constant contacts. Transfar's staff who went to Japan have been deeply impressed by Kao's logistics where daily chemical delivery is counted by inner pack, while in China it is counted by piece, which is a large box. This logistics center supplies products for 300,000 stores. "There are only three operators in the logistics center, with every operator running constantly, putting products into a container according to the orders. Every operator runs about 10,000 of meters in the two working hours." Xu Guanju who had a strong impression of Kao's strength from his six-day stay in Japan said: "We need a partner who will be advanced worldwide in the next few decades." Xu Guanju's visit to Kao led to the establishment of the joint venture.

A common characteristic of joint venture failures in the domestic chemicals industry — Chinese firms could not get the controlling interest, but in the case of Transfar & Kao, Transfar got 65% of the stakes with more than three board seats. Transfar's controlling interest derived from the plan Transfar drafted for the next 10 years and indeed it was Transfar's strategic positioning of the Chinese rural market which impressed Kao.

The joint venture would highly rely on Transfar's distribution power in rural and town markets. Indeed, the Chinese rural market is a mystery for multinational companies. They have realized the obvious brand demand in Chinese rural areas, while local brands gained huge success in the rural market and thus they extended into urban areas. But, the foreign brand needed a media through which to enter this vast market, and Transfar became a strong supporter for Kao by its penetration into the rural market. The most important fact is that Transfar has gained the controlling interest of the joint venture.

The successful cooperation with Kao made Transfar go global. On April 9, 2004, Hangzhou Ground Biotechnology Co., Ltd. of Transfar Group and Japan Kirin Corporation signed a "Strategic Cooperation Agreement". This was the first time for a Chinese horticultural company to have all-round, close cooperation with international giants, and Transfar Agriculture started its internationalization from then on. Through this cooperation, Transfar's Ground experienced a great progress in the aspects of technology, management, marketing, ability to acquire resources, etc. This is another strategic cooperation with the Fortune 500 enterprises after Transfar's cooperation with Kao. Xu Guanju, Transfar's president, stated that "Cooperation with Kirin is a specific method for Transfar Agriculture to explore and practice modernization of the Chinese agricultural industry". Transfar entered the high-tech agriculture industry a few years ago, and now the agriculture industry has become one of the four major industries for Transfar. Matsushima, president of Kirin, argued that the two reasons why Kirin chose Transfar: On one hand, Transfar was a well-known POE with a certain level of technology in agriculture; on the other hand, Transfar's Ground-Zhejiang High-tech Agricultural Demonstration Zone which was a good platform to transfer Kirin's biotechnology and improve its biotechnological structure.

7.3.2 Internationalization strategy

According to the external environment theory, newly-founded enterprises are not equipped with basic experience and knowledge of internationalization and they must acquire them gradually through international business. In 1990, Xu Guanju after nearly 1,000 experiments developed

"901" for dyeing de-oiling by the traditional method, a textile auxiliary which received a national invention patent, putting the history of importing "171" to an end in the Chinese dyeing industry. Transfar's sales revenue soared from CNY 2–3 million to CNY 20 million, which was the first bucket of gold. The "901" — the core technology built the prototype of a modernized industrial enterprise, Transfar, and made it well-known. Transfar was taking a leading role in China, but if it wanted to go global, the international business environment must be taken into consideration. The detergent industry is fully competitive worldwide due to its low demand for technology. If Transfar chose exporting first, domestic advantages in cost and technology would be sure to disappear. So, Transfar chose to import the silicone oil technology from American "Dow Corning" to improve its own technological level. According to competition strategy theory, because Transfar had no technological and cost advantages internationally, it adopted an internal internationalization strategy, that is to say making use of foreign capital to help it expand market shares and enhance the technological level in an effort to develop the international market in the future. To be specific, Transfar's internationalization pattern included introduction of technology, establishment of joint ventures and Japanese materials processing, of which the most important was the relationship with foreign capital.

After the cooperation with Kao, Transfar mainly adopted price differentiation strategy. Transfar has insisted the price of CNY 1.7 for its 320 g Fragrance washing powder ever since its first launch in 2003, which faced tremendous pressure later. In 2004, the price of sulphonic acid, the main material of washing powder, increased from CNY 6,000 per ton to CNY 8,000 per ton and the price of a major surfactant also increased by 20%. From a list provided by Transfar, the price of its 320 g Fragrance washing powder had to be increased to CNY 1.8 in an effort to avoid a loss. The public relations department of Transfar & Kao stated that the price should remain unchanged. It was only a one-time difference to customers, but the price hike would ruin the distribution channels that have been for many years. In order to handle the problem, Transfar & Kao launched a more expensive ultra-concentrated washing powder, but the market did not react positively. Staff from Kao concluded from a study of Shanghai's market that price was the most influential factor for Chinese customers when choosing washing powder. Transfar faced fierce competition from other manufacturers. In 2005, NICE, another domestic chemicals manufacturer in Zhejiang Province, also launched a new product: "Diaopai" transparent washing powder. And P&G, Uniliver, German Henkel and other high-end brands developed a low-end market after they have occupied large cities, to fight for the market in the second and third tier Chinese cities and rural areas. Managers of Transfar & Kao had no effective solution to meet the strong competitions. Currently, the competition in Chinese detergent industry has been tense; in which brand and capital power are the core competitive strengths. The brand could be improved by investments on commercials. In 2004, Kao neither proposed any specific plan, which could face the fierce market competition, nor any products that could generate higher gross profits. But Transfar deliberately developed a natural green tea detergent and launched it afterwards. This detergent made of green tea extract can not only eliminate oily and fishy smells, but also remove the pesticide residues on fruits and vegetables quickly. Transfar & Kao used "experiential marketing" to explore customers' needs for fresh experiences. The cooperation between Transfar & Kao laid a solid foundation for experiential marketing, for its quality has already gone beyond the basic demands for the products, focusing more on fresh feeling and physical and mental happiness of customers.

7.3.3 Determinants of internationalization

Transfar's internationalization strategy is to make use of joint ventures to absorb the advanced technology and management experience from foreign enterprises, and finally after the integration with the overseas market, to expand the international market. In terms of internationalization timing, Transfar adhered to an implication in PTI theory, as mentioned earlier, that the later internationalizer survive more easily than the earlier internationalizer in the internationalization movement, because the enterprise is usually risk-averse, and a later internationalizer has more chances to survive for it could accumulate resources as time goes by. So, this type of internationalization has its own advantage — less risk, and enterprises can make decisions according to the market situation; It also has disadvantages, for example the uncertainty of joint ventures, including price strategy, sales channels and even technological terms, which are somewhat all-influential factors in internationalization.

First, the uncertainty of a joint venture was a big obstacle for Transfar's internationalization which has been demonstrated in the case of Kao. These two companies did not maximize their own benefits. For example, Kao did not become a well-known brand in China through the cooperation with Transfar, but its market positioning in Chinese market contained a certain risk. With the change of the market strategies of other multinational giants in China, some local enterprises even believed Kao; quality image has been damaged and the adverse effect will appear gradually. However, the marketing manager of Daily Chemicals of Transfar, believed that the reason Transfar cooperated with Kao was to improve product quality while maintaining a low price, and effectively explore and consolidate the rural market. Transfar conducted a special in-depth market survey and it showed in 2020, the Chinese urban population will overtake the rural population for the first time. That is to say, the rural population will decrease from 70% at present to less than 50%, which means 20% of the rural population will move to urban areas in 10 years and their brand awareness will be cultivated more easily. As for brand awareness, Transfar wants to create a fashionable image in the 2-CNY washing powder markets for rural consumers by collaborating with a foreign brand. According to a survey issued by Shanghai Foresight Consulting Corporation, given that the price is low enough, foreign brands are more acceptable to rural consumers, because whenever Unilever reduces its price of Omo, the sales increase dramatically. Rural consumers prefer "foreign brands" which launched lots of advertisements, only if the price is low. Transfar wanted to cope with the low-price advantage of Diaopai of Nice Group by taking advantages of foreign brands and high quality of products. On November 4, 2011, Transfar merged with Kao, which was the first joint venture in the Chinese domestic chemicals industry in which Transfar held 65% of stake, and occupied a majority of three seats in the new company worth USD38.7 million. Xu Guanju, Transfar's president, believed that Transfar's controlling interests derived from Kao's consent of the plan drafted by Transfar for the next 10 years, and Transfar's strategic positioning in China's rural market. In this plan, the future joint venture relies on Transfar's power in rural and small urban markets and Transfar is qualified to be the supporter of Kao.

In fact, Transfar had desire to expand the domestic chemicals business. In 1997, Transfar's fine chemical business had already taken a leading role in the industry and its chemical products enjoyed brand and resource advantages in the rural market, but much to regret that Transfar did not seize this opportunity. Nice group swept the national market by advertisements and low price advantages in a short period. Xu Guanju also admitted, "We were very contradictory in 1997, losing the chance to make Transfar become a national top brand of daily use chemicals."

Later, Transfar entered into agriculture and logistics industries and tested the water in the capital markets. However, five years later, Transfar decided to expand the daily-use chemicals business again. At that time, Transfar was worried that Kao had less stakes and less commitment in the joint venture. Consequently, Kao could achieve low costs and high returns for it could enter Transfar's marketing network at low costs and receive a royalty fee for its technology that had been monopolized by Kao. In the joint venture, Kao monopolized the technology and China monopolized the sales channels, which created the risk for Transfar that the provider of technology would raise the fee after the establishment of the sales/marketing channels, while the risk for Kao that Transfar would cut off the sales channels after the joint venture was mature.

In addition, the poor performance in rural market and the difference of marketing strategy with Kao consisted of two big concerns for Transfar. According to the psychological distance theory mentioned earlier, enterprises will usually start from nearby markets and then extend the market range. Internationalization is regarded as a passive response to changes of the internal and external environment in an effort to avoid risk. Transfar's market strategy selection departed from the normal psychological distance, conquering urban areas after rural areas, but the result was not optimistic. Transfar attributed its passive position in market development to Kao's ambiguous strategy in China. Kao did not stick to China's rural low-end market and its localization strategy in China swung back to the high-end market. In March 2004, Kao's Japanese headquarters announced that it would launch its high-end brand Sofina in Shanghai, planning distribution in Beijing and other cities in 2005. Kao once stated, by the 2007 fiscal year, its sales revenue in China would try to reach USD9.4 million. Kao was a world-known daily commodity enterprise, listed No. 358 in the

Fortune Top 500 enterprises in 2003. Unfortunately, Kao whose domestic sales revenues occupied 70% of its total sale revenues did not attain great brand improvement and growth even when the Japanese economy began to recover. In 2004, its rank fell to No. 385 with a market value of USD13.782 billion. In recent years, Kao still focused its overseas market in South East Asia, but actively integrated global brand resources to cover the Chinese high-end market and consciously gave up some low-end markets. Intensive attention was paid on the Shanghai first-class market as the mainstream profit market. Unfortunately, Kao did not become famous in this line.

Finally, Kao's product line was excessively long which led its brand structure to be in a disadvantageous position in the Chinese market. For example, Kao's Shifen shampoo intentionally used the prefix "Kao" to expand its influence, but its capacity to improve brand awareness was weak for the limited popularity of its own brand. Moreover, Kao's brand image in China had already been regarded as a consumer-packaged product due to its promotion in low-end markets and its strategic cooperation with Transfar, leading to a dilemma that there was no condition for it to explore the high-end market. In fact, all of the products of Transfar & Kao used "Transfar" as trademark, rather than "Kao". At the end of 2004, a liquid detergent of "Transfar" was awarded "China Famous Brand", but Transfar & Kao produced this product. The Public Relations (PR) manager of Transfar & Kao stated that in 2003 the sales revenue was CNY 0.255 billion, which did not reach the goal sales of CNY 0.3 billion but still increased by 12%. The primary reason was that the price of major raw materials of washing powder increased but the price of the product did not increase. The second reason lied in the nature of the limited liability joint venture; Transfar & Kao neither increased investment nor offered cash flow support. The narrow production line without production capacity would surely lead to a loss amidst fierce competition. Some observers also pointed out that Transfar & Kao were seemingly in harmony but actually at variance. In terms of cooperation pattern, their cooperation stayed only at the capital level, and Kao's subsidiary in Shanghai still stayed independent in operations. Kao was in rich global capital resources, Kao consequently chose mere logistics platform cooperation, rather than entire brand integration. Kao did not offer its core and high-end brand for cooperation and still retained its claim to position, promote and expand its own brands. Due to the dual-branding model in joint ventures, in terms of the mutual use of marketing resources, the distribution network advantages of Transfar's daily use chemicals were not that strong. Thus, Transfar would not exert a fundamental, comprehensive influence on changing Kao's competitive situation in the Chinese market. But the PR manager believed that Transfar was qualified to represent all Kao's brands in China. He cited the argument "Transfar's development strategy concentrated on the socialization of management and the internationalization of capital" proposed by Xu Guanju. Transfar's cooperation with Kao, Kirin and the other Fortune Top 500 enterprises was an inevitable choice for achieving its international development.

7.4 Holley Group: A Typical Example of Diversified Investment

Established on September 28, 1970, Holley Group is a multi-industry corporation with Holley Worldwide Holdings, as the parent company and with pharmaceuticals as its core business. Holley has been involved in diversified businesses across pharmaceuticals, power metering instruments and power automation system, wireless and wide-band telecommunication, electronic materials, real estate, agriculture, petrochemical and mining, etc.

Holley enjoys a strong employee force of over 10,000 people around the globe, and has established an international presence with manufacturing bases and branches in the US, France, Russia, Argentina, India, Thailand, and the Philippine, and representative offices in more than a dozen countries in Africa.

Holley Group had controlling interest of four listed companies in domestic A-share market (Holley Pharmaceutical, Holley Technology, Kunming Pharmaceutical, and Wuhan Jianmin). Its main R&D and production bases are located in Zhejiang, Shanghai, Chongqing, Yunnan, Hubei, Sichuan, Guangdong, Hainan, etc., and it also has manufacturing factories, companies and research institutions in Hong Kong (SAR of China), Thailand, the US, Canada, France, Israel, Argentina, India, Nigeria, etc. In 2005, its total business revenue was CNY 11 billion within which pharmaceuticals were around CNY 5 billion, instrumentation nearly CNY 3 billion and real estate nearly CNY 1.5 billion. "Holley" and "Jianmin" are two Famous Chinese Brands; Holley's electric energy meter is a "Famous Chinese Product" and an export inspection-exempted product. Holley is one of the largest electrical instruments manufacturers worldwide. In 2005, the business revenue of the Holley pharmaceutical industry made up nearly 40% of the revenue of the whole group. In the future, attentions have been paid on the electro-technical instruments industries, Holley will also focus on the pharmaceutical industry including herbal medicine and Chinese medicine.

Holley Group adopts three major strategies: technological innovation, capital operation, and internationalization. Holley advocates technological innovation strategy and insists that technological innovation is the "growth engine" of its sustainable development. The implementation of this strategy made Holley form its technological advantages in different industries to achieve the maximum added value of products and services. Scientific researchers from all over the world consisted of Holley's technological innovation team, working in the US, Canada, and provinces like Hangzhou, Beijing, Shanghai and Shenzhen in China. Holley's annual research fund accounted for 5% of its annual sales revenue. Holley insists on technological innovation by improving its self-learning and self-adaptation ability. Different technological development strategies have been made according to their own industry features. On one hand, Holley group establishes research institutions and technological centers to develop an R&D team and to enhance it R&D capacity; in the meantime, the group actively seeks technology cooperation with famous foreign enterprises, international research organizations and universities. In 2001, Holley acquired Phillip's Code Division Multiple Access (CDMA) cell phone chip design and the overall design solution department and became the first enterprise who mastered core technology through overseas capital operations in Chinese information industry, entering a new industry from a high starting point.

Holley's development is closely linked with a capital operation strategy, which is the important way for its fast growth. In order to get through the bottleneck of a single financing channel and cash flow shortage for traditional manufacturing enterprises, Holley has begun to seek direct financing channels in the capital market since 1994. In 2001, Holley Holding (America) Co., Ltd. acquired and reorganized Pacific Systems

Control Technology, Inc (PFSY), a NASDAQ listed company. In 2002, Holley Group acquired Kunming Pharmaceutical to continue the integration of capital market operations. A pharmaceutical production platform of more than CNY 2 billion was established within only 3 years, which became a miracle for a Chinese enterprise achieving great expansion by using the capital market. In the future, Holley will continue to implement its capital management strategy by focusing its major business on capital allocation on a global basis, and achieve synchronous development between industrial management and capital management. As China entered the WTO, Holley took active measures to plan the industry development from a global view, implementing its internationalization strategy. In the new century, Holley promotes technological innovation, capital management, and internationalization strategies, comprehensively achieving the shift from traditional to a modern multinational high-tech company full of global competitiveness.

7.4.1 Internationalization process

In 1998, Holley initially exported electric energy meters to Thailand and other countries, and its exports accounted for less than 1% of its total exports. From 1998 to 2001, its annual income was around CNY 2 billion. According to insiders, two factors triggered Holley's internationalization during this period of time: First, the demand of foreign market, the economic globalization determined the internationalization of Holley; Second, in order to obtain a better development and to avoid the recession, Holley established a wholly-owned company in 2000, Holley Holdings (US) Co., Ltd., in Silicon Valley of California. In October 2000, after a careful study of Thailand and ASEAN markets, Holley Thailand production base was founded in Bangkok with an initial investment of USD1.2 million. The local electricity department for its advantages in performance and qualified service soon accepted the base. It integrated into the local market rapidly, especially its electric wire carrier remote meter reading system, gaining obvious competitive advantages in the fierce local competition and also the Philippines, and other ASEAN markets. Subsequently, Holley had made investment in South Asia, South America,

Africa, and East Europe, building a global production and sales system for electronic instruments before 2005. These two investment projects were conducted within the same year, which was the first move in Holley's overseas investment.

In terms of international cooperation, as early as 1989, Holley established the first local joint venture with an Italian enterprise, producing copper foil board. In 1999, Holley cooperated with Israel meter manufacturer Nikos to establish the joint venture "Zhejiang Holley Nikos Electric Co., Ltd." to produce electronic meters. In terms of exports, Holley established Zhejiang Holley Import and Export Co. Ltd. as early as 1990. In 1997, an overseas business department was founded which became the business platform of internationalization. In terms of market status, Holley's meters have occupied first place in the market since the mid-1990s.

In 2001, Holley founded a company in the US and soon acquired two NASDAQ listed companies PFSY and PACT. In September 2001, Holley's subsidiary in the US officially acquired Phillips CDMA mobile information communications department in San Jose (including the R&D branches in Las Vegas and Vancouver), obtaining the entire intellectual property, research equipment, R&D tools and a large number of experienced researchers of CDMA. Based on this, Holley founded American Holley Communication Company. The acquisition of the CDMA mobile communications department of Philips in San Jose is clearly different from other overseas acquisitions that Holley experienced, being not only assets but also advanced core technology.

Holley had formed a resource allocation pattern in the form of obtaining overseas high-end technology, realizing industrialization in China, meeting the demands of the markets at home and abroad. It aimed at developing into a multinational company allocate resources (market, labor, capital, and technology) globally. On May 12, 2005, Holley (Thailand) Electric Company held an opening ceremony in honor of the new factory with more than 100 million baht investment which was the first Chinese mainland enterprise in the Thailand Amata industrial zone. In the opening ceremony, Wang Licheng, president of Holley, said that Holley had established a firm foothold in Thailand and the Thailand subsidiary would be developed into Holley's center that allocates its production, sales and resources in South East Asia.

7.4.2 Internationalization strategy

According to PTI theory, given the existence of psychological distance, enterprises should develop international business in small steps. But Owita and McDougall (1994) challenged PTI theory by pointing out that blocked communication and transportation channels limited international market information collection in the past, raising the risk of overseas business. But in recent years, improved international communication, transportation and the homogeneity of the international market have simplified and shortened the internationalization process. These changes minimize the influence of psychological distance on internationalization. Enterprises can jump over some phases, which is exemplified by Holley's internationalization process. First of all, Holley built the first local joint venture with an Italian enterprise to produce copper foil board and later exported electric meters to Thailand and other countries. The internationalization pattern of investing in developed counties first and then exporting to developing countries jumped over the phase of internationalization process with psychological distance, which identified the view about psychological distance and the internationalization order proposed by INV theory from another angle: technological and economic development can both minimize psychological distance and shorten, simplify or leap the processes of internationalization. Wang Licheng, chairman of Holley Group, once stated, "Holley's internationalization strategy is not to merely sell products to foreign markets, but is a comprehensive strategy which combines market exploration, technological cooperation, financing and manufacture. Holley's internationalization is to achieve resource allocation on a global basis, including market resources, capital resources, technology resources and talent resources. Holley wants to participate in the global labor division, transfer comparative advantage to competitive advantage and adapt to globalization." Specifically, there were four internationalization strategies:

The first strategy was to establish an overseas holding company. According to the external environment of internationalization theory, if domestic and foreign markets are integrated and homogeneous, enterprises' performance in the domestic market will be very similar to that in the foreign market. The best way to improve the homogeneity of domestic and foreign markets is direct investment and Holley's overseas holding company is an effective way of internationalization. In 2000, Holley entered the US market and established a wholly-owned company, Holley Holding (US) Co., Ltd. in Silicon Valley California. Holley made clear description of its function: Based on Holley's overall strategy for industry development, US subsidiary should make use of capital operations to acquire high-tech enterprises at low cost, to quickly integrate all technological resources, to achieve optimal resource allocation mode "R&D bases in North America, industrial bases in China", and to offer an access for Holly's quick entrance into high-tech industry. In 1998, Holley's total export was less than 1% of total sales revenue. In 2000, the Dean of the International Trade Department concluded the two reasons why Holley established its first overseas factory in Thailand related to entrepreneurship and international trade barriers. In 2001 and 2002, the export products were rejected by Chile and Brazil, which had been accepted when packed in Thailand. Local protectionism is quite serious in this industry with various requirements concerning certificates of origin and production standards. So Holley achieved sales in the origin market by foreign investment and established regional development platforms (e.g. taking Thailand as a center, Holley developed market of electronic instruments in other southern East Asian areas). Holley has another sales company in Nigeria which also serves as regional development platform.

The second strategy is to choose the proper time to acquire overseas listed companies at a low price. In September 2001, Holley's subsidiary in US officially acquired Philips CDMA mobile information communications department in San Jose. The acquisition conducted right after "9.11" when the stock market crashed and Philips hurried to seek buyers. By integrating the R&D centers in three different countries in half a year, Holley formed an interactive industrial chain in which the R&D department in Dallas is in charge of set solutions, Silicon Valley in charge of chip design, Vancouver in charge of system software, and Hangzhou in charge of external design and product integration.

The third strategy is to increase the profitability of acquired companies and revive their financing capability in the capital market. Holley enhanced profitability, capital operation capability and the capability to integrate the acquired companies by improving core competitiveness. Acquisition exerts a positive influence on the development of Holley's core competitiveness for it can obtain the sustainable R&D ability. Simply speaking, Holley's pattern can be concluded as follows: In the international market, the enterprise directly acquires overseas companies or departments of certain enterprises in the form of capital acquisitions to obtain the resources that are scarce in China, such as technology and talents. Just as Wang Licheng, the president of Holly, said, "Once the acquisition succeeds, what I need to do is to combine the business of the acquired company with Holly. By doing so, the profitability will be improved, the stock price will rise and its financing function on the NASDAQ will recover and then we can use the money to do business in the US."

The fourth strategy is to acquire core technology and talents by capital operations. Holley obtained what they needed in developed countries and thus achieves optimal allocation of resources.[5] The US market was Holly's first target, while it was not to establish factories, but to obtain technology, personnel capital. Holley departed from the general pattern of investment for it acquired an American listed company by capital operations and established Holley Holding (US) Co., Ltd. Wang Licheng, president of Holly, believed that the biggest advantage of acquisition of listed companies was to transfer investment into start-up capital. "If it works, we could make full use of the financing function in the capital market in America." In September 2001, Holley acquired Philip's CDMA mobile communications department, entering the high-end mobile communications market. Besides, the Holley Group has proven the success in personnel internationalization. Wang Licheng said, "Internationalization is the global allocation of resources rather than exports or the establishment of an overseas company . . ." At present, Holley has primarily achieved global allocation of personnel, technology, markets and capital. In the communication company of Holley Group, more than 50% of the staff is American and Canadian, because they mastered core technology. Even though the labor costs of such staff are high, the company achieved optimal allocation of human resources.

---

[5] Shi Huiping, Capital operation in the process of internationalization — interview with Wang Licheng, Holley's chairman, Zhejiang Fiscal Tax and Accounting, 2002 (6).

7.4.3 Determinants of internationalization

Wang Licheng, president of Holly, contributed a lot to Holley's success. According to the argument of limited entrepreneurship mentioned above, entrepreneurs play a significant role in internationalization. When doing business in international markets, enterprises may face relative disadvantages compared with local markets, including trade barriers, unfamiliarity with the law, language, and business code. Facing the advantages and disadvantages of internationalization entrepreneurs have to decide whether, when and how to enter the international market. Holley's final decision was overseas acquisition to achieve internationalization by capital operations. But it is not always successful, and there are at least two influential factors as follows:

First, Holley's acquisition of Philip's CDMA project met troubles due to the lack of unsystematic integration. In 2001, Holley acquired Philip's CDMA project in America, which surprised the media that Chinese enterprises initiated to go global. It would not be long to break Qualcomm's monopoly of CDMA and even the American media paid great attention to this acquisition. In 2001, Wang Licheng was named Chinese Businessman of the Year by Fortune, an American magazine. But in later years, 3G, the third generation of mobile telecommunications technology, was coming, while Holley's CDMA project stagnated. It reported the motivation for the acquisition of Philip's R&D department was to maintain rapid growth through diversified business. After the acquisition, there was an illusion that Holley had bought and mastered the core technology of CDMA and could fully compete with Qualcomm who had patented technology of CDMA. However, Holley failed due to some secret and authorization agreements. After acquisition, Holley only got the technologies of CDMA 95A, and 20001X at first, while the CDMA patent related to 3G was still controlled by Qualcomm. Thus, it was obvious that if Holley wanted to develop CDMA, it must get new authorization from Philips and Qualcomm to acquire the new CDMA patent. It was reported that the annual investment was more than USD10 million to maintain the original technological team and continuously update the system. More annoying is that products developed by Holley always fell behind Qualcomm and were limited by Qualcomm's patents. Holley's CDMA technology could not dominate the market.

Unicom and other domestic major mobile and systems manufacturers all adopted Qualcomm's technological products and Holley had to target the low-end wireless telephone market or sell chips to minor manufacturers abroad. As Holley was a newcomer and its previous technology resources accumulated in the meter industry could not offer necessary background support to the CDMA project. Holley was trapped in a dilemma: Extracting huge amounts of money from meager profit of electric meters sales to hire American personnel, buy American machines, and compete with a much stronger American competitor in the US in a brand new field. Four years later, Holly could not afford the CDMA project and began to transfer its focus: Holley Information Industry Development Co., Ltd. (a subsidiary of Holley Information Industry Group) signed a TD-SCDMA terminal cooperation agreement with Datang Mobile Communication Equipment Co. Ltd. Holley and Datang would develop TD-SCDMA business based on a joint solution of Datang Mobile, and participate in a pre-business test held by the Information Industry Department.

Secondly, from the aspect of multi-industry integration, Holley lacked control on core technologies and sales channels, and its underestimation of competitors led to internationalization difficulties. Holley has been involved in diversified businesses across pharmaceuticals, power metering instruments and power automation system, wireless and wideband telecommunication, electronic materials, real estate, agriculture, petrochemical and mining, etc. With pharmaceuticals as its core business, Holley Pharmaceuticals is founded to serve the new strategy of Holley Group — to enter the pharmaceutical market. Most attention was exerted on its establishment. By acquisition and integration, Holley reorganized and acquired a new industrial chain — the artemisinin chain. Artemisinin is the only Chinese medicine that is recognized by the World Health Organization (WHO) to be consistent with Western medical standards, and it is mainly used for treatment of malaria. It is reported that arteannuin extracted from the Chinese plant Artemisia is recognized as the safest and most effective medicine to treat malaria and its major export destination is Africa. Since 2000, Holley Holding Corporation has began to integrate the artemisinin industry. Within four years, Holley made great efforts in artificially cultivating the best seeds by huge investment which resulted in the improvement of average arteannuin content from 0.8% to 1%. It acquired Hunan Jishou pharmaceutical, placing a control of over 80% of Chinese artemisinin production, and established Beijing Holley–Cotec Pharmaceuticals Co., Ltd. (Holley–Cotec), setting up a professional marketing department. Holley finally established a complete industrial chain from seed cultivation to international marketing.

There was a great chance for artemisinin. Global medical institutions finally changed their minds to take Chinese medicine artemisinin as the first treatment choice for malaria. At the end of July 2004, the WHO stated that it planned to purchase artemisinin for 100 million servings in Chongqing Youyang; donating countries including the US, United Kingdom (UK), etc. and United Nations International Children's Emergency Fund (UNICEF) and the World Bank who used to oppose artemisinin welcomed this new medicine. Chongqing Youyang is the artemisinin production base of Holley Holding. As to the plantation of artemisinin, it was not optimistic for Holley Holding, although it controlled 80% of mainstream plantations. Holley aimed to be enrolled in WHO's purchase catalog, which asked it to meet the requirements of the WHO.

It is reported that there are only two artemisinin-based high-end compound drugs in the world, one is Coartem of Novartis, and the other is Artekin of Holley Group. Novartis has been the supplier to WHO and its collaborator. And Kunming Pharmaceutical Corporation, a subsidiary of Holley Group, is the supplier of artemether, which is the major ingredient of Coartem. The terminals are still controlled by Novartis, and hence the Kunming Pharmaceutical Corporation has a limited say in the price setting.

Holley's Artekin has entered WHO public procurement channels in September 2006, being the world's second WHO supplier of the antimalarial as well as Novartis. Artekin has been included in the WHO public procurement, and consequently Holley can extend sales to African countries in which malaria is still rampant, and Holley Group will also change its previous status as a raw material supplier, and become medicine sellers. Holley–Cotec Pharmaceuticals Co., Ltd., a subsidiary of Holley Pharmaceutical Co., Ltd., has possessed a complete artesunate production chain, stretching from raw materials to the circulation. Holley–Cotec artemisinin-based antimalarial has become a best-seller in more than 40 countries of Africa and Southeast Asia, for its high efficiency and low toxicity.

Holley–Cotec has setup subsidiaries in Kenya, Tanzania, Uganda of Africa, French subsidiaries in Europe to service the terminals of the drug promotion. These two cases of Holley's acquisitions with an international background encountered troubles after the acquisitions: The former acquisition left Holley trapped in a situation where Holley used huge amounts of money to compete against technology; the latter shows that even though Holley has upstream material and medical materials, because the core technology and sales channels are controlled by foreign companies and organizations, Holley is weak in pricing, and limited by others.[6] Holley's internationalization makes us think that different internationalization patterns lead to different internationalization processes and predicts the difficulty of internationalization to some extent.

7.5 Youngor Group: A New Version of China's "Pierre Cardin"

Youngor Group founded in 1979 is one of the Fortune 500 Chinese enterprises, and has gradually formed a diverse and specialized business mode with garment, real estate development and financial investment as its major operation. In 2011, the group's total sales were CNY 36 billion and its total profit total CNY 3.3 billion. And the total value of import and export was USD2.7 billion. The group's net asset was more than CNY 16 billion and it had more than 50,000 employees. As a leading garment enterprise in China, its key product shirts had occupied the largest market share for 17 consecutive years, and its suits also had occupied the largest market share for six years. Its subsidiary Youngor Group Co., Ltd. is a listed company of Shanghai stock exchange. As China's largest garment enterprise, Youngor endeavors to improve quality with new technology and new facilities.

Youngor's international trade developed rapidly. In 1999, Ningbo Foreign Trade Co., Ltd., which was controlled by Youngor, was successfully restructured. It incorporates production and trade. The trade company's exports of textile and apparel grew rapidly, and the Group's value of import and export reached USD1.3 billion in 2005. The brand "Youngor" were chosen by the Commerce Department as one of the "Top 10 Exports Brand".

---

[6]Anonymous, Holley series: Acquisition and trail out of internationalization impulsion, *Zhejiang Business Net.*

One of Youngor's business aims is to promote international trade and to build its international marketing system so as to help develop related business. Youngor has setup international trade organizations in Ningbo, Shanghai, Hong Kong (SAR of China), and cities in Japan. These trade organizations expand Youngor's imports and exports, and help strengthen its business relationship with other international trade enterprises. In 1999, Youngor invested in China's export commodity base in Ningbo, which is directly controlled by the Ministry of Foreign Trade. The newly established firm, Zhongji Ningbo Foreign Trade Co., Ltd., became the first cross-industry, cross-regional, cross-trade, and cross-ownership foreign trade companies. Backed up by Youngor's capital strength, reputation and international trade system, the company successfully built trade relations with 112 countries and regions and its total imports and exports reached USD778 million in 2004. The trade amount is 8.3 times higher compared to that in the pre-restructure year of 1999. The registered capital of the company increased to CNY 120 million, 20 times of that in the pre-restructure period. Real estate is Youngor's new focus of entry industries. In 1992, Youngor founded a real estate company together with Macao (SAR of China) Nanguang Company. Since then Youngor has committed to property market. Youngor extended into the security investment in 1999 and became the second largest shareholder of CITIC Securities. Youngor also undertook investment in the infrastructure, public welfare and the mass media.

7.5.1 Internationalization process

Youngor deepened its internationalization process mainly in the form of investment in technology. In 1990, the newly formed joint venture — Youngor Garment Co., Ltd. — invested millions of dollars to introduce more than 300 pieces of advanced equipment from Germany, Japan, and the US. Youngor shirts soon attracted consumers with its high quality and opened a new market for high-end products. In 1994, Youngor introduced the HP Wrinkle Free Shirt technology from Japan. In October, five ministries and commissions (including National Science and Technology Commission) recognized the Youngor non-iron Shirt as the first new product in the shirt industry in China. Thereafter, other firms started to use the HP technology and the new wrinkle free shirt soon became even more prevalent in China than that in Japan. Four years later, Youngor introduced the most advanced VP wrinkle free shirt technology from the US, and the wrinkle free shirts became popular because they were both environmentally friendly and comfortable. The five ministries and commissions recognized it again as a national new product. In 2004, Youngor introduced the world's leading nano-technology from the US and developed its nano VP wrinkle free Shirt.

Youngor's suit is the second main product. In 1994, Youngor introduced the latest suit production lines from Germany, Italy, Japan etc., and men's suit pattern from an Italian company who was the best in design at that time. One year later, Youngor's new casual Italian style suit became popular on the market. Since then, Youngor consecutively introduced first-class automatic preshrinking shaping and Computer-Aided Design (CAD) system to ensure the precision and speed in material selection and cutting. It also setup the world's most advanced suit stereotyping center. These equipment and technology not only ensured the quality of the suit, they also shortened the cycle of new product development from one month to one week. In addition, they improved Youngor's competitiveness on the suit market. Owing to years of efforts, Youngor's suit dominated the market. Youngor's annual investment in R&D was over CNY 50 million. With the R&D investment, Youngor now is equipped with almost all the most advanced manufacturing facilities. In addition, it also established a modern marketing network system and a global quality control system. The company relied on flexible ownership structures such as alliances or networks to obtain resources. Youngor Group sped up the process of overseas market exploration through cooperation with well-known foreign firms. Cooperation aimed to establish manufacturing base of high-end products, to introduce advanced technology and internationalize the firm's brand.

In February 2005, Youngor Group Co., Ltd setup a joint venture — Yaxin Shirt Co., Ltd. — with Kellwood Asia Ltd., a subsidiary of American apparel sales giant Kellwood. The new joint venture mainly engaged in the production and export of the shirts so as to further consolidate Youngor's overseas market. Total investment in the joint venture was USD6 million and the company scheduled to export 5 million to 7 million pieces of shirts in three years. This cooperation was a comprehensive and multi-level one. It not only obtained funds, more importantly, it helped to build Youngor's overseas channels by adopting the brand, management and operation, customer resources, advanced technology and human capital from Kellwood. In early May 2005, the first shipment of Yaxin's shirts was exported to the US via Hong Kong (SAR of China). At the same time, Youngor also established a Textile City together with Japan Itochu, Nissin Spinning, and other famous enterprises. The yarn-dyed fabric and knitting fabric projects have been put into operation.

Youngor's Textile City aims at building a high-grade fabrics manufacturing base in which Youngor can improve its product quality by using high-grade fabrics and lay a foundation to further explore the international market by the overseas sales networks. In order to get more involved in the world market, Youngor adopted the strategy of "market exchanges" in which distribution channel exchange was the key point. In 1997, when Japan was affected by the Asian financial crisis and the Japanese economy was in recession, Youngor acquired a Japanese company to establish a subsidiary in Japan. It was the first try of Youngor's overseas manufacturing. Youngor's subsidiary in Japan was not only a sales company; but also a bridge to promote Youngor's culture and brand. At present, the Youngor Group has set up representative offices in the US, France, Italy, etc. Youngor segmented different overseas markets. For instance, the Japanese market is taken as a sales market because Japan and China share a lot of similarities in culture. Almost 80% of Japan's clothing is imported. Adequate capital in Japan also makes it possible to start capital cooperation with Japanese firms. The European market is considered as a technology center because Europe is the origin of fashions and trends, and it takes the lead in the fabric, designs, and innovation worldwide, while the US is mainly a consumer market.

7.5.2   Internationalization strategy

Youngor started its internationalization process after some achievements have been made in the domestic market. In order to obtain international market recognition, Youngor set a new goal: To create an international brand, to build an established enterprise. Youngor decided to increase its exports as early as in 1997 when demand for Youngor shirts and suits from the domestic market was huge. They built close contacts with businesses in Japan and Hong Kong (SAR of China), hiring local elites to explore the market and manage firms. When the Japanese economy was in recession because of the Asian financial crises, its Japanese company grew unexpectedly: Total sales were more than USD50 million and total profit was USD800,000 in 2001. In order to create an international brand, Youngor hired Mr. Marty, the founder of Paris Fashion Studio and the former art director of the US-based "Paris Fashion Design Institute", as brand consultant. Youngor spent CNY 50 million to build China's largest design center and recruited many world-renowned designers. At the same time, Youngor spent CNY 50 million on its digital process cooperating with the Chinese Academy of Sciences. In order to maintain sustainable growth and internationalize the quality and style of its clothing, Youngor built the world first-class Youngor International Textile City with companies from Japan and Hong Kong (SAR of China) in an effort to iron out the difference textile fabric lagged behind garment production and meet the demand for high grade, high quality, small orders, short process and multiplicity. Youngor's efforts were rewarded after years of endeavor: The brand was gradually recognized by consumers in Japan, Europe, and the US. Youngor ranked 268th among the most potential 1,250 firms, according to an official Japanese journal. In October, 2004, Youngor setup a branch in the US and hired an American as its marketing director. By doing this, Youngor established its overseas marketing channels and laid a foundation for building a world-class enterprise. Youngor's international strategy played a decisive role in all these achievements.

It is a trend for Chinese firms to internationalize, though firms differ in their own circumstances, timing and modes. Research shows that there are different modes of overseas expansion: (1) domestic production by using foreign brands; (2) domestic production by using domestic brands; (3) overseas production by using foreign brands; and (4) overseas production by using domestic brands. At present, the major mode of Chinese firms' overseas strategy is "domestic production by using foreign brands" because it is relatively suitable for Chinese firms. Youngor advocates promoting internationalization steadily by cooperation with world renowned clothing enterprises. The five strategies adopted are:

First, market exchange strategy: Youngor cooperated with famous foreign companies to establish a high-end manufacturing base and avoid producing or processing low-grade clothing. By cooperating with famous foreign firms, Youngor learned their technology and improved its brand. These efforts laid a foundation for Youngor to build an international brand. By cooperation, Youngor helped foreign companies to develop the Chinese market and they helped Youngor to develop the international market, the so-called "market exchange for market" facilitated the integration into the world's market system. At present, the major way of implementing "market exchange for market" strategy is "distribution network exchange". It is difficult for Chinese firms to expand marketing channels abroad and it is costly and time-consuming. Foreign companies faced the same problem when they developed China's market. Youngor's large stores have clear business mode: They not only sell Youngor's clothes, but also sell clothes and related goods of other famous brands around the world, thus improving Youngor's brand image. As a reward, Youngor uses these foreign companies' sales channels to promote its products and brand overseas. This was a win–win situation as it meets the interests of both sides and resources on both sides are fully utilized. In fact, this is a process of "internationalization without going abroad". Youngor took the opportunity to internationalize its product first because the whole internationalization process in general is terribly long. Youngor used to cooperate with Maxim's of Pierre Cardin, the world top men's clothing brand, in the form of being its franchiser in China. Youngor was in charge of both processing and marketing. The cooperation resulted in mutual recognition, and the introduction and assimilation of technology. The history of industrialization process in the developed countries resulted in the accumulation of cultures and thoughts. Connection with foreign companies has benefited Chinese companies, for OEM provided Youngor an opportunity to get to know world-class brands and to integrate more quickly into the international market.

Second, foreign market segmentation strategy: Despite Youngor being a relatively late internationalizer, it was a successful internationalizer. In the late 1990s when Japan's economy was in recession Youngor entered the Japanese market and its sales revenue in the second year reached over USD50 million. Youngor setup a branch in Japan, which is not only a sales company, but also a platform to promote Youngor's culture and brand. In addition, it also had representative offices in the US and Hong Kong (SAR of China). Export sales increased almost by 50% annually. The main difficulty in Youngor's internationalization process lies in its procedures. There are few qualified personnel available who are capable of exploring the foreign market. So in the coming years, Youngor's was to promote Youngor brand and build up business relations with foreign friends.

The fast growth in exports also brings risks to internal management and it is difficult to adjust. Youngor has differential priorities in overseas market. Its top priority is the Japanese market. In the 2000s, 70% of Youngor's exports went to the Japanese market. Japan has a high reliance in import, and Japan and China are Asian countries with similar cultural background. In addition, Japan's adequate capital makes it easy for Youngor to initiate capital cooperation, joint ventures, and technical communication. The second overseas market is the European and US market. Youngor chose the European market for its fabric and technology because Europe is the origin of apparels and the world is now fascinated with the European style. Its fabric development, it is taking a leading role in the world's trends of product design and innovation. The US market is targeted mainly for the large population of consumers.

Third, setting up modern marketing network: In 2002, Youngor shifted its goal of strategy from "creating a world renowned brand, building a multi-national group" to "creating an international brand, building an established enterprise". Youngor's unique sales network and its efforts to build the brand images by Mega marketing strategy contributed tits core competitiveness. Youngor constantly adjusted its marketing strategies, introducing the latest marketing theory, implementing the MID theory in domestic stores and Youngor promoted its brand and deepened its market exploration by forming its brand strategy taking stores as the major sales channel. It also integrated its marketing network with information technology. In 2011 Youngor had over 2,632 sales outlets, including over 772 proprietary outlets. To smooth linkage between the logistics, the internal supply chain, information collection and feedback, and the production response system, Youngor spent over more than CNY 50 million on a "digitalization project" which realized mass customization and online sales.

Fourth, to make full use of international resources: Youngor regards high investment, high technology as important ingredients in improving product quality and implementing its brand strategy. Therefore, Youngor continuously made huge investment to purchase the world's most advanced equipment. Total investment in the ninth "Five-Year Plan" Period (1996–2000) exceeded CNY 400 million. In 1990, Youngor spent millions of dollars to introduce more than 300 sets of advanced machines and facilities from Germany, Japan, the US, etc. In 1994, Youngor invested a huge amount of money and introduced suit production lines from Germany, Italy, Japan, etc. Youngor introduced first-class automatic preshrinking shaping and CAD system to ensure the precision and speed in material selection and cutting. It also setup the world's most advanced suit stereotyping center in which equipment and technology shortened the cycle of developing new products from one month to one week. The center became the largest and the most successful applied software base in Asia. It also introduced German's computer-controlled hanging workstations, automatic warehouse system, and ironing hanging delivery system. At present, Youngor owns world-class production facilities and it is the pioneer in domestic industry in introducing equipment and technology, which provides a guarantee for Youngor's high quality and high output. At the same time Youngor also emphasized on the training of technician and managers. Youngor hired specialists in the clothing industry to instruct technicians on the spot. In addition, Youngor sent technical personnel abroad for training and recruited a large number of technicians from mechanics, electronic engineers, and other textile related fields.

Fifth, to integrate into international quality control system: Based on international standards, Youngor adopted a set of internal control standards that were even stricter than national standards. It had a set of sophisticated production management procedures and complete quality control manuals. The manual splits the entire production procedure into hundreds of steps such as materials selection, pre-shrinking, cutting, accessories, ironing, delivery, and testing. The manual specified 88 items for standardized management alone and 180 key points for standardized operations, forming a four-level standardized quality control system that ensured strict control of quality and exterior appearance. Youngor's target was to build an international brand. In order to improve product quality, Youngor introduced the latest edition of International Quality Management System in 1997 and 2001, and implemented full quality management across the company.

With the improvement in quality, Youngor shirts and suits were the first in the industry to pass the ISO9001:2000 appraisal in 2002. Youngor's entire production process is incorporated into the quality management operating system. Youngor monitored its customer satisfaction as to evaluate the quality of management system.

In all, Youngor's internationalization process is as follows: It started with OEM processing to get familiar with the international market and seek overseas partners. After obtaining some experiences, it looked for opportunities to enter the international market. At present, Youngor has accumulated its advantages in foreign trade: Mass production, advanced equipment, advanced technology, and famous brand image across the nation, and good relations in international business. Its disadvantages: Weak competitiveness in pricing of the processing, lower capability to deal with small orders, long delivery time because the fabric factory is not completed yet, lack of international network impeded Youngor's foreign trade. To further deepen its international process, Youngor plans to focus on four aspects: (1) Develop target products for target markets. A fatal weakness in China's exported clothing is the fabric. Because of the shortage of good fabrics, the added value of exported clothing is greatly reduced. Youngor is now building a shirt factory, a pure wool suit fabric factory, a knitted fabrics factory and water washing cloth factory. Youngor cooperated with the best international fabrics manufacturers and introduced the most advanced equipment and technology. It also hired foreign experts to improve its R&D, cooperated with the best trade companies and used their international networks to explore overseas sales channels for fabrics and garments. (2) Follow the trend of multiplicity and small orders on the international market. After the establishment of a textile city, Youngor plans to shorten the time between fabric production and clothing so as to satisfy consumers' demand for small orders. (3) Use the market as the guide and produce what is needed in the market. Youngor's marketing strategy will be based on trends. It will also learn more of international trade, including knowledge about the export markets and circulation systems. Youngor hopes to cultivate a group of talents with cross-cultural communication ability. (4) Setup representative offices in France and Italy. Youngor's Japan Company, regional offices in the US and Hong Kong (SAR of China), will help collect the latest information of trends in fabrics and cloth, and dynamics of the development of local firms. In addition, they will also be exposed to advanced brand management information.

7.5.3 Determinants of internationalization

According to the external business environment theory, domestic and foreign business environments are increasingly tied and homogeneous. After obtaining a large market share on the domestic market, Youngor began to enter into the international market. According to the INV theory, cost advantage is one of the prerequisites for the success of firm internationalization. There are various ways to obtain cost advantage and Youngor chose to cooperate with the best foreign counterparts in an effort to realize economies of scale. Specifically, the two important factors that influence Youngor's internationalization are:

Firstly, market positioning of a high-end market is the key to Youngor's success for all these years. As early as in the mid-1990s, Youngor introduced modern production lines including world-class automatic pre-shrinking shaping equipment, CAD system, automatic hanging system and intelligent ironing equipment from Germany, Italy, Japan, etc. Visiting experts from China Clothing Association said that Youngor was the best experimental base for introduction of clothing technology. Even Pierre Cardin also made high compliments after visiting Youngor International Clothing City and that he believed was one of the best in terms of facilities and scale. Youngor established the world's most advanced suit model center where suits sales increase dramatically once they were put into the market for it integrated both western clothing styles and eastern cultures. Youngor also expatriated its employees abroad to study the techniques, procedures, and quality control systems of world-class brands that are consistent with international standards. At the beginning of 2003, Youngor Group and Japan's Itochu, the world's largest textile seller, spent USD40 million setting up a comprehensive worsted wool company that covered 60,000 square kilometers. The joint venture imported world-class dying, textile, weaving machines, and other advanced equipment. It was soon put into production and gained competitiveness on the international market.

Secondly, cooperating with the clothing giants for mutual benefits, Youngor continuously introduced advanced techniques and products while enhancing its independent R&D capacity. In recent years, Youngor has communicated frequently with world leading clothing giants in Italy, Japan, France etc, and explored its own overseas sales channels by establishing joint sales ventures in America, Japan, Hong Kong (SAR of China) etc. Observers believed that collaboration with Itochu and Marzotto is one of Youngor's strategies to enter the high-end market. Marzotto will provide its exclusive technique and know-how to the joint venture of Youngor and Itochu through new investment, technological transfer and marketing channel provision thus to enhance the competitiveness of all the three companies.

7.6 Summary

7.6.1 Comparison of internationalization modes

The previous four enterprises, Wanxiang, Transfar, Holley, and Youngor, become international companies eventually, but patterns and degrees vary. Finnish scholars Welch and Rothstein believe that enterprise's internal internationalization will influence its external internationalization and the effect of internal internationalization will be decisive to the success of its external internationalization. The cross theory of internationalization also believes that internal internationalization will affect external internationalization. In other words, the import pattern is more important than the export pattern. But at the beginning of their internationalization processes, the four companies chose different patterns.

Take Wanxiang, Transfar, and Holley as examples. In these three enterprises, Wanxiang and Holley chose to export first and then import, while Transfar chose to import first and turned to export after getting larger and obtaining a certain market share in China. The choice of patterns is not accidental. Based on cross theory, internationalization is a gradual process. It starts from simple participation in international trade, establishing overseas agencies and branches, and then transforming to building international marketing networks. At the initial stage, firms normally adopt a single entry strategy. This model applies to Chinese small and medium size enterprises, because implementation of this strategy is simple. Moreover, it is less risky and does not require a large amount of resources. The choice between import and export depends on the firms' own competitiveness in the world market and their technology. In 1984, for the first time Wanxiang exported 30,000 sets of joints to the US, becoming the first Chinese firm entering the US market. In 1998, Holley exported electric meters to Thailand and other countries, though revenues from export accounted for less than 1% of its total sales. Careful analysis of these two enterprises shows that they did not take imports as their only strategy because their products are high-tech products that are competitive on the world market. Through exporting, the companies got to know products' technology at international level and operation patterns as well. This knowledge enhances their competitiveness and contributes to their internationalization process. On the contrary, since Transfar's products are not technology-oriented, the company chose to import technology as its first step for internationalization.

According to the network theory of internationalization, an industrial system consists of enterprises engaging in production, sales, services, and other activities. Division of activities of enterprises demonstrates that enterprises are interdependent. They may have cooperation through interactions in the network. The internationalization process of these three enterprises follows this rule but the directions are different. Wanxiang's major business is auto parts despite of its large-scale. Wanxiang's network is horizontal specialization, which helps improve technology and reduce reliance on upstream and downstream foreign enterprises. The network pattern enhances Wanxiang' control on the international auto parts market. Transfar's internationalization direction is the same as Wanxiang's horizontal specialization because its production line is relatively simple. Holley's network pattern is special and its internationalization strategy is not simply selling products to overseas markets, rather it adopts a multi-dimensional strategy that incorporates market exploration, technology cooperation, capital raising, and manufacturing. The product line of Transfer now covers pharmaceutical, instruments and systems, information technology, electronics, chemicals and engineering, real estate, and other areas. Because of its different positioning, Holley chose a vertical diversification strategy in its international network for better risk sharing and enhancing of its overall strength.

According to the technology innovation theory, technical innovation is the key for entrepreneurs to seize potential profitable opportunities in the market. With the aim of profit maximization, entrepreneurs reorganize production conditions and factors, and setup more effective, more efficient production and operating systems at lower costs. Innovation also helps produce new products, new production techniques and explore new markets. Further, it also helps entrepreneurs to obtain raw materials or semi products and helps create new business organizations. Technology innovation becomes the core of economic activities. It enables firms to adapt to the changing environment. Therefore, enterprises should closely hold this endogenous power which is particularly important for enterprises. Wanxiang's innovation is legendary. At the beginning, Wanxiang put its exposition booth at the gate of conferences in order to attract foreign firms. The Group always regarded independent innovation as its lifeline and insisted on independent R&D of core technology. The Group kept doing independent technology innovation to enhance its core competitiveness. Wanxiang adheres to its unique concept in its patent competition with other firms, i.e. "external patent creation, patent introduction, patent purchase and cooperative development in patent creation." However, traditional patterns of cross-industry acquisition impede Wanxiang's international process. Same problems happened to Transfar. In its cooperation with Kao, Transfar relies on Kao's technology despite its absolute control. Transfar's innovative capacity was restricted by its inability in R&D development and technological barriers as well. As for Holley, it has formed a resource allocation pattern characterized by importing high-end technology from foreign countries, putting into production in China and opening both domestic and global markets. Holley's innovations are exactly what Wanxiang and Transfar lack, namely, capital operations, and acquisition of potential enterprises. Nevertheless, Holley also made some mistakes. The acquisition of Philip's CDMA project turned out to be a failure because Holley failed to integrate the firm due to lack of system support. In spite of these failures, Holley's international acquisition mode is worthy of learning from and imitating. Other development modes such as Youngor can also be summarized using the previous theories. Generally speaking, the patterns of international market operation of these four enterprises can be summarized from Table 7.3.

Table 7.3. International market operation patterns of sample enterprises.

Internationalization pattern	Network pattern	Innovation pattern	Cross pattern
Transfar Group	Horizontal Specialization	Technology Introduction	Import–Export
Youngor	Horizontal Specialization	Technology Introduction	Import–Export
Holley	Vertical Diversification	Capital Acquisition	Export–Import
Wanxiang	Horizontal Specialization	Patents	Export–Import

7.6.2 Determinants of internationalization

The theoretical analysis and empirical studies in previous sections show that six factors play important roles in firms' internationalization process: External business environment and the timing, understanding of opportunities, initial resource requirements, psychological distance, internationalization steps, competition strategy and duration. According to PTI and INV theories, these factors affect firms differently. As a result, firms exhibit different patterns in their internationalization process. PTI theory posits that internationalization is a gradually evolving process which is a sequential form of incremental commitment to foreign markets. INV theory emphasizes the analysis of the influence of entrepreneurs and resources and weakens the role of psychological distance. To China's private firms, patterns of and factors affecting internationalization might be more complicated. It should be noticed that the relationship between international duration and performance was not clear in the previous cases and this section will mainly explore the other five factors.

As can be seen from the cases of the previous four firms, the internationalization patterns of China's private firms fit the predictions of PTI and INV theories. However, since China's private firms expand rapidly in a short time period, these private firms are different from foreign companies in the internationalization process. Specifically, we think that the limited entrepreneurship mentioned in Chapter 6 cannot be ignored. The entrepreneurship is rooted in domestic business environment and may play an important role in a certain stage in the internationalization process.

I. Generality of PTI theory

A common problem facing China's private firms is the shortage of resources. In addition, echoing China' economic development, firms' understanding of the external business environment and business opportunities takes a long time. These firms chose to enter the international market step by step because they are faced with such problems as psychological distance. In this sense, PTI theory well explains the internationalization patterns of China's private firms.

(1) The effect of the external business environment and the timing

The PTI theory states that at the beginning of firms' international process, lack of experience and knowledge about international business environment is a big obstacle. In previous cases, except for Wanxiang, other enterprises did not rush to enter the international market. Rather, they chose to focus on domestic market first and expand internationally after gradually adapting to external business environment. Transfar first became a national brand and then established joint ventures with foreign companies. Based on the domestic success, Transfar then went to the global markets. Holley started to export electric meters to other countries in 1998 and sales revenue at that time accounted for less than 1% of its total sales. Youngor focused on building its brand and importing technology at the initial stage, and then sped up its internationalization process. For instance, Youngor introduced from German, Italy, Japan, and other countries modern production lines, including world-class automatic pre-shrinking shaping equipment, CAD system, automatic hanging system, and intelligent ironing equipment, etc. Youngor also aimed at world-class brands and sent its employees abroad to study. The techniques, procedures and quality control system are comparable to international standards, setting a good starting point for the firm.

(2) Psychological distance and internationalization steps

According to the psychological distance assumptions in PTI theory, firms carry out their international business step by step. They will enter new markets with expanding psychological distance, and gradually increase their control. Except for Holley Group, other enterprises were all influenced by this factor. With this assumption of psychological distance, Wanxiang expanded its overseas market. Youngor started its internationalization process after having achieved some success on the domestic market. Although Youngor started late to explore the overseas market, it had some success. Youngor's steps in its internationalization process are as follows: Starting with OEM processing to get familiar with the international market and seek overseas partners. After obtaining some experience, look for opportunities to enter the international market. Youngor setup a subsidiary in Japan, and offices in America and Hong Kong (SAR of China) which serve as windows to promote Youngor's brand and culture.

(3) Initial resource requirements in internationalization

According to PTI theory, when firms begin to go global, they need resources to learn international experience and knowledge, as have not been proven by the cases shown before. These companies, except Wanxiang Group, started their internationalization strategies after obtaining enough resources. In the early 1980s, China was still in the era of a planned economy and demand from within the country was weak. Due to these environment and policy constraints, Wanxiang had to resort to overseas market.

(4) International competition strategy

According to PTI theory, internationalization is a process of constantly adjusting to changing environment, as has been proved by Wanxiang. When Wanxiang gradually gained a firm foothold on the overseas market, it started to change its internationalization strategy, trying to win more space for survival and development. Other enterprises began internationalization at different stages, which was also an adjustment to external environment Transfar explored further internationally after its successful cooperation with Kao. And Holley's strategy was more active.

II. INV, a supporting theory explaining the internationalization of China's private firms

(1) External business environment

Unlike PTI theory, INV theory states that entrepreneurs consider the domestic market and international market as a whole and start to internationalize as early as when they setup their firms. For example, Wanxiang began to implement its internationalization strategy in the late 1970s and actively explored the international market. The reason for aiming at overseas market was the market condition and policy constraints. Exporting was Wanxiang's optimal choice after considering its cost advantage and overseas demand for its products.

(2) Psychological distance

In recent years, international communication and transportation have seen great improvement and the international markets have become more homogeneous. These changes shorten firms' internationalization process. The changes reduce the influence of psychological distance and firms can even pass some stages, or they might even not have to follow the conventional order. Holley's internationalization process supports this theory. It did not wait, but rather took initiatives to allocate resources globally and implement an internationalization strategy.

(3) Internationalization competition strategy

According to INV theory, exclusive technology and differentiated localized strategy help firms implement their internationalization strategy. Firms have disadvantages in their international business compared with local business management. One way out is to obtain exclusive technology and to apply the technology to realize differentiation or cost advantages. So INV theory believes that exclusive technology is the source of differentiation and cost advantages. For instance, Holley advocated technology innovation strategy, regarding innovation as its engine. It established its advanced position and obtained maximum added value through the implementation of technology innovation strategy.

(4) Entrepreneurs' understanding of international business opportunity

According to INV theory, the entrepreneur plays an important role in internationalization. Facing the advantages and disadvantages of internationalization, entrepreneurs must decide whether, when, and how to enter international markets. The influence of the entrepreneur is more evident in China's private firms, as have been on the entrepreneurs of the previous four Chinese firms.

III. The influence of limited entrepreneurship on internationalization

The PTI theory states that entrepreneurs have little influence. The theory focuses only on the decision making system rather than the decision makers. On the contrary, INV theory considers that entrepreneurs play important roles in internationalization. These two theories seem unable to explain some features of entrepreneurs in China's private firms. These features could explain the different characteristics in the internationalization process of China's private firms from foreign companies. Therefore, importing the theory of entrepreneurship will make current internationalization theories more convincing, as have been evidenced by China's experience.

Take Wanxiang as an example. In the early 1980s, due to restrictions on exports, few entrepreneurs in township enterprises realized the need of exports or had the courage to export. It takes great courage and resolution to make the decision. Lu Guanqiu, the spiritual leader of the group and current chairman of the board, pushed the group internationally. Because of his persistence, Wanxiang's first batch of products was exported to the US. Another example is Holley. Holley chose to invest in developed countries first and then export to developing countries, passing the stage of psychological distance. Holley's success was to a large extent attributed to its chairman Wang Licheng. The internationalization process of Youngor and Transfar was all backed up by the strong will power of their entrepreneurs.

Generally speaking, entrepreneurs from private firms are constrained by relatively lower levels of education, insufficient experience, limited technology, management skills, and language. As mentioned in Chapter 6, when faced with limited rationality and a relatively huge domestic market, entrepreneurs in China's private firms tend to look more into the domestic markets. However, with firms' rapid expansion, entrepreneurs' own will power sometimes dominates firms' strategies, as has been characterized by some private firms in their internationalization process.

Chapter 8

Pattern Selections

Various theories of enterprise internationalization and empirical studies of the internationalization in China's POEs show that the enterprise will get a better internationalization performance if it starts internationalization earlier and faces a domestic business environment which is close or homogenous to their international counterparts. Besides, internal factors, such as qualities of the entrepreneur, the size of the enterprise, the competitive strategy applied and years of internationalization, will significantly affect the performance of internationalization. The analysis of the internationalization of domestic enterprises and successful experiences of internationalization of enterprises in the developed countries in the previous chapters further confirm the conclusion.

During the past more than 30 years, some of the privately-owned enterprises (POEs) have enjoyed a rapid growth in their export-oriented business, and they have committed to diverse international operation mode flexibly, including processing trade in the initial period, export sales, cooperative leasing and direct overseas investment which is the higher forms of internationalization. Export-oriented POEs have become an important growth engine of China's foreign trade, and hence they have become a vital part of China's foreign trade strategy. Zhejiang Province was the cradle and the pioneer of private enterprises in China, and it has some prototypes of multinational companies with certain scale and international competitiveness, such as the Feiyue Group that has 18 international branches in countries like Japan, Germany, the Holley Group that acquired the core technology of Philips CDMA mobile phone chips which made it enter the field of CDMA core technology monopolized by

Qualcomm. These private enterprises have a good reputation at home and abroad and provide successful international models and examples for the internationalization of private enterprises.

In spite of the fact that China's private enterprises do enjoy a golden opportunity in the process of world globalization, we cannot deny that barriers to internationalization are also obvious. With regard to how enterprises should start and promote the process of internationalization, there are two sharply different opinions. One is the gradual international-ization development pattern which means internationalization is a gradual process; the other is radical development pattern, in which enterprises can start the internationalization abruptly by skipping some certain stages. Enterprises should choose their ways of internationalization according to their scale, resources accumulated and the entrepreneur's ability. This chapter will discuss private enterprises' internationalization patterns by private enterprises' operating management and development strategy.

8.1   Gradual Pattern of Internationalization

According to Psychic distance hypothesis of PTI theory, the presence of psychological distance will make enterprises take small steps to develop the international management gradually, and they will enter new markets where the psychological distance is constantly expanding and they can constantly expand their control. This shows that the gradual internationalization pattern is the path for enterprises when they are affected by psychological distance factors. In the early 1970s, Johanson, Finn Wiedersheim-Paul, the Swedish economist, used enterprise behavior theory to do empirical research on some European enterprises' internationalization experiences, and found that enterprise internationalization was a successive process of multiple stages, and thus put forward the theory of gradual internationalization. This research lays a solid foundation for the gradual internationalization development pattern. According to the theory of gradual internationaliza-tion, enterprise internationalization is a gradual process, including double evolutions: One is the expansion of enterprise managements' geographical space or the expansion of the market; the other is the evolution of the enterprise management pattern. With respect to the expansion of the market, most enterprises have been taking the pattern of "a decreasing importance of proximity and familiarity", and the geographical expansion of market usually takes place in the following four phases: (1) from the local market to the regional market; (2) from regional market to the national market; (3) from the national market to the neighboring foreign market; and (4) to the global market. The progressive international management pattern has the following features: most enterprises take the pattern of "from the easy to the difficult" to participate in the international market gradually. And the development path of international management is generally constituted by the following steps: domestic market sales; indirect export *via* independent agent; direct export, setup sales departments abroad; setup production facilities overseas.

8.1.1 Gradual internationalization process

Under the gradual internationalization development pattern, an enterprises' internationalization is a long process. No matter whether it is the direct export-driven internationalization or the outsourcing-driven internationalization, POEs more frequently participate in international market competition in the internationalization process.

The optimization of external environment plays a crucial part in the internationalization of POEs. The following factors: simplification of investment authorization procedure, deregulation of foreign trade, perfection of the overseas investment related laws and regulations, and growing concern on the enterprise's overseas investment, will greatly stimulate private enterprises to implement the going-global strategy and even further the process of internationalization.

Czinkota (1982, 1991) and Cavusgil (1980, 1982) argue that multinational management activities are the result of collaboration of two mechanisms, the external "push mechanism" and the internal "pull mechanism". The external push mechanism includes changes of market environment and market structure. The internal pull mechanism includes the factors of institutional innovation as well as the ownership advantages etc. Czinkota holds that an enterprise internal "pull mechanism" is the most important one for it determines whether an enterprise can develop the international management from an initial stage to a higher stage, such as starting from indirect exports and jumping to more international market involvement. For China's POEs, one of the direct motivations to develop international management, especially the one that takes foreign direct investment, is to acquire foreign advanced technology, managerial skills and company philosophy. And it can explain, to a large extent, the enterprises internationalization practice, which chooses developed market economy countries as host countries. Zheng Kebin (2003) investigated the internationalization practice of the Wanxiang Group and believed that one motive of the Wanxiang Group's internationalization was to learn and take advantage of foreign advanced technologies.

For enterprises in developing countries, the technology innovations in the process of internationalization often accompany the strong characteristics of "learning by doing" and imitation. The enterprise makes use of its late-mover advantages to master and develop production technology by learning and imitating technologies in developed countries. The internationalization in developing countries creates a shortcut for "learning by doing" in technology innovation. Technologies and other internationalization knowledge, especially market knowledge and managerial knowledge, can be acquired by the way of "learning by doing". For SMEs who are in the early period of international development, their abilities to learn and realize the late-mover advantage of imitative innovation by the way of "learning by doing" plays a key role in their growth potential to be multinational companies.

There are apparent differences between multinational enterprises in developing countries and multinational enterprises in developed countries. Compared with the multinational enterprises in developed countries, the multinational enterprises in developing countries have the following three features: (1) a rapid follower who has a clear goal of catching up; (2) a technology imitator who can make full use of various resources to achieve a new combination advantage; and (3) an enterprise who has strong ability to learn, absorb and digest the technology, and to realize the effective distribution of resources according to the local market conditions. Undoubtedly, China's POEs should make use of their late-mover advantages to explore the road of "learning by doing" when they take the gradual internationalization pattern.

8.1.2 Gradual internationalization: The traditional pattern selection

The POE in China has a rather brief internationalization history, so its early pattern is still in the exploratory stage. Specifically, when it comes to the gradual internationalization pattern, the path selection at present is mainly to commit to gradual internationalization via international trade. The implementation of business internationalization is a gradual process, that is to say, the gradual path starting from simply participating in the import and export trade to setting up a marketing agency, then to establishing a foreign production base. Most privately-owned enterprises adopted this method to conduct the internationalization, Wanxiang, Transfar and Holley take this method in their internationalization processes. As to the form of international trade they take, enterprises will choose between import and export according to the industry's international competitiveness and the technology level of products, for example, Wanxiang and Holley chose export as a priority and then an import strategy, while Transfar and Youngor chose import as a priority and turn to exports only after their imports have a certain market scale at home.

According to the deduction of the gradual internationalization theory, the internationalization process of an enterprise is generally divided into five stages (take export priority as an example): (1) the domestic market stage: at this stage, the enterprise has little reputation in the market and possesses initial "naïve" features in aspects of production management, product development and marketing etc. An enterprise mainly devotes to opening the domestic market and improving product reputation in the domestic market at this stage. The private enterprises mentioned in this book, except Wanxiang Group, did not rush into the international market at the initial stage, instead they took different approaches to consolidate the domestic market, and gradually adapted to the external business environment, in order to make preparations for the internationalization strategy in the future. (2) The stage of products' indirect export: As the enterprise's domestic market share and products' popularity increase, it naturally attacks attention from foreign trade agents or foreign customers, which makes export through foreign trade agents logically. (3) The stage of products' direct export: The stable developments of an enterprise's direct exports increase opportunities for enterprises to connect with international markets. The enterprise starts to apply its research and development, production and management in accordance with international rules, and become more involved in the international market to a larger extent, and eventually avoid the agent to export directly. (4) The stage of investment in different countries: Generally, setup branches in neighboring countries or the most important regional market, and expand gradually from a sales center to production base. (5) The stage of global investment: At this stage, the enterprise is no longer a small and medium enterprise. It has accumulated considerable strength and formed the framework of a multinational corporation. Its international investment and management are in accordance with its global strategy.

The POE is generally weak in its initial period, with the poor ability to avoid risk and the limited knowledge of the international market. Consequently, it is appropriate for the privately-owned enterprise to take the development path of a gradual internationalization pattern via foreign trade. In the process of internationalization, enterprises should first choose import and export trade as a priority, thus enhancing interaction with the international market by trade and consequently laying the foundation for exploring the international market and further development. Then they can consider developing towards a higher stage and such pattern selection can maximize the success of their internationalization strategy. In the five stages of internationalization, direct export is a key step, which is the manifestation of enterprises' real contacts with the international market. The advantages of direct export-led internationalization strategy are:

First, direct export is a starting point of internationalization. By direct export, enterprises can gradually establish a fixed contact with the international market. At present, many private enterprises export their products to the international market mainly in the following two forms: one is that foreign buyers come to China to buy and order products directly, especially via various national or regional trades fairs; another is through professional foreign trade companies which will sell products to foreign markets. It shows that private enterprises have not established regular and direct contact with the international market, and the export is, to a great extent, dependent on others, which will bring much contingency and uncertainty. With direct export, enterprises can connect with the international market directly and establish stable sales channels. It helps to improve dependence on the international market and thus to strengthen enterprises' international management wittiness.

Second, direct export enables enterprises to organize production according to the international market requirements, participate in the international labor division directly, and accumulate experiences of international business, thus laying a solid foundation for further international management. Generally, private enterprises in China lack international management experience and talents, so it is obviously unrealistic for enterprises to invest overseas directly and implement multinational management. But in the case of indirect exports, the enterprise does not face the international market directly, and rarely participates in specific international trade activities. To some extent, there is no big difference from purely domestic enterprises. So, direct export can avoid business risks incurred by excessive contrasts of the management environment in overseas investment, and it can also help the enterprise contact with international business, understanding the international market and international practices, and accumulating international management experience in the process of direct export.

Generally speaking, after a period of sustainable export, the scale of the enterprise will be somewhat expanded; the strength will be enhanced; the dependence on the overseas market will be increased. Then they will setup sales agencies in order to expand the market, even to build or acquire local enterprises in the host country to take part in international production, realizing the conversion from products export to foreign direct investment. It is proven that China's enterprises which obtained foreign trade management autonomy in the period of reform and opening up went abroad step by step in this way.

The foreign-trade-driven internationalization process has a special method called outsourcing. Since the 1980's, there has been a new trend in the internationalization of multinational companies and many important products or services are no longer produced or managed directly by branches in foreign countries, but produced by other countries' international outsourcing enterprises. The enterprises themselves only purchase and check the products or services as the outsourcing corporation, and then assemble products or provide final service for users. So, a corporation can also form a network of internationalized production and management. With the network, the company can optimize the allocation of resources more effectively on a global scale, and provide products that are more competitive in the quality price ratio. This way of realizing internationalization through business outsourcing is called "external sourcing", "outsourcing" or "externalization".

China's private auto parts makers achieved their successful internationalization mostly by the means of outsourcing. The auto part is a typical product of multinational corporations' outsourcing. A major trend in auto products exports in Zhejiang is that more and more corporations are brought into the outsourcing system of western multinational corporations, and become the main suppliers of outsourcing business for giant American and European auto components distributors. It is consistent with the products' comparative advantages of "light, small, labor intensive" in Zhejiang, thus greatly promoting the rapid development of the auto components industry in Zhejiang. For auto parts manufacturers in Zhejiang Province, participating in the outsourcing system of multinational corporations was the first step on the way to internationalization. Wanxiang Group's experience was the most successful and also the most typical one. Wanxiang Group is recognized as the typical successful case of international management of private enterprises. In the 1990s, it began its internationalization strategy and so far it has setup, merged and held a stake in more than 20 corporations in 8 countries including the United States, Britain, Australia and Canada, and has preliminarily formed the framework of a multinational corporation. Wanxiang Group generally followed the route of shifting from low-end outsourcing contractors to international producers. Specifically, the internationalization of the Wanxiang Group experienced four key steps. The first step: Contracting the outsourcing orders from foreign auto component dealers. According to the history of the Wanxiang Group, the factory received its first auto order from overseas in 1984, and from then began to set foothold in the international market. In the following decade, Wanxiang Group entirely relied on foreign orders to expand exports. Most of these orders come from the outsourcing business of auto components distribution enterprises in Europe and the United States. Scheler Corporation was the most important outsourcing procurement buyer in the American market.

The second step: Setting up overseas marketing institutions, selling products in the target market directly. In 1994, Wanxiang Group setup its first marketing institution in the United States, establishing a closer link with the American outsourcing distributors of auto components, and realizing the preliminary internationalization. The third step: changing the position: It acquired foreign auto component distribution corporations to shift from being a low-end outsourcing contractor to middle-end procurement buyer, and take part in the outsourcing purchasing system of the leading car enterprises in the United States. In 2000, Wanxiang Group acquired the famous American auto components distribution corporation — Scheler Corporation, which made it join in the outsourcing intermediary link between auto manufacturers and components manufacturers. The fourth step: Choosing auto component as its core business, realizing a multi-national and diversified expansion, and establishing the framework of a transnational corporation. In 2001, Wanxiang succeeded in acquiring 21% stake of UAI which was a listed corporation on the NASDAQ, becoming the first major shareholders. The acquisition allowed Wanxiang to gain patent technologies of the acquired corporation and to enhance its manufacturing capacity and product quality. What is more, with the help of the acquired corporation's original brand and sales channels, Wanxiang could have access to the western mainstream market and its brand became popular gradually.

Wanxiang Group finally realized internationalization in the way of outsourcing, which shows that auto enterprises can start from outsourcing and then realize internationalization. For POEs, they should draw lessons from the successful experience of Wanxiang and seize the present "outsourcing" opportunity of multinational corporations, starting from the low-end suppliers, and then gradually entering the middle and high-end supporting system; starting from the overseas after-sales market and then to OEM business, and finally realizing radical internationalization.

8.2 Radical Pattern of Internationalization

Most early multinational corporations followed a gradual internationalization pattern, and their expansion starting from domestic markets until their global strategy was ultimately realized. In the early 20th century, many corporations in Japan, R.O. Korea and Singapore broke the tradition and realized radical internationalization in which the firm skipped or jumped stages to hasten the internationalization process, which provided a new development pattern for internationalization and multinational operations. The rapid emergence of these corporations also proved that, in the situation of new international labor divisions, the leap forward development pattern is feasible and effective. The leap forward development pattern can be called leap forward internationalization development pattern, which means that even with little internationalization practice, corporations can suddenly "go global" by merging or investing directly. Since the 1980s, with the soaring development of economic globalization, the great breakthrough in information and network technology and its intensive worldwide use, the relations between corporations and the international market has been much closer. The transmit speed of international market information, especially investment and operation information has accelerated and the demonstration effect of enterprises internationalization has expanded, which made corporations try to join in the billowing tide of internationalization. In practice, these corporations increasingly abandoned the traditional pattern of "a decreasing importance of proximity and familiarity", skipping one or more processes, trying to expand radically. Thus, a radical or leap forward development pattern of internationalization became more and more prevalent.

The theoretical basis of radical internationalization pattern is the radical internationalization theory. Simply speaking, this pattern is manifested as being radical in the process of internationalization. The explanation of this theory is very complex for there are several versions among which the argument of the Swedish scholar, Forsfren, is relatively comprehensive. His theory includes four propositions: First, the increment of overseas investment, the enterprise's overseas investments increase incrementally; second, the blindness of overseas investment, enterprises sometimes even invest overseas with little experience and little knowledge; third, the uncertainty of corporations' decision making in overseas investment, if enterprises believe that the risk of investing overseas is lower than not doing so, they would invest even with no experience or knowledge; fourth, enterprises' overseas investment strategy is radical, the gradual accumulation of market knowledge does not conflict with the enterprises' radical overseas investment strategy. Forsfren argues that, for a large-scale multinational enterprise, it is hard to predict the speed and structure of its international development. Therefore, the use of the gradual theory of internationalization is quite limited when it comes to explaining large-scale multinational enterprises.

8.2.1 Main pathways of radical internationalization

In the era of global business, time has become a key strategic weapon. The gradual internationalization theory cannot provide enterprises with efficient ways to survive in the international market neither can they explain the survival or growth pattern of high-tech enterprises. On one hand, these enterprises do not have sufficient prerequisite resources, such as capital, to initiate the internationalization. On the other hand, neither do they have unlimited time to acquire resources. To seize the opportunity to be the early movers in international competition, enterprises should no longer follow the gradual pattern by which they internationalize step by step. However, the next urgent problem is how enterprises can efficiently and successfully take the radical internationalization path? We hold that when SMEs take the radical path to commit internationalization, they should involve themselves into the business networks of other enterprises, by which they can make use of other enterprises' power, but without losing flexibility or adaptability. Specifically, they can have two combinations: One is the vertical combination that is to combine SMEs with large enterprises; the other is horizontal combination that is to combine similar-sized SMEs, forming enterprise clusters.

8.2.1.1 *The symbiosis of SMEs and large enterprises*

German biologist De Bary put forward the concept of "symbiosis" in 1897, which meant that two different species of organisms live together. According to symbiosis theory, symbiotic mode is also called a symbiotic relationship that refers to the interaction or combination between symbiotic units. It reflects both the interaction between symbiotic units and the intensity of the interaction, as well as information on substance exchange and an energy exchange relationship between symbiotic units. Symbiosis theory in biology was soon introduced into sociology, management and economics.

The competition pressure in the globalization environment forces large enterprises to reduce costs through stronger specialization, which has prompted them to acquire specialization by outsourcing or value chain specialization, so that small and medium-sized private scientific enterprises can be integrated into the large enterprises' value chains giving them access to the global market, thus forming a symbiotic relationship. Symbiotic cooperation can appear in any place of the value chain, and the partnership can appear in many modes. The purpose of symbiotic cooperation between two or more enterprises is to increase the output value by reducing costs, shortening marketing time or improving customer service, and allow all parties to obtain benefits. Therefore, each party relies on and complements each other in the cooperation arrangements in a sustainable way. For large enterprises, they increase their flexibility and efficiency through the integration with SMEs, and at the same time they provide SMEs with opportunities in the network. For SMEs, the symbiotic cooperation with large enterprises facilitates their development and internationalization process mainly in the following ways: First, enterprises need "energy" exchange with the outside world in the growing processes, through the extension of internal resources advantages and introduction of external resources so as to achieve the maturity of the internal system. Enterprises need to make full use of the symbiotic pattern to achieve the growth of internationalization in the condition where their own strengths are limited. Small enterprises cooperate with large enterprises in a symbiotic pattern in the process of internationalization, providing large enterprises with higher elasticity and efficiency, making themselves more specialized, and forming economies of scale in production. Second, the cooperation between small enterprises and large enterprises in the symbiotic relationship is an important means for private enterprises' symbiotic leapfrog, and in this way private enterprises can expand the international market for their products in a more rapid and lower-cost way than they can alone, which brings them to internationalize more rapidly and effectively. Third, as SMEs are restricted by many factors, their ability to reduce risks is poor when they develop international management. In particular, if they want to skip stages in their internationalization process, the risks they face are bigger. Enterprises enter the international market rapidly by forming symbiotic relationships with large multinational corporations, which can minimize risks and initiate internationalization at the fastest possible pace.

For China's SMEs, their symbiotic cooperation model with big corporations has two variations in the process of internationalization. First, there is a symbiotic cooperation with multinational corporations, such as establishing strategic alliances, the manufacturing of original equipment or participation in the division of the global value chain. By cooperation with multinational corporations, small and medium-size private enterprises can gain partial protection in the symbiotic network to avoid fierce competition. Bonaccorsi, Dana and Estemad have analyzed how SMEs rely on large corporations in the process of internationalization via the "scale-up" process. They can make use of the leverage of network resources to shorten the time, to reduce the cost and to avoid the internationalization risk. Similarly, commitment to some special functions of big corporations encourage small private enterprises to speed up their learning curve and gain more special internationalization skills, thus eventually becoming more competitive. Second, there is a symbiotic cooperation with big domestic corporations, that is to say, combining with large enterprise groups. On the one hand, small and medium-sized private enterprises establish cooperative relationships with big corporations. With the advantage of flexibility, they produce related products and parts for big corporations and become the subcontracted enterprises in the big corporations' production support system. In this process, they have access to big corporations' capital and technological support. On the other hand, with the following-up strategy, small and medium-sized private enterprises rely on corporations, which have successfully internationalized to enter into the international market by using their overseas marketing channels and management ability.

When POEs establish a symbiotic cooperation with big corporations, it is of great significance to evaluate and decide on the relationship involved. The essence of the symbiotic model is to benefit all parties. Therefore, in the process of internationalization, the symbiosis between private enterprises and big corporations must be commensalism or mutualism.

The symbiosis at first is mutualism. The survival of private enterprises relies on the development of big corporations while symbiosis is needed for big corporations' further development. However, the relationship is unstable, for big corporations have a much wider range of selection. Thus, private enterprises should have complementarities in resources with symbiotic corporations, and strong learning ability in the internationalization process to make full use of shared knowledge. Thus private enterprises can reduce the dependence on large enterprises, and keep a lasting relationship. The relationship commonly starts with mutualism and then develops into commensalism.

In the symbiotic model, it is possible to obtain efficiency but also it is easy to lose partial independence. That is to say, there appears a somewhat negative correlation between efficiency and the controlling interest. For example, many R.O. Korean corporations have attempted to enter the international market by only using their own resources and brands. However, they soon realized that they lacked brand credibility and the internal resources needed in the process of quick internationalization. They re-allocated their resources to become the original equipment manufacturers for multinational corporations headquartered in America or Europe. With the help of large corporations' brands, their final products were able to be sold all over the world, but it also led to a much higher reliance on single customers. Though large corporations rely on small enterprises to some extent, they still can diversify their supply of resources to reduce the reliance. For example, large corporations are able to take advantage of bargaining power to eliminate the possibility that small enterprises may provide products for other potential customers. Therefore, POEs should clearly acknowledge that they should make great efforts to improve their capabilities rather than be content with participation in the global value chain or alliances with large corporations.

8.2.1.2 *Cooperative development in the cluster of SMEs*

In the process of international development, small and medium-sized private enterprises can promote their competitiveness by establishing enterprise clusters. As defined by Porter, the cluster refers to the geographical agglomeration of enterprises and organizations that are interrelated in some specific field. United Nations Conference on Trade and Development (UNCTAD) holds that the cluster of SMEs is one of the most efficient ways to promote the technology, management and marketing strategies of small and medium-sized private enterprises. Since the 1980s, Silicon Valley, Italy, Bangalore, Hsinchu, where the cluster of small and medium-sized technology enterprises play a leading role, have achieved great economic success, and enterprise clusters have become the highlights of economic development. Porter thinks that there are neither international strategies nor international divisions of labor in most of the weakest industrial clusters; the involved industry must be internationalized to gain the permanent competitive advantage of industrial clusters; similarly, even though industrial clusters are disintegrating, the industries which are able to confront fierce competition and have customers at home and abroad can avoid domino effects. Enterprises that can gain a competitive position in the international market are often agglomerated instead of dispersed. Internationalization of China's industrial clusters is mostly limited to export without international labor divisions, and the international competitive power of individual enterprise is not strong enough. Such industrial cluster is rather weak. Therefore, to encourage China's privately-owned enterprises to go global, internationalization strategy should be carried out, and enterprises should take part in the international labor division. The effects of enterprise cluster on promoting the international development of small and medium-sized private enterprises are mainly manifested in the following aspects.

First, industry cluster is beneficial to advance SMEs' production efficiency and improve their response to international market changes. In the industry cluster, a large number of specialized enterprises agglomerate geographically, which introduces an economy of scale. Accordingly, an industry cluster creates a larger marketplace and there is an increasing potential demand for products and services introduced by a more specific labor division and higher specialization. Owing to proximity and mutual trust, the market information concerning products, technology, and competition can be quickly collected and widely spread among enterprises in the industry cluster with a low communication cost. Prompt responses to market information are the premises for small enterprises to take advantage of their flexible mechanism. Confronted with urgent orders, small and of variety, the industry cluster can help the cooperative enterprises to be well prepared in the fastest way. As the cooperative foundations have been set up in the past, it is not necessary for SMEs to bargain and sign agreements.

In the era of the changing international market, the ability to provide a quick response can bring a particularly competitive advantage for SMEs.

Second, an industry cluster is beneficial in forming the mechanism of competitive pressure. In the industry cluster, enterprises in the same industry gather in one place, and consequently the evaluation indexes of price, quality and product differentiations bring competitive pressure for enterprises. Competition is a manifestation of maintenance or expansion of market share not only by reducing production costs, but also by the quality and differentiation of products. Enterprises with product differentiation use the advantage of market competition and gain a larger proportion of market share. Through interior competitive pressure, enterprises in the cluster obtain the advantage of product differentiation based on quality. As Porter has mentioned, industries with the international competitive advantage develop the advantage from the mutual competition in the industry cluster, rather than the national champion enterprises.

Third, the industry cluster is beneficial in improving the innovation ability. The industrial cluster is the catalyst for the birth of new enterprises. The healthy atmosphere of both cooperation and competition among SMEs promotes the birth of new enterprises, and creates a high survival rate for new enterprises. Concentrated customer groups can reduce the investment risk for new enterprises and it is easier for investors to seize market opportunities. In the region of concentrated industries, it is easier for entrepreneurs to find out the deficiencies in the products or services and be inspired to setup new enterprises. Regional concentration of competitive industries can attract talent and other production factors, and even workers from depressed industries (Wang, 2001). Its contribution to innovation also exists in the informal communication within the same industry. There are essential differences between informal communication and interior communication in highly-integrated organizations. Informal communication brings in the latest market information, management experience, technical skills, and inspires innovation.

Fourth, an industry cluster is beneficial in forming a mechanism of differentiation advantage. By gathering together, enterprises can make full use of the power of advertising, the group effect, which can form the "regional brand". Through the "regional brand" effect, on the one hand, it is beneficial for individual enterprises to eliminate economic externality, change the situation in which an individual enterprise is not willing to actively participate due to the high advertising costs. On the other hand, compared with an individual enterprise's brand image, a "regional brand" is more vivid and more direct; it is the concentration and the refining essence of many enterprises' brands. Compared with enterprise clusters, an individual enterprise's life cycle is relatively short, and the brand effect is difficult to maintain. While enterprises in the cluster follow the law of the survival of the fittest, the regional brand effect is more likely to last as long as the cluster lasts, unless the cluster undergoes recession or transition because of external conditions such as technical or natural conditions.

8.2.2 Radical internationalization: The new pattern selection

The radical pattern shortens the time of enterprise internationalization and makes its products capture the international market rapidly. This pattern has attracted the extensive attention of private enterprises in coastal areas in recent years, and it creates demonstration effect for these kinds of enterprises' internationalization. Some industries such as the lighter and glass industries in Wenzhou, position their target markets at the foreign market at the very beginning, skipping the parts of "local market-regional market-national market". With respect to international management style, they skipped the stage of domestic management and went directly to the export stage (Lin Li, 2003). In addition, the typical examples of China's POEs internationalization, such as Wanxiang group and some other enterprises, had the features of gradual internationalization development pattern in the early period, starting from export via agencies to setting up overseas marketing centers, while they have manifested a more and more radical internationalization tendency in recent years. Some POEs such as BOE and Holley Group of Zhejiang are not large enterprises according to international standards, but their internationalizations directly started from acquiring foreign enterprises. BOE acquired the TFT LCD business of Modern Display Technique Joint-Stock Company of R.O. Korea and Holley acquired CDMA mobile phone technology of Philips in 2001, all above are attempts to take the leapforg internationalization development pattern for the radical features.

Theoretically, large enterprises are more suitable for taking the radical internationalization development pattern. The international managerial experience and strong innovation ability are favorable conditions and a basis for large enterprises to develop international businesses as they rely on their own power to develop markets independently and obtain absolute control and all the profits from overseas investment. In the context of China, large enterprises are the "vanguard" and "main force" of enterprises internationalization.[1] Of course, large enterprises should also choose a suitable internationalization development path according to their external environment including the industry's development and internal characteristics including the accumulation of managerial resources. At present, the large enterprises in China that can afford to promote internationalization can be divided into several types as follows:

(1) The professional foreign trade corporations with a good internationalization foundation and strong managerial ability, and Chinese-funded trade groups in Hong Kong (SAR of China) and Macao (SAR of China): Professional foreign trade corporations have been engaged in export trade for a long time, and they gradually mastered proficient international marketing skills and flexible trade modes, and have had complete information systems, stable long-term customers, many overseas representative offices, high reputation and convenient financing channels. Most of their subsidiaries overseas belong to "trading enterprises". These companies can make use of those above-mentioned advantages, gradually establish production enterprises overseas, forming comprehensive multinational companies with both international trade and international production.

(2) The enterprise or enterprise group with considerable technical strength and managerial ability: With their long-term accumulated economic power, special technical resources, talents and management ability, these enterprises can circumvent competitive fields with giant multinationals in developed countries and penetrate each local market, different levels of technology, different processes of production and different types of products. Some of these enterprises have started their

---

[1] Jin, R. (1999) *Multinational Companies and Global Strategy of China's Enterprises Internationalization*. Beijing: Higher Education Press.

outward foreign direct investment, but most of them made horizontal integration investment in the domain of standardized products and mature technology. Along with the shortened product life cycle and the devaluation of the existing technology, they were required to speed up the product development and technology development. These large enterprises or enterprise groups have a certain amount of international management experience, if they can cooperate with large domestic foreign-funded companies, acquire and merge with some enterprises, or collaborate with some foreign companies with strong R&D ability or marketing ability, they could become strong multinational enterprises.

(3) The so-called industrial trade, technology trade, agricultural trade companies or groups: Take the technology trade companies as an example. The companies own patent technology or trademark ownership, so they can participate in international business in the form of technology licensing. But as technology is a kind of intermediate product whose market is an incomplete competition market and there are many uncertainties in technology licensing or technology transformations, it is difficult for the technology licensors to control the licensees' use of technology, product quality and service standards, so they would internalize technologies rather than licensing. That is to say, transfer the technology into product and then export or conduct international production through outward foreign direct investment.

(4) The financial companies or service companies with substantial capital strength: The financial industry and service industry are the highlights of multinational companies' investments. China's financial and service companies can completely participate in the international competition. At the same time, the internationalization of financial and service industries can provide service and backups for the internationalization of manufacturing industries, boosting the export of domestic goods and services.

However, from the facts of enterprise internationalization in China, it is not difficult to find that the radical development pattern is gradually becoming the inevitable choice for private SMEs' internationalization. It is mainly due to the appearance of many small and medium-sized private scientific and technological enterprises. Enterprise internationalization is often described as a gradual process.[2] The stage theory assumes a considerable time span through which enterprises obtain experience and accumulate resources and the managerial abilities for international operations. This kind of gradual internationalization is very appropriate for manufacturing enterprises. But the rapid internationalization of the market and competition are shortening the time span significantly, which restrains private SMEs' abilities to control their own growth paths somewhat. The changing circumstances are urging private SMEs (especially scientific enterprises) to deviate from the gradual internationalization pattern. Coviello and Martine once pointed out that small-sized high-tech enterprises rarely did internationalization through a gradual process. The born global enterprises theory put forward by Tage, Koed, Madsen and Per Servais also believes that, driven by constantly developing new technologies, new markets and constantly emerging new innovation talents, small-sized high-tech enterprises have been devoted to international management since early in their establishment; they improved their international competitiveness by establishing strong R&D centers in the areas which are close to sales markets, skipping several successive development stages. In the circumstances where the industry entry cost is high, the scale of the domestic market is too small and the product life cycle is shortening, enterprises have no choice but to internationalize.

The industry cluster of private enterprises can take three routes to realize the internationalization: First, attracting foreign direct investment; in order to adapt to changes of the external environment, only when the industry cluster becomes a dynamic and open system and by realizing exogenous innovation can it keep the prevalent vitality. The industry cluster should attract the multinational corporations' investment, and the forward and backward linkages produced by multinational corporations' value chain can enhance the technical level of the cluster's upstream and downstream enterprises related to the multinational corporations, then promoting the strength of multinational corporations' purchase and investment. Relying on the dynamic, open system and the exogenous innovation it incurred, international competitiveness of private enterprises

---

[2] Johanson, J. and Wiesersheim, P.E. (1975) "The Internationalization of the firm four Swedish cases." *Journal of Management Studies* 12:305, 322.

will be improved considerably. Second, copying the industrial chain: For private enterprises without outward foreign direct investment, they can enter the path of copying the industrial chain to enter the overseas market. That is to say, some of the upstream and downstream production enterprises, which have industry linkage, invest abroad, and maintain the original production connection. This kind of bounded group investment pattern can form advantages of scale economy and complete industrial chain, reduce dependence on local suppliers of the host country, making enterprises operate in a relatively familiar business environment. Using reasonable group investment can also play a role in supporting production, reducing production costs, shortening the time to entering the international market. Third, network combination: Along with the continuous development and maturity of enterprise clusters, we can further consider building a private enterprise group. That is to say, develop from "enterprise clusters" to a "cluster enterprise", reaching the effects of scale economy and global competitiveness. With private-enterprises group in which one or two connected enterprises in the cluster act as the leader, using the "cluster effect" such as unifying sales promotion, regulating quality standards, identifying specific techniques, promoting common trademarks, sharing cluster credit, POEs can acquire an advantage that an individual SME cannot possibly acquire. Economy of scale can be an important factor that determines the competitiveness of an enterprise. Only by a moderate scale can the enterprise put itself in an invincible position in the fierce market competition. Generally, the scale of China's privately-owned enterprises is generally small, and many private enterprises have to take the radical pattern to promote internationalization, they should be encouraged to build a private-enterprises group to increase the benefits from a scale economy in an effort to acquire the ability to cope with the changing and fierce competition in the international market.

8.3 Summary

Chinese multinational enterprises have diverse choices in the international target markets. According to Luo and Tung (2007), China's privately-owned multinational enterprises were divided into niche market type and global type from the dimensions of target market selection.

Niche market type: Refers to the private enterprise that enjoys a high concentration in the international market from the aspects of regional and product distribution. These kinds of enterprises are neither aided by the government nor possessed with rich experience. They focus on a narrow product line and a regional market to strengthen their own advantages. Thus Zhongxing Telecom Equipment (ZTE) Corporation sets up a laboratory and production base in Dallas, USA, in an effort to develop the market for mobile phones and telecommunications in North America. Ausnutria Dairy Group holds a 51% stake in Dutch Hyproca Dairy Group through the acquisition in 2011, by which it has obtained a qualified milk supply and production base in Europe.

Global type: Refers to the private enterprise that has a wide range of product lines in the international market and arranges its production and sales on a global basis. This kind of enterprise depends on its core cost advantage to become a competitive participant in the global market, although it has not developed a similar market position with multinational companies in developed countries in terms of scale and profit. Haier group has developed into a strong brand in the world of the domestic appliances market, and has covered the world. Huawei Technologies was the second largest telecommunications equipment suppliers in the world in 2011. However, in North America and the European market, its market share is much lower than the world's first big communications equipment supplier, Ericsson.

8.3.1 The internationalization mode for niche market type enterprises

China's early internationalizers preferred the gradual internationalization mode, because of the lack of internationalization experience and the intensive global industrial competition. Consequently, they were forced to take the internationalization mode of "exporting prior to foreign direct investment", "joint venture investment prior to wholly owned investment" in an effort to avoid uncertain political and business risk.

Niche market enterprises should give priority to gradual internation-alization, unless entrepreneurs with international experience and external network resources can adopt the radical internationalization mode. In the internationalization mode selection, owing to limited strength and ability, a niche type of market should be better to use as an innovation model. For the core business it should strengthen its innovation and competitiveness. Conversely, for non-core business, it can imitate and copy but avoid intellectual property protection resulting from dispute.

Radical internationalization mode: New international enterprise theory was developed in the 1990s, and it paid attention to the natural features of globalization of SMEs. The SMEs prefer to take the radical mode in international expansion, where they initiate internationalization development soon after their establishment, and participate in foreign direct investment and international business. Niche market type enterprises that are knowledge-intensive and technology-intensive often take the radical internationalization path. In the past more than 10 years, in the Yangtze River delta and Pearl River delta region a large number of global enterprises have emerged. Their characteristics are mainly embodied in the following: (1) The founder and top managers have abundant international experiences, so that the enterprise is willing and able to develop the markets in several countries soon after the early stage, committing to exporting or direct investment activities. (2) Entrepreneurs or core managers can maintain cooperation with a large number of external network organizations, and develop overseas markets through customers or suppliers. (3) They aim at the global niche market even from the beginning of their foundation; to create value for customers with high quality differentiated products and customized products and services. Although enterprises can quickly enter the international market, due to lack of resources and limited ability, their international expansion is often limited to export-oriented activities, and it is difficult to become a multinational enterprise that can realize resource integration on a global basis.

8.3.2   The internationalization mode for global type enterprises

Before 2001 when China entered the WTO, Chinese enterprises usually took a gradual internationalization mode. Only a few high-tech enterprises in the Yangtze River delta and Pearl River delta took a radical internationalization path, and consequently became global enterprises. Global type enterprises mainly take a gradual internationalization path. Haier group started its internationalization in 1991. At that time its early strategy was to export a large number of products overseas, Haier successively established production bases and sales companies in the United States, Europe and developing countries from 1998. In 2006, Haier officially launched its globalization brand strategy which integrated procurement, manufacturing, design, sales and so on, after nearly 15 years of international exploration.

In the 21st century, especially since China's government promoted its "going global" as a national strategy, TCLs acquisition of Thomson in France in 2004, Lenovo's acquisition of IBM's PC business in 2005 and other such large acquisitions have introduced a new high tide of Chinese enterprises' internationalization. Especially after the outbreak of the global financial crisis in 2008, both state-owned enterprises and POEs have flocked overseas, and mergers and acquisitions have peaked. The enterprise may be neither a born global enterprise nor an enterprise that follows gradual growth, but takes a radical growth path, often growing by mergers and acquisitions (M&A) with other national enterprises.

Private global enterprises can follow gradual internationalization or a combination of gradual and radical internationalization. In a familiar area, they can make acquisitions or direct investment by the radical mode; in an unfamiliar area they can follow gradual internationalization. In the internationalization mode selection, the enterprises can decide according to the nature of the industry, service enterprises can develop business channels and improve customer management systems and global service systems in the form of strategic alliances or direct investment. Manufacturing enterprises select the value-chain development mode to purchase the upstream or downstream enterprise. Retailers can follow a global resource integration model, just like Haier, to optimize the value chain in the global market by exploiting the comparative advantages of different host countries.

References

Aldrich, H. and Zimmer, C. (1986) Entrepreneurship through social networks, in Sexton, D. L. and Smilor, R. W. (eds.), *The Art and Science of Entrepreneurship*. Cambridge: Ballinger.

Ali, A. J. and Camp, R. C. (1993) "The relevance of firm size and international business experience to market entry strategies." *Journal of Global Marketing* 6(4):91–108.

Anderson, P. (2002) "Connected internationalization process: The case of internationalizing channel intermediaries." *International Business Review* 11:365–381.

Anderson, S. (2000) "The internationalization of the firm from an entrepreneurial perspective." *International Studies of Management & Organization* 30:63–92.

Anderson, S. (2004) "Internationalization in different industrial contexts." *Journal of Business Venturing* 19:851–875.

Anderson, V. and Skinner, D. (1999) "Organizational learning in practice: How do small businesses learn to operate internationally?" *Human Resource Development International* 3:235–259.

Arenius, P. M. (2002) *Creation of Firm-Level Social Capital, Its Exploitation, and the Process of Early Internationalization*. Helsinki: Helsinki University of Technology.

Arndt, C., Buch, C. M. and Mattes, A. (2012) "Disentangling barriers to internationalization." *The Canadian Journal of Economics* 45:41–63.

Autio, E. (1995) Symplectic and generative impacts of new technology based firms in innovation networks: An international comparative study. Doctorial Dissertation, Helsinki University of Technology.

Autio, E. (2005) "Creative tension: The significance of Ben Oviatt's and Patricia McDougall's article 'toward a theory of international new ventures'." *Journal of International Business Studies* 36:9–19.

Autio, E., Sapienza, H. and Almeida, J. (2000) "Effects of age at entry, knowledge intensity, and imitability on international growth." *Academy of Management Journal* 43(5):909–924.

Axinn, C. N. (1988) "Export performance: Do managerial perceptions make a difference?" *International Marketing Review* 5(2):61–71.

Barney, J. B. (1991) "Firm resources and sustained competitive advantage." *Journal of Management* 17(1):99–120.

Beamish, P. W. (1990) The internationalization process for smaller Ontario firms: A research agenda, in Rugman, A. M. (ed.), *Research in Global Business Management*, Volume 1, Greenwich, CO: JAI Press, pp. 77–92.

Bell, J. (1995) "The internationalization of small computer software firms — A further challenge to "stage" theories." *European Journal of Marketing* 29(8):60–75.

Bell, J. (2009) "The internationalization of small computer software firms: A further challenge to 'stage' theories." *European Journal of Marketing* 29:60–75.

Benito, G. R. G. and Gripsrud, G. (1992) "The expansion of foreign direct investments: discrete rational location choices or a cultural learning process?" *Journal of International Business Studies* 23(3):461–476.

Bilkey, W. J. and Tesar, G. (1977) "The export behaviour of smaller-sized Wisconsin manufacturing firms." *Journal of International Business Studies* 93–98.

Bloodgood, J. M., Sapienza, H. J. and Almeida, G. J. (1996) "The internationalization of new high-potential U.S. ventures: antecedents and outcomes." *Entrepreneurship: Theory and Practice* 20(4):61–76.

Boddewyn, J. J. (1988) "Foreign direct divestment and investment decisions: Like or unlike?" *Journal of International Business Studies* Winter: 23–35.

Bonaecorei, A. and Dalli, D. (1992) Internationalisation process and entry channels: evidence from small Italian exporters, in Cantwell, J. (ed.), *Proceedings of the 18th Annual EIBA Conference*, University of Reading, pp. 509–526.

Buckley, P. J. (2002) "Is the international business research agenda running out of steam?" *Journal of International Business Studies* 33:365–374.

Buckley, P. J. and Casson, M. C. (1976) *The Future of the Multinational Enterprise*. London: Macmillan.

Campbell, D. T. (1975) "Degrees of freedom and the case study." *Comparative Political Studies* 8:178–193.

Carlson, S. (1975) How foreign is foreign trade? Working Paper, The University of Uppsala.

Caves, R. E. (1971) "Industrial corporations: the industrial economics of foreign investment." *Economica* 38:1–27.

Caves, R. E. (1982) *Multinational Enterprise and Economic Analysis*. Cambridge, MA: Harvard University Press.

Cavusgil, S. T. (1980) "On the internationalization process of firms." *European Research* 8:273–281.

Cavusgil, S. T. (1982) *Some Observations on the Relevance of Critical Variables for Internationalization Stages, Export Management, An International Context*, Czinkota, M. R. and Tesar, G. (eds.). Praeger: New York, pp. 276–288.

Chakravarthy, B. S. and Perlmutter, V. (1985) "Strategic planning for a global business." Columbia Journal of World Business, Summer:5–6.

Chandler, A. D. (1962) *Strategy and Structure*. Cambridge: The MIT Press.

Chen, F. (2004) "Learning doctrine of enterprise internationalization." *Factory Management* (12):56–65.

Chen, H. and Zhang, K. (2006) "Analysis of wealth effect on M&A of China's listed companies." *The Journal of World Economy* 12:74–80.

Chen, H. *et al.* (2008) "Empirical analysis of national innovation system on firm's international competitiveness." *The Journal of World Economy* 1:90–96.

Chen, H., Yang, C. and Pan, X. (2008) "Empirical analysis on the relativity between economic internationalization and governmental service innovation and expenditure." *Journal of International Trade* 2:80–85.

Chen, L. and Cao, Z. (2007) *Institution and Ability: The Explanation of 20 Years of Growth of China's Private Enterprises*. Shanghai: Shanghai Renmin Publish House.

Chetty, S. and Campbell-Hunt, C. (2004) "A strategic approach to internationalization: A traditional versus a 'born-global' approach." *Journal of International Marketing* 12:57–81.

Chetty, S. and Holm, D. B. (2000) "Internationalization of small to medium-sized manufacturing firms: A network approach." *International Business Review* 9:77–93.

Chetty, S. and Wilson, H. (2003) "Collaborating with competitors to acquire resources." *International Business Review* 12:61–81.

Child, J., Ng, S. H. and Wong, C. (2002) Psychic distance and internationalization: Evidence from Hong Kong firms." *International Studies of Management & Organization* 32:36–56.

Clercq, D. D., Sapienza, H. J. and Crijns, H. (2005) "The internationalization of small and medium-sized firms." *Small Business Economics* 4:409–419.

Coviello, N. E. (2006) "The network dynamics of international new ventures." *Journal of International Business Studies* 37:713–731.

Cui, X. (2001) "The decision-making model of FDI mode." *Foreign Economies and Management* 10:6–11.

Czinkota, M. R. (1982) *Export Development Strategies: US Promotion Policies.* New York: Praeger Publishers.

Czinkota, M. R. and Ursic, M. (1991) "Classification of exporting firms according to sales and growth into a share matrix." *Journal of Business Research* 22(3): 243–153.

Daniel, S. and Bauerschmidt, A. (1990) "Incremental internationalization: A test of Johanson and Vahlne's thesis." *Management International Review* 30:19–30.

De Wit, B. and Meyer, R. (2004) *Strategy: Process, Content, Context.* London: Thomson Learning.

Dhanaray, C. and Beamish, P. W. (2003) "A resource-based approach to the study of export performance." *Journal of Small Business Management* 41:242–261.

Ding, Q. (1997) "Ownership choice and foreign direct investment in the People' Republic of China." Dissertation, University of Miami.

Du, Y. (2003) "Haier's survival strategy to compete with world giants." *Chinese Economic and Business Studies* 1:259–266.

Dunning, J. H. (1988) "The eclectic paradigm of international production: A restatement and some possible extensions." *Journal of International Business Studies,* 19:1–31.

Eisenhardt, K. M. (1989) "Building theories from case study research." *Academy of Management Review* 14:532–550.

Ellis, P. (2000) "Social ties and foreign market entry." *Journal of International Business Studies* 31:443–463.

Eriksson, K., Johanson, J., Majkgard, A. and Sharma, D. D. (1997) "Experiential knowledge and cost in the internationalization process." *Journal of International Business Studies* 28:337–360.

Erin, A. and Gatignon, H. (1986) "Modes of foreign entry: A transaction cost analysis and propositions." *Journal of International Business Studies* 17:1 26.

Erramilli, M. K. (1991) "The experience factor in foreign market entry behavior of service firms." *Journal of International Business Studies* 22(3):479–502.

Fan, T. and Phan, P. (2007) "International new ventures: Revisiting the influences behind the 'born-global' firm." *Journal of International Business Studies* 38:1113–1131.

Fernández, Z. and Nieto, M. J. (2005) "Internationalization strategy of small and medium-sized family businesses: Some influential factors." *Family Business Review* 18:77–89.

Fletcher, R. (2001) "A holistic approach to internationalization." *International Business Review* 10:25–49.

Fletcher, M., Harris, S. and Richey, R. G. (2013) "Internationalization knowledge: What, why, where, and when?" *Journal of International Marketing* 21:47–71.

Forsgren, M. (2002) "The concept of learning in the Uppsala internationalization process model: A critical review." *International Business Review* 11:257–277.

Forsgren, M., Holm, U. and Johanson, J. (1995) "Division headquarters go abroad: A step in the internationalization and the multinational corporation." *Journal of Management Studies* 32(4):475–491.

Fu, J. (2005) "The cluster strategy of small and medium-sized private enterprises internationalization." *Modern Finance & Economics* (7):41–44.

Gabrielsson *et al.* (2008) "Conceptualizations to advance born global definition: A research note." *Global Business Review* 9:45–50.

Glaser, B. and Strauss, A. (2004) *The Discovery of Grounded Theory.* Chicago: Aldine.

Hagg, I. and Johanson, J. (eds.) (1982) *Foretag i natverk — ny syn pa konkurrenskraft.* Stockholm: SNS Forlag.

Haleblian, J. and Finkestein, S. (1999) The influence of organizational acquisition experience on acquisition performance: a behavioral perspective. *Administrative Science Quarterly* 44(1):29–56.

Hammarkvist, K.-O., Hakansson, H. and Mattsson, L.-G. (1982) *Marknadsforing for konkurrenskraft.* Malmo: Liber.

Han, M. (2004) "The core competitiveness and the theory and practice of private enterprises' transnational operation." *International Business* (5):47–50.

Hashai, N. and Almor, T. (2004) "Gradually internationalizing "born global" firms: An oxymoron?" *International Business Review* 13:465–480.

Herriott, R. E. and Firestone, W. A. (1983) "Multisite qualitative policy research: Optimizing description and generalizability." *Educational Researcher* 12:14–19.

Horst, T. (1972) "The industrial composition of U.S. exports and subsidiary sales to the Canadian market." *The American Economic Review* 62(1/2):37–45.

Hymer, S. H. (1960) "The International Operations of National Firms: A Study of Direct Foreign Investment," Ph.D. Dissertation. Published posthumously. Cambridge, Mass: The MIT Press, 1976.

Hymer, S. H. (1960) "The international operations of national firms: a study of direct foreign investment." Ph.D. thesis, MIT, Cambridge.

Ietto-Gillies, G. (1998) "Different conceptual frameworks for the assessment of the degree of internationalization: an empirical analysis of various indices for the top 100 transnational corporations." *Trans Corp* 7(1):17–40.

Jae, C. J. and Bansal, P. (2009) "How firm performance affects internationalization." *Management International Review* 49:709–732.

Johanson, J. and Mattsson, L.-G. (1988) Internationalisation in industrial networks — A network approach, in Hood, N. and Vahlne, J.-E. (eds.), *Strategies in Global Competition*. London: Croom Helm, pp. 287–314.

Johanson, J. and Sharma, D. D. (1987) "Technical consultancy in internationalization." *International Marketing Review* 4:20–29.

Johanson, J. and Vahlne, J. E. (1977) "The internationalization process of the firm: A model of knowledge development and increasing foreign market commitments." *Journal of International Business Studies* 8:23–32.

Johanson, J. and Vahlne, J. E. (1990) "The mechanism of internationalization." *International Marketing Review* 7:11–24.

Johanson, J. and Vahlne, J. E. (2009) "The Uppsala internationalization process model revisited: From liability of foreignness to liability of outsidership." *Journal of International Business Studies* 40:1411–1431.

Johanson, J. and Wiedersheim-Paul, F. (1975) "The internationalization of the firm — four Swedish cases." *The Journal of Management Studies* 12(3):305–322.

Johanson, J. U. and Nonaka, I. (1983) "Japanese export marketing structures, strategies, counter strategies." *International Marketing Review* 1(2): 12–25.

Jones, M. V. and Coviello, N. E. (2005) "Internationalization: Conceptualizing an entrepreneurial process of behaviour in time." *Journal of International Business Studies* 36:284–303.

Karafakioglu, M. (1986) "Export activities of Turkish manufacturers." *International Marketing Review*: 3443.

Keupp, M. M. and Gassmann, O. (2009) "The past and the future of international entrepreneurship: A review and suggestions for developing the field." *Journal of Management* 35:600–633.

Kim, W. C. and Hwang, P. (1992) "Global strategy and multinationals' entry mode choice." *Journal of International Business Studies* 23(1):29–53.

Kindieberger, C. P. (1969) *American Business Abroad: Six Lectures on Direct Investment*. New Haven: Yale University Press.

Knight, G. A. and Cavusgil, S. T. (2004) "Innovation, organizational capabilities, and the born-global firm." *Journal of International Business Studies* 35:124–141.

Kogut, B. and Zander, U. (1993) "Knowledge of the firm and the evolutionary theory of the multinational corporation." *Journal of International Business Studies* 24:625–645.

Kotha, S., Rindova, V. P. and Rothaermel, F. T. (2001) "Assets and actions: firm-specific factors in the internationalization of U.S. Internet firms." *Journal of International Business Studies* 32(4):769–791.

Laage-Hellman, J. (1989) "Technological development in industrial networks." Ph.D. thesis, Uppsala University, Department of Business Studies.

Lall, S. (1983) "Determinants of R&D in an LDC: The Indian engineering industry." *Economics Letters* 13:379–383.

Larson, A. (1992) "Network dyads in entrepreneurial settings: A study of the governance of exchange relationships." *Administrative Science Quarterly* 37:76–104.

Li, C. (2005) "The network marketing and private enterprises internationalization." *Economic Tribune* (4):55–57.

Li, H. (2005) "The unfavorable factors and countermeasures of private enterprise internationalization." *Group Economics Research* (20):35–37.

Li, L. (2003) "A study of the "Going Global" Mode of the Private enterprises in Wenzhou." *International Economics and Trade Research* (4):81–84.

Li, L. (2004) Driving mode of "going global" of private enterprises in Wenzhou." *International Business* (3):23–25.

Li, Y. and Xu, Z. (2008) *Report on Competitiveness of China's Private Enterprises*. Beijing: Social Sciences Academic Press.

Li, Y. *et al.* (2008) "The analysis of ODI dual selection model." *Commercial Times* 7:49–50.

Liesch, P. W. and Knight, G. A. (1999) "Information internalization and hurdle rates in small and medium enterprise internationalization." *Journal of International Business Studies* 30(1):383–394.

Linder, S. B. (1961) *An Essay on Trade and Transformation*. New York: Wiley.

Lindqvist, M. (1988) Internationalization of small technology-based firms, three illusive case studies on Swedish firms. Research Paper 88/15, Institute of International Business, Stockholm School of Economics.

Lippman, S. and Rumelt, R. (1982) "Uncertain instability: an analysis of interfirm differences in efficiency under competition." *Bell Journal of Economics* 13:418–438.

Liu, H. and Li, K. (2002) "Strategic implications of emerging Chinese multinationals: The Haier Case Study." *European Management Journal* 20:699–706.

Liu, K. (2006) "Analysis of multinational investment of China's privately owned firms." *Group Economic Research* 2.

Liu, Q. (2003) "Restricting factors and countermeasures of private enterprise internationalization." *Modern Enterprise* (8):20–21.

Liu, X., Xiao, W. and Huang, X. (2008) "Bound entrepreneurship and internationalization of indigenous Chinese private-owned firms." *International Business Review* 3:488–508.

Liu, Y. (1992) *Multinational Companies and Chinese Enterprise Internationalization*. Shanghai: CITIC Press Group.

Low, S. P. and Jiang, H. (2004) "Estimation of international construction performance: Analysis at the country level." *Construction Management and Economics* 22(3):277–289.

Lu, J. W. and Beamish, P. W. (2001) "The internationalization and performance of SMEs." *Strategic Management Journal* 22:565–586.

Luostarinen, R. (1970) "Foreign operations of the firm: their quantitative structure and the factors behind them." Licentiate Thesis, Helsinki School of Economics and Business Administration, Helsinki.

Luostarinen, R. (1979) "Internationalization of the firm." Doctoral thesis, Marketing Department, International Marketing, Helsinki School of Economics and Business Administration, Helsinki (Series A: 30).

Ma, R. (2003) "New patterns of private enterprise internationalization operation." *Science & Technology Progress and Policy* (11):98–99.

Ma, Y. and Zhang, Y. (2003) "Technical advantages and foreign direct investment: an analysis framework of technology diffusion." *Nankai Economic Studies* (4):11–19.

Madsen, K. and Servais, P. (1997) "The internationalization of born globals: an evolutionary process?" *International Business Review* 6(6):561–583.

Maitland, E. Rose, E. L. and Nicholas, S. (2005) "How firms grow: Clustering as a dynamic model of internationalization." *Journal of International Business Studies* 36:435–451.

Mariotti, S. and Piscitello, L. (2001) "Localized capabilities and the internationalization of manufacturing activities by SMEs." *Entrepreneurship & Regional Development* 13:65–80.

Mathews, J. A. (2006) "Dragon multinationals: New players in 21st century globalization." *Asia Pacific Journal of Management* 23:5–27.

Mayer, T. and Ottaviano, G. I. P. (2008) "The happy few: The internationalization of European firms — new facts based on firm-level evidence." *Intereconomics* 43:135–148.

McDougall, P. and Oviatt, B. (2000) "International entrepreneurship: The intersection of two research paths." *Academy of Management Journal* 43:902–908.

McDougall, P., Shane, S. and Oviatt, B. (1994) "Explaining the formation of international new ventures: The limits of theories from international-business research." *Journal of Business Venturing* 9:469–487.

Melin, L. (1992) "Internationalization as a strategy process." *Strategic Management Journal* 3:99–118.

Ministry of Commerce and State Statistical Bureau (2004) *China's Outward Direct Investment Statistical Report.* Beijing: Ministry of Commerce and State Statistical Bureau.

Mintzberg, H. (1994) "The fall and rise of strategic planning." *Harvard Business Review* 13(1):107–114.

Mitchell, R., Smith, B., Seawright, K. and Morse, E. (2000) "Cross-cultural cognitions and the venture creation decision." *Academy of Management Journal* 43(5):974–993.

Moen, O. and Servais, P. (2002) "Born global or gradual global? Explaining the export behaviour of small and medium-sized enterprises." *Journal of International Marketing* 10:49–72.

Mudambi, R. and Zahra, S. A. (2007) "The survival of international new ventures." *Journal of International Business Studies* 38:333–350.

Nan, C. (2004) "Globalization and the new engine of private enterprises in China." *Proceedings of the 12th China Quality Conference.*

Nelson, R. R. (1987) *Understanding Technical Change as an Evolutionary Process.* New York: Elsevier Science Publishers B. V.

Nelson, R. R. and Winter, S. G. (1982) *An Evolutionary Theory of Economic Change.* Harvard: Harvard University Press.

Nigel, P. (1981) "Company internationalisation: active and reactive exporting." *European Journal of Marketing* 15(3):26–40.

Ohlin, B. (1933) *Interregional and International Trade.* Cambridge: Harvard University Press.

Oviatt, B. M. and McDougall, P. (1997) "Challenges for internationalization process theory: The case of international new ventures." *Management International Review* 37:85–99.

Oviatt, B. and McDougall, P. (1994) "Toward a theory of international new ventures." *Journal of International Business Studies* 25:45–64.

Oviatt, B. and McDougall, P. (1995) "Global start-ups: Entrepreneurs on a worldwide stage." *Academy of Management Executive* 9:30–44.

Oxelheim, L., Gregorič, A., Randøy, T. and Thomsen, S. (2013) "On the internationalization of corporate boards: The case of Nordic firms." *Journal of International Business Studies* 44:173–194.

Pandit, K. (2009) "Presidential address: Leading internationalization." *Annals of the Association of American Geographers* 4:645–656.

Pederson, T. and Petersen, B. (1998) "Explaining gradually increasing resource commitment to a foreign market." *International Business Review* (7):483–501.

Peng, M. (1997) "Firm growth in transitional economies, three longitudinal cases from China, 1989–1996." *Organisation Science* 18:385–413.

Peng, M. (2001) "The resource — based view and international business." *Journal of Management* (6):803–829.

Peng, Z. and Li, Y. (2004) "Manufacturing enterprise international operation and economic benefit." *World Economy Study* (6):42–47.

Penrose, E. T. (1959) *The Theory of the Growth of the Firm.* Oxford: Basil Blackwell.

Pettigrew, A. M. (1990) "Longitudinal field research on change." *Organisation Science* 3:267–292.

Porter, M. E. (1985) *Competitive Advantage: Creating and Sustaining Superior Performance.* New York: Free Press.

Prahalad, C. K. and Doz, Y. (1987) *The Multinational Mission: Balancing Local Demands and Global Vision.* New York: The Free Press.

Prahalad, C. K. and Hamel, G. (1990) "The core competence of the corporation." *Harvard Business Review,* 68(3):79–91.

Preece, S. B., Miles, G. and Baetz, M. (1998) "Explaining the international intensity and global diversity of early-stage technology-based firms." *Journal of Business Venturing* 14(3):259–281.

Ren, H. (2002) "Zhejiang privately owned enterprises transnational operation." *Economic Management* (15):21–24.

Ricardo, D. (1817) *The Principle of Political Economy and Taxation.* London. John Murray, Alber-marle Street. J. McCreery Printer, Black Horse Court.

Rogers, E. M. (1962) *Diffusion of Innovations.* New York: The Free Press.

Root FR. (1982) *Entry Strategies for International Markets.* Lexington, MA: Lexington Books.

Ruigrok, W. and Wagner, H. (2003) "Internationalization and performance: An organizational learning perspective." *Management International Review* 43:63–83.

Sapienza, H. J., Autio, E., George, G. and Zahra, S. A. (2006) "A capabilities perspective on the effects of early internationalization on firm survival and growth." *Academy of Management Review* 31:914–933.

Shi, J. (2006) *Report on the Development of China's Private Economy.* Beijing: Economic Science Press.

Shi, J., Jin, X., Zhao, W. and Luo, W. (2002) *Institution Change and Economic Development: Study on Wenzhou Mode.* Hangzhou: Zhejiang University Press.

Smith, A. (1776) *Wealth of Nations.* London: Methuen & Co., Ltd.

Stevenson, H. H. and Jarillo, J. C. (1990) "A paradigm of entrepreneurship management." *Strategic Management Journal* 11:17–27.

Strandskov, J. (1985) "Towards a new approach for studying the internationalization process of firms." Presented at the *Annual Conference of European International Business Association*, Glasgow, Scotland, 15–17 December.

Sullivan, D. G. (1994) "Measuring the degree of internationalization of a firm." *Journal of International Business Studies* 25(2):325–342.

Tsang, E. W. K. (1999) "Internationalization as a learning process: Singapore MNCs in China." *Academy of Management Executive* 13:91–101.

Tsang, E. W. K. (2001) "Internationalizing the family firm: A case study of a Chinese family business." *Journal of Small Business Management* 39:88–94.

Tsao, S. M. and Lien, W. H. (2013) "Family management and internationalization: The impact on firm performance and innovation." *Management International Review* 53:189–213.

Turnbull, P. W. A. (1987) Challenge to the stages theory of the internationalization process, in Rosson, P. J. and Reid, S. D. (eds.), *Managing Export Entry and Expansion*, New York: Praege, pp. 21–40.

Turnbull, P. W. and Valla, J.-P. (eds.) (1986) *Strategies for International, Industrial Marketing*. London: Croom Helm.

Tyagi, P. (2000) "Export behavior of small business firms in developing economies: Evidence from the Indian market." *Marketing Management Journal* 10:12–20.

United Nations (2000) *World Investment Report*. Geneva: UN.

Vernon, R. (1966) "International investment and international trade in the product cycle." *Quarterly Journal of Economics* 80(2):190–207.

Vernon, R. and Wells, L. T. (1990), Economic Environment of International Business, Shanghai Joint Publishing Co, Ltd.

Very, P. and Schweiger, D. M. (2001) "The acquisition process as a learning process: evidence from a study of critical problems and solutions in domestic and cross-border deals." *Journal of World Business* 36(1):11–31.

Wang, X. and Chen, H. (2002) "The internationalization of small and medium-sized enterprises: an approach of resource base and network capacity." *Foreign Economies & Management* (6):23–28.

Wang, X. and Tian, C. (2005) "Analysis on the internationalization of private companies based on inter-organizational network: The case of Zhejiang province." *International Trade Journal* (10):66–72.

Wang, Y. (2001) "The global profit distribution and the Chinese government's new role in the era of knowledge economy." *Shanghai Economic Review* (12): 8–20.

Wang, Z. (2003) "Government's thoughts about business orientation for privately-owned firms."*Economics Frontier* 12.

Wang, Z., Zhuang, G. and Fan, X. (2005) "Influence factors and framework of Chinese manufacturing firms' internationalization: TCL as a case." *Nankai Business Review* (3):88–94.

Wei, Z., Gu, G. and He, Y. (2006) "Outward FDI and China's technological progress: mechanism analysis and tentative empirical analysis." *Management World* (7):53–60.

Welch, D. E. and Welch, L. S. (1996) "The internationalization process and networks: A strategic management perspective." *Journal of International Marketing* 4(3):11–28.

Welch, L. S. and Luostarinen, R. (1988) "Internationalization: evolution of a concept." *Journal of General Management* 14(2):34–55.

Welch, L. S. and Luostarinen, R. K. (1993) "Inward and outward connections in internationalization." *Journal of International Marketing* 1:46–58.

Wells, L. T. (1983) *Third World Multinationals: The Rise of Foreign Investments from Developing Countries*. MIT Press Books.

Westhead, P. and Wright, M. (2001) "The internationalization of new and small firms: A resource-based view." *Journal of Business Venturing* 16:333–358.

Williamson, O. E. (1975) *Markets and Hierarchies: Analysis and Antitrust Implications*. New York: The Free Press.

Wolf, B. M. (1977) "Industrial diversification and internationalization: some empirical evidence." *Journal of Industrial Economics* 26(2):177–191.

Wolf, J. A. and Pett, T. L. (2006) "Small-firm performance modeling the role of product and process improvements." *Journal of Small Business Management* 44(2):268–284.

Wu, B. and Zhen, T. (1997) "Two-phase theory: A new analysis model of foreign direct investment." *Economic Research Journal* (7):25–31.

Wu, S. (2005) "Empirical study on the impacting issues on Chinese SMEs' international involvement." *Journal of Jinan University* (5):22–29.

Wu, X. (2005) "International production system of TNCs & internationalization of Chinese enterprises: Discussion about patterns & paths." *Business Economics and Administration* (1):58–61.

Xia, Q. (2003) "Internationalized strategy and performance of Chinese enterprises." *China Soft Science* (7):64–69.

Xian, G. and Yang, R. (1998) "Technology accumulation, competition strategy and foreign direct investment in developing countries." *Economic Research Journal* (11):56–63.

Xiao, R. (2006) "General process of enterprise internationalization and its influence factor: a literature summary." (2):126–129.

Xiao, W. and Chen, Y. (2008) *A Study on the Influencing Factors and Pattern Choice of the Internationalization of Chinese Private-Owned Firms.* Hangzhou: Zhejiang University Press.

Xiao, W., Chen, Y. and Lin, G. (2009) "Analysis of performance of Chinese private-owned enterprise." *Zhejiang Academic Journal* 2:193–198.

Xiao, Y. (2005) "Problems and solutions of internationalization of enterprises in Zhejiang." *Enterprise Economy* (12):70–71.

Xie, J. (2005) "Wenzhou pattern of internationalization of regional economic and enterprise management." *Finance & Trade Economics* (12):86–89.

Xie, S. and Xue, Q. (2004) "Thread of thoughts and mechanism of Chinese enterprises' global learning strategy — from the perspective of the two-way approach of internationalization." *Fudan Journal* 3:86–93.

Xu, M. (2003) "The challenge for the Chinese enterprise internationalization." *World Economy Study* (2):4–9.

Yang, J. (2004) "The theoretical basis of China's foreign direct investment." *Contemporary Finance & Economics* (5):105–108.

Yeoh, P. L. (2004). "International learning: Antecedents and performance implications among newly internationalizing companies in an exporting context." *International Marketing Review* 21(4/5):511–535.

Yin, R. K. (2003) *Case Study Research: Design and Methods*, 3rd edn. London: Sage Publications.

Yli-Renko, H., Autio, E. and Tontti, V. (2002) "Social capital, knowledge, and the international growth of technology based new firms." *International Business Review* 11:279–304.

Yong, J. (2003) "The internationalization of Private enterprises." *Reform of Economic System* (4):65–67.

Zahra, S. A. A. (2005) "Theory of international new ventures: A decade of research." *Journal of International Business Studies* 36:20–28.

Zahra, S. A. and Dess, G. (2001) "Defining entrepreneurship as a scholarly field." *Academy of Management Review* 26:8–10.

Zahra, S. A. and Garvis, S. (2000) "International corporate entrepreneurship and company performance: The moderating effect of international environmental hostility." *Journal of Business Venturing* 15:469–492.

Zahra, S. A., Korri, J. S. and Yu, J. F. (2005) "Cognition and international entrepreneurship: Implications for research on international opportunity recognition and exploitation." *International Business Review* 14:129–146.

Zeng, M. and Williamson, P. J. (2003) "The hidden dragons." *Harvard Business Review* 10:92–99.

Zettinig, P. and Benson Rea, M. (2008) "What becomes of international new ventures? A coevolutionary approach." *European Management Journal* 26:354–365.

Zhang, Q. and Li, J. (2001) *International Operation of Small and Medium-Sized Firms — Facing Challenges from the New Economy*. Beijing: Democracy and Construction Press.

Zhao, C. (2003) "The operation strategy mode and selection of Nanjing private enterprises transnational." *Social Sciences in Nanjing* (9):145–150.

Zhao, P. (2005) "Chinese enterprise internationalization business strategy." *Academic Exchange* (10):69–72.

Zhao, W. (2004) *China's Firms "Going Globally": Government Policy Choice and Representative Case Study*. Beijing: Economic Science Press.

Zhao, W. (2005) "Internationalization of Chinese private-owned enterprises: Comment on current situation and suggestion on development path." *International Economic Cooperation* 8:10–12.

Zhao, W. and Gu, G. (2006) *Internationalization of Chinese Private-Owned Enterprises*. Beijing: Economic Science Press.

Zhao, Y. (2003) "*Status quo*, problems and development countermeasure of internationalization of small and medium-sized private enterprises in Zhejiang." *International Economic Cooperation* (10):27–30.

Zhao, Y. (2005) *The Internationalization of Medium and Small Sized Firms — Theory and Practice*. Shanghai: Fudan University Press.

Zheng, K. (2003) "The motivation of China's private enterprise internationalization — case study from Wanxiang Group." *China Non-Governmental Science Technology and Economy* (8):9–11.

Zheng, Y. (2005) "Brand internationalization of Chinese enterprises." *Audit & Economy Research* (6):89–91.

Zhu, Y. (2005) "China's enterprise internationalization: weakness and countermeasures." *International Economic Cooperation* (2):12–15.

Index

Printed in the United States
By Bookmasters